Federico Alvarez Igarzábal, Michael S. Debus, Curtis L. Maughan (eds.)
Violence | Perception | Video Games

Studies of Digital Media Culture | Volume 11

The series is edited by Gundolf S. Freyermuth and Lisa Gotto.

Federico Alvarez Igarzábal is a postdoctoral researcher at the Institute for Frontier Areas of Psychology and Mental Health in Freiburg, Germany, working in the EU-funded project VIRTUALTIMES. His research focuses primarily on the temporality of video games from a formalist and cognitive-scientific perspective. He obtained his PhD at the Institute of Media Culture and Theatre of the University of Cologne and the Cologne Game Lab of the TH Köln in 2018 with his thesis »Time and Space in Video Games«.
Michael S. Debus conducted his PhD research as part of the Making Sense of Games project at the Center for Computer Games Research at the IT University of Copenhagen from 2016-2019. His research focuses on the analysis and synthesis of existing game ontologies into a clearer terminology for the study of games. He has published papers about the ontology of navigation in videogames and metagames.
Curtis L. Maughan is a PhD candidate in the Department of German, Russian and East European Studies at Vanderbilt University. From 2016-2019, Curtis managed the Master's program in *Game Development and Research* at the Cologne Game Lab. His research interests include surveillance and interactivity, narratology and digital games, and the novellas of Thomas Mann and Heinrich von Kleist. His dissertation project examines *flanerie* in the context of open world gameplay trends and game design practices.

Federico Alvarez Igarzábal,
Michael S. Debus, Curtis L. Maughan (eds.)
Violence | Perception | Video Games
New Directions in Game Research.
Young Academics at the Clash of Realities 2017-2018

[transcript]

TH Köln-University of Technology, Arts, and Sciences supported the publication of this volume.

**Technology
Arts Sciences
TH Köln**

This publication has received funding from the European Research Council (ERC) under the European Unions Horizon 2020 research and innovation programme (Grant Agreement No [695528] MSG: Making Sense of Games).

Bibliographic information published by the Deutsche Nationalbibliothek
The Deutsche Nationalbibliothek lists this publication in the Deutsche Nationalbibliografie; detailed bibliographic data are available in the Internet at http://dnb.d-nb.de

© 2019 transcript Verlag, Bielefeld

All rights reserved. No part of this book may be reprinted or reproduced or utilized in any form or by any electronic, mechanical, or other means, now known or hereafter invented, including photocopying and recording, or in any information storage or retrieval system, without permission in writing from the publisher.

Cover concept: Kordula Röckenhaus, Bielefeld
Cover illustration: Matan Gantz
Printed by Majuskel Medienproduktion GmbH, Wetzlar
Print-ISBN 978-3-8376-5051-8
PDF-ISBN 978-3-8394-5051-2
https://doi.org/10.14361/9783839450512

Contents

Preface | 7

Introduction | 11

REFRAMING THE VIOLENCE AND VIDEO GAMES DEBATE

Real Violence Versus Imaginary Guns.
Why Reframing the Debate on Video Game Violence is Necessary
Christopher J. Ferguson | 17

Avatars Don't Kill People, Players Do! Actor-Network-Theory, Mediation, and Violence in Avatar-Based Video Games
Frank Fetzer | 29

The (American) Way of Experiencing Video Game Violence
Natali Panic-Cidic | 39

Video Game Violence from the Perspective of Cognitive Psychology. Role Identification and Role Distancing in A WAY OUT
Christian Roth | 53

The Playing Voyeur.
Voyeurism and Affect in the Age of Video Games
Ahn-Thu Nguyen | 63

The Spectacle of Murder.
Over-Aestheticized Depiction of Death in Horror Video Games
Cornelia J. Schnaars | 77

Designing Rituals Instead of Ceremonies.
The Meaningful Performance of Violence in Video Games
Rüdiger Brandis & Alex Boccia | 93

Damage over Time.
Structural Violence and Climate Change in Video Games
Derek Price | 105

PERCEIVING VIDEO GAMES

A Cyborg, If You Like.
Technological Intentionality in Avatar-Based
Single Player Video Games
Frank Fetzer | 115

Player Perception of Gameworlds and Game Systems:
Load Theory as Game Analytic Tool
Nikolay Mohammad-Hadi | 127

On Character Analysis and Blending Theory.
Why You Cried at the End of THE LAST OF US
Natali Panic-Cidic | 137

Depression and Digital Games.
An Investigation of Existing Uses of Therapy Games
Leonie Wolf | 151

Perceived Behaviors of Personality-Driven Agents
Alberto Alvarez & Miruna Vozaru | 171

From Pixelated Blood and Fixed Camera Perspectives to VR
Experience. Tracing the Diversification of Survival Horror
Video Games and Their Altered Mode of Perception
Cornelia J. Schnaars | 185

Survival Horror and Masochism.
A Digression from the Modern Scopic Regime
Shunsuke Mukae | 199

Epiphany Through Kinaesthetics.
Unfolding Storyworlds in Immersive Analog Spaces
Agnes K. Bakk | 213

Authors | 225

Preface

GUNDOLF S. FREYERMUTH

"Civilization is but a thin blanket," Auschwitz survivor Ella Lingens once remarked.[1] The blanket of human knowledge seems even thinner; though today we at least have a growing awareness of how little we now know. Macrohistory teaches us that the cognitive revolution through which we acquired language dates back roughly 50-70,000 years; the invention of writing systems some 3,500 years; the scientific revolution barely 500 years. These few recent centuries in which humanity established modern culture—particularly the academic way of thinking, rigorous scholarship, and the scientific method—look, in the words of Yuval Noah Harari, like "the blink of an eye compared to the tens of thousands of years during which our ancestors hunted and gathered."[2]

Games, or at least playfulness, are known to reach back to these distant beginnings of human civilization and beyond, as several higher animal species have long been at play.[3] Nevertheless, we know very little about games, particularly their latest incarnation. The scholarly investigation of digital games began—under the label of Game Studies—less than a quarter of a century ago. Establishing a new academic discipline has been compared to exploring un-

---

[1] Korotin, Ilse (ed.): *"Die Zivilisation ist nur eine ganz dünne Decke ..."*: *Ella Lingens (1908-2002). Ärztin–Widerstandskämpferin–Zeugin der Anklage*, Wien: Praesens Verlag, 2011.

[2] Harari, Yuval Noah: *Sapiens: A Brief History of Humankind*, London: Harvill Secker (Kindle Edition), 2014, p. 40.

[3] Huizinga, Johan: *Homo Ludens: A Study of the Play Element in Culture*, Boston: Beacon Press (Kindle Edition), 1955 (*1938); see also Chris Crawford: THE PHYLOGENY OF PLAY, (2010), http://www.erasmatazz.com/personal/videos/the-phylogeny-of-play.html

known territory. When the *Clash of Realities* Conference was first held in 2006, the lack of games knowledge manifested itself in both the Academy and the general public as a sweeping mistrust of—and even an outright hostility toward—this new medium, which was mischaracterized as inherently violent and highly seductive to a targeted group: the youth.

Considering these circumstances, it seems all the more astonishing that the conference did not create a space dedicated to the promotion of young researchers. Nothing changed in this respect in 2015, when the Cologne Game Lab (CGL) became the guiding hand of the conference and reframed it as the *Clash of Realities—International Conference on the Art, Technology and Theory of Digital Games*. We—my colleague Björn Bartholdy and I—decided to respond to the growing enthusiasm around digital games by boosting the frequency of the once biannual conference; the *Clash* became a yearly event. We also broadened the once singular focus on media pedagogy to include approaches from the humanities and transmedia research, while also advancing a strong artistic emphasis. However, we did not take that extra step of offering a specific forum for young researchers. It took the initiative of young academics themselves to remedy this regrettable shortcoming.

For the 8th *Clash of Realities*, which took place in November 2017, two CGL research assistants, Federico Alvarez Igarzábal and Curtis L. Maughan, along with Michael S. Debus of the IT University of Copenhagen, came up with the idea of a "Young Academics Workshop." They developed a convincing concept characterized by diversity of both perspectives and participants—an initiative which Björn and I were happy to support. Starting with the first workshop (which I had the pleasure to attend) and ever since, the organizers have succeeded in bringing together a wide variety of both scholarly and artistic research. Side by side with game developers, young academics from a dozen disciplines have discussed digital games in a variety of contexts, from literature and film studies, to art history and game design theory, to theatre and performance studies, as well as pedagogy and cognitive science, among others. At each workshop, a large student audience filled the entire lecture hall to the last row. The young audience's free, open, and active participation distinguished itself from their engagement in other summits of the conference, where senior academics set the tone.

Through the *Clash of Realities* conference, the Cologne Game Lab, which Björn and I founded in 2010, has gained international visibility as an educational institution and games research hub. The Young Academics Workshop was an essential puzzle piece missing from the conference. One of the many benefits of the workshop is its broad appeal to potential participants. In addition to the numerous international guests, CGL's own students of all levels—from Ph.D. candidates to particularly talented Bachelor's students—get the exciting opportunity to present their research in front of a diverse audience and to publish their findings in the pages of this book, which for some will be their first academic publication.

Knowledge, its influence and its fate, has always depended on being passed down through the generations. Presently, such transmission seems especially tenuous. Even the relatively small sum of knowledge that we have thus far accumulated is in constant danger from social and political forces that fear we have already gone too far down the path leading to enlightenment. Knowledge is power; it has the potential to bring about great change. But like all power, it also frightens; both those in charge who should know better and those whom our modern societies have kept in the dark. The present shift in political culture puts not only basic values of liberal democracy at stake but also our hard-won "scientific mindset."[4] Given the global resurgence of anti-Enlightenment forces, significant challenges await the scholars of today and tomorrow. In the field of games research, the Young Academics Workshop actively faces these challenges, pursuing new paradigms in the search for—and the sharing of—knowledge.

---

4 Harari, *Sapiens*, p. 286.

Introduction

Establishing the Young Academics Workshop

FEDERICO ALVAREZ IGARZÁBAL, MICHAEL S. DEBUS,
& CURTIS L. MAUGHAN

The present volume compiles papers presented at the Young Academics Workshop (YAW) at the Clash of Realities (COR) conferences of 2017 and 2018. For years, the COR—an internationally recognized conference—invited prominent academics and game developers to the Cologne Game Lab in order to share their unique perspectives on the subject of digital games. Prior to 2017, however, the COR lacked a space in which exclusively young scholars—BA and MA students, PhD candidates, and postdocs—could present and discuss their research.

In 2017, we—the workshop organizers—set out to address this gap by hosting The Young Academics Workshop at the COR. We also wanted to provide an environment where participants could gather (first) experiences in a conference setting without the pressure of presenting alongside seasoned scholars and industry professionals. To add extra value to the proceedings, we would invite an accomplished guest scholar or professional to the workshop, someone who could bring their knowledge and experience to the table in an advisory role.

It should be noted that we too are young academics. When we founded the YAW, we were all PhD candidates and today we are either in the postdoctoral phase or transitioning into it. Therefore, it has never been our goal to counsel participants as their seniors but to learn with and from them. With all of this in mind, we decided that the focus of the discussion would not only be placed on content, but also on form; exchanging advice on how to best communicate the results of one's research in addition to a deep discussion of the research proper.

Furthermore, we strove to foster an interdisciplinary exchange by inviting researchers from all areas of academia. Though the title of the workshop addresses "Young Academics," we expressly encouraged game development students and young developers to share their research as well. In line with the spirit of the COR, research was broadly understood as scholarship and praxis, academic as well as creative.

The topics of the first two workshops, the presentations of which are featured in these pages, were "Violence and Video Games: Reframing the Debate" (2018) and "Perceiving Video Games" (2017).

The 2018 workshop established alternative perspectives on the still controversial topic of violence and video games. Specifically, we sought to elevate the discussion beyond the well-worn discourse that games with violent content, such as MORTAL KOMBAT, are responsible for eliciting violent behavior—a spurious claim lacking the support of legitimate scientific research. In light of this, we encouraged participants to submit presentations that reframed this discussion in novel and productive ways. Instrumental in achieving this goal, Christopher J. Ferguson joined the proceedings as our distinguished guest speaker. Professor Ferguson's work as a social psychologist and science communicator is a testament to the dire need to bring high academic standards and intellectual rigor to the debate concerning violence and video games. His text in this anthology provides an excellent summary of the research on this controversial topic, as well as the shortcomings of his own field, which were exploited to stoke the fire of moral panic around video games that continues to burn even to this day.

Frank Fetzer's contribution applies phenomenology and Latourian theory to examine the dynamic between the player and the game, specifically representations of guns as an extension of the gameworld. Natali Panic-Cidic argues that violence in the United States of America is, first and foremost, a social problem that can be illuminated by the study of video games as they relate to human emotions. Christian Roth applies a model of ludonarrative meaning-making to explore the moral implications of a particular sequence of violence from A WAY OUT. Anh-Thu Nguyen criticizes the imprecision of the term violence in the context of video games, while exploring the concepts of voyeurism and affect as tools for a more nuanced examination of the relationship between video games and the player. Cornelia Janina Schnaars discusses the spectacle of murder in THE EVIL WITHIN 2, placing special emphasis on aestheticized depictions of violence. Borrowing from Turner's work on ceremonies and rituals, Rüdiger Brandis and Alex Boccia develop new terminology for discussing—and designing—sequences of combat and violence in video games. Finally, Derek Price explores the complex matrix of environmental violence in video games, which often overlook the consequences of such harm as well as the means of resistance.

The 2017 YAW benefitted from the presence of Cologne Game Lab cofounder and co-director, Gundolf S. Freyermuth, who also serves on the board of the COR. As a guest moderator, Professor Freyermuth demonstrated how to constructively critique and collaborate in a conference setting, while imparting years of academic and professional expertise to the attendees of the workshop. He also authored the preface of this volume and played an integral role in the realization of this publication.

The 2017 workshop aimed to explore different aspects of perception, from lower-level sensory processes to higher-level meaning-making, all in the context of (digital) games. We were aware the topic of perception would include a wide array of research areas, from phenomenology to aesthetics to emotional engagement. The expansive reach of this topic, however, resonated with the COR goal to bridge the gap between industry and academia. In this light, our broadly-scoped workshop allowed us to set truly impressive precedents both in terms of its interdisciplinarity and diversity. Indeed, our 2017 workshop was globally inclusive and featured academics as well as game designers and artists.

In his contribution, Frank Fetzer explores the video game as a bodily experience, relying on the notion of the cyborg to conceptualize the player-avatar relationship. Nicolay Mohammad-Hadi examines how the audiovisual layer of video games affects player perception through the lens of Load Theory and the psychological notions of sensation, perception, and cognition. Natali Panic-Cidic explores the emotional bond created between the player and the characters in THE LAST OF US through Blending Theory. Leonie Wolf reviews the state of the research on treating depression with video games and offers potential pathways forward for this burgeoning discipline. Alberto Alvarez and Miruna Vozaru present their study on the design and programming of AI agents with a focus on behavioral believability. Cornelia Janina Schnaars examines how technological developments have impacted the evolution of the survival horror genre. Shunsuke Mukae analyzes the survival horror genre as well, coming from the perspective of Deleuzian masochism in relation to film. Finally, Ágnes Bakk draws parallels between video games and DAS HEUVOLK, an immersive theater play by the SIGMA company, investigating the audience's experience of agency and immersion.

This anthology is a testament to the dream the YAW team has had right from the start: to offer a diverse array of participants the opportunity to share their research in a setting that fosters intellectual and professional growth. Correspondingly, this book granted participants the chance—for some, the first chance—to present their work in an academic publication, along with all the labor that such a process entails. By publishing the proceedings of both YAW 2017 and 2018 together, we strive to bring about more of the interdisciplinary connections and intellectual constellations that emerged from the interpersonal dynamics of both workshops. On that note, we would like to acknowledge the crucial role played by the YAW audience, whose number and level of active participation greatly exceeded our expectations. And we hope that this book forms a new audience, one that matches the intellectual curiosity and discoursal civility that characterized the exchanges between workshop participants and audience members at the 2017 and 2018 Young Academics Workshops.

We are deeply grateful to the entire network of people who made this publication and the 2017-2018 workshops possible. First and foremost, we would like to thank the team at the Cologne Game Lab—the venue of the workshop—for all of their help. We are especially grateful for the ongoing support we have received from Gundolf S. Freyermuth and Björn Bartholdy, co-directors of CGL and board members of COR. We would also like to thank the COR board, as well as the conference organizing team: Judith Ruzicka-Grote, Judith Neumann, Katharina Klimek, Alexandra Hühner, Tobias Lemme, Sebastian Felzmann, Su-Jin Song, Rüdiger Brandis, and the CGL "Events" Student Work Group. As intellectual diversity is a primary goal of our workshop, we are grateful for the transinstitutional support from the Center for Computer Games Research of The IT University of Copenhagen. We are also grateful for the support from the sponsors of the Clash of Realities conference, in particular the TH Köln—University of Applied Sciences (Cologne, Germany).

And certainly we would also like to thank all of our workshop participants and contributors for their impressive efforts: Frank Fetzer, Ágnes Bakk, Shunsuke Mukae, Cornelia Janina Schnaars, Alberto Alvarez, Miruna Vozaru, Thiago Gatti, Thomas Constant, Diego Saldívar, Nicolay Mohammad-Hadi, Natali Panic-Cidic, Hanns Christian Schmidt, Leonie Wolf, Ahn-Thu Nguyen, Alex Boccia, Rüdiger Brandis, Carman Ng, Anja Wodzinski, Derek Price, Christian Roth, and Christopher Ferguson. We are inspired by the relevance and significance of your contributions, the intellectual rigor of your research, and the dedication you have brought to the completion of this volume, which we see as a continuation of an already robust relationship that will stretch far into the future.

The Young Academics Workshop will continue in the fall of 2019, the 10th anniversary of the Clash of Realities, with an edition on "Play, Games, Mental Health." This year we are happy to welcome a new member to the organizing committee: game scholar and producer Su-Jin Song. With her input, we look forward to further innovations in research and global collaboration, as well as the many new directions the Young Academics Workshop will pursue in the years to come.

Reframing the Violence and Video Games Debate

Real Violence Versus Imaginary Guns
Why Reframing the Debate on Video Game Violence is Necessary

CHRISTOPHER J. FERGUSON

The debate on whether video game violence does or does not have an influence on players remains a heated one in the general public and among scholars. Naturally, we see one influence the other. For instance, after the 2018 Parkland shooting in the United States, President Trump initially invoked video games as a cause. Some Republican politicians and Trump administration officials invoked statements by the American Psychological Association linking video games to aggression, although his administration later backed down from such claims after official hearings during which evidence was prevented.[1] Many of the misunderstandings regarding the current nature and strength of video game violence research come from the difficulty in distinguishing violence from aggression. At the same time, scholars may inadvertently miscommunicate or fail to recognize the weaknesses within aggression research, eliciting/generating more confidence about the research on violent video games in the general public than is warranted from current data. At this juncture, the weaknesses of aggression research are well known. Current controversies now focus on the use and misuse of meta-analysis, the related issue of psychology's "crud factor," and the misuse of near-zero effect sizes. In this essay, I will briefly summarize the evidence for effects of games on violence (which society cares about). I will then spend more time focusing on the effects of games on prank-level aggression (which society argu-

---

1 School Safety Commission: "Final Report of the Federal Commission on School Safety" (2018). https://www2.ed.gov/documents/school-safety/school-safety-report.pdf, retrieved April 16, 2019.

ably does not care about), including "crud factor" results, misuse of meta-analysis, and "death by press release." I will conclude by observing that psychological science has gradually reduced the standard of evidence for the link between games and aggression over the course of 20 years, arguably in a defensive reaction to preserve the ostensible value of psychological science itself.

THE EVIDENCE REGARDING VIOLENT CRIME

Space constraints preclude an exhaustive summary of this data, but several pools of evidence highlight an increasingly clear lack of evidence for an impact of violent games on societal violence, ranging from mild bullying behaviors all the way to mass shootings. This evidence comes from several sources, none of them perfect, but all pointing in the same direction. These include:

Inverse Correlation Between Violent Video Game Sales and Violence. Most of the data in this realm comes from the US, where the inverse relationship between violent video game sales and significant reductions in youth violence, homicides, and other outcomes is clear and has been known for some time.[2] Such correlational data must be interpreted with caution, given the potential for ecological fallacies. However, other data does suggest that the release of very popular violent games is associated with immediate declines in crime.[3]

Little Evidence that Mass Homicide Perpetrators Consume High Amounts of Violent Media Including Games. This particular pool of evidence dates as far back as 2002 with a US Secret Service report that noted that school shooters tend to consume less rather than more violent media than the amount expected for males of their age group.[4]

---

2   Ferguson, Christopher J: "Does Media Violence Predict Societal Violence? It Depends on What You Look at and When," in: *Journal of Communication* 65 (2015), pp. E1–E22.

3   Markey, Patrick M./Markey, Charlotte/French, Juliana: "Violent Video Games and Real-World Violence: Rhetoric versus Data," in: *Psychology of Popular Media Culture* 4 (2015), pp. 277–295. McCaffry, Kevin/Proctor, Ryan: "Cocooned from Crime: The Relationship Between Video Games and Crime," in: *Social Science and Public Policy,* In Press.

4   United States Secret Service and Department of Education: "The Final Report and Findings of the Safe School Initiative: Implications for the Prevention of School Attacks in the United States (July 2004). https://www2.ed.gov/admins/lead/safety/preventingattacksreport.pdf, retrieved April 16, 2019.

Cross-National Comparisons Find High Game-Consuming Countries are Low Violent Crime Countries. The first analyses along these lines came from the Washington Post following the 2012 Sandy Hook shooting, but a recent update with Patrick Markey confirmed these conclusions.[5] Essentially, high game-consuming countries such as Japan, South Korea, and the Netherlands are among the least violent on the planet.

All the above data are societal in nature. Intriguingly, the psychological research field has seldom engaged with this societal-level data and, for the most part, ignores its existence. Unfortunately, this creates a situation in which the psychological science remains largely divorced from the real world. To the extent that psychological research may disagree with the real world (although that itself is a matter of interpretation, as I will show in a moment), scholars may often come across as implying that the real world is less important than what happens in psychological laboratories.

THE EVIDENCE FROM PSYCHOLOGICAL STUDIES

Psychological studies can be either experimental or correlational/longitudinal. We'll consider each in turn.

Experimental Studies. Experimental studies of violent video game effects typically take individuals (often, though not always college students) and randomize them to play violent or non-violent games in an artificial, laboratory setting. So long as the games are equal on all levels other than violence, this provides an argument for causal effects. Because it would be unethical or even illegal to cause individuals to behave violently, the aggression measures are, by nature, prank-level aggression—such as giving someone hot sauce when they do not like spicy food or putting someone's hand in a bucket of ice water. Such measures can certainly be interesting, though likely tell us little about violent crime. Nevertheless, this pool of studies has been known to suffer from a number of flaws.

Publication Bias. First, it is now well-understood that experimental studies of video games and aggression suffer from publication bias and, when such bias

---

5 Markey, Patrick M/Ferguson, Christopher J: *Moral Combat: Why the War on Violent Video Games is Wrong,* Dallas, TX: BenBella Books 2017.

is controlled for, effects drop pretty close to zero.[6] Further, more recent preregistered studies[7] of violent game effects have returned non-significant findings.[8] Thus, despite some claims to the contrary, it is not clear that experimental studies of violent game effects have provided evidence for causal effects.

Poor Matching of Video Game Conditions. For about a decade, it has been understood that a common confound of video game experiments has been a failure to match video games carefully on factors other than violent content.[9] Other factors such as game difficulty, frustration, and competition may differ systematically between mainly violent and non-violent games, introducing critical confounds.

Use of Unstandardized Aggression Measures. Unstandardized aggression measures allow for researchers to pick and choose outcomes that fit their hypotheses while ignoring those that do not. It has been demonstrated that such unstandardized aggression measures result in upwardly biased effect size estimates.[10]

Demand Characteristics. In many designs, the close pairing of the game condition with measures of aggressiveness makes the study hypotheses obvious. Under such conditions, participants may be able to guess the study hypotheses and change their behavior accordingly.

---

6   Hilgard, J/Engelhardt, CR/Rouder, JN: "Overstated evidence for short-term effects of violent games on affect and behavior: A reanalysis of Anderson et al (2010)," in: *Psychological Bulletin* 143 (2017), pp. 757-774.

7   i.e. Those in which the analysis plan and hypotheses are published in advance of data collection to reduce questionable researcher practices.

8   Ferguson, CJ/Trigani, B/Pilato, S.et al.: "Violent video games don't increase hostility in teens, but they do stress girls out," in: *Psychiatric Quarterly* 87 (2016), pp. 49-56. McCarthy, RJ/Coley, SL/Wagner, MF/Zengel, B/ Basham, A.: "Does playing video games with violent content temporarily increase aggressive inclinations? A preregistered experimental study," in: *Journal of Experimental Social Psychology* 67 (2016), pp. 13-19.

9   Adachi, PJC/Willoughby, T.: "The effect of violent video games on aggression: Is it more than just the violence?" in: *Aggression and Violent Behavior* 16 (2011), pp. 55-62.

10 Elson, M/Mohseni, MR/Breuer, J.et al.: "Press CRTT to measure aggressive behavior: The unstandardized use of the competitive reaction time task in aggression research," in: *Psychological Assessment* 26 (2014), pp. 419-432.

CORRELATIONAL/LONGITUDINAL DESIGNS

Correlational and Longitudinal designs do not control video game exposure, thus limiting causal attributions, but do allow for the assessment of more serious aggression or violent behavior. However, they too are known to experience a number of critical issues.

Failure to Adequately Control for Relevant Variables in Longitudinal and Correlational Studies. Many studies fail to control for important variables that may explain links between violent games and aggressiveness, ranging from gender to trait aggression to genetics. Studies that control for such variables suggest that actual socialization effects for violent games (or other media) are minimal.[11]

Unstandardized Self-Report Measures. As with experimental studies, many correlational and longitudinal studies use poorly-designed self-report measures. This problem is compounded by their self-report nature. Most studies do not include checks for unreliable or mischievous responding, both of which can cause spurious correlations.

Demand Characteristics. As with experimental studies, the close pairing of questions about video games with measures of aggression or violence (or worse still, asking participants to rate the violent content of the games they play) create significant demand characteristics and potential spurious positive results.

Researcher Expectancy Effects. One curious effect that has been observed is the presence of researcher expectancy effects. In particular, it has been observed that studies that employ citation bias (citing only studies favorable to the authors' personal views) tend to have higher effect sizes than those with more balanced literature reviews.[12] As with experimental studies, preregistration can help remove some researcher expectancy effects. Thus far, preregistered correlational studies, as with experimental studies, have not been encouraging of violent game effects[13]—aside from one study with college students.[14]

---

11 Schwartz, JA/Beaver KM: "Revisiting the association between television viewing in adolescence and contact with the criminal justice system in adulthood," in: *Journal of Interpersonal Violence* 31 (2016), pp. 2387-2411.

12 Ferguson, CJ: "Do angry birds make for angry children? A meta-analysis of video game influences on children's and adolescents' aggression, mental health, prosocial behavior, and academic performance." *Perspectives on Psychological Science* 10 (2015), pp. 646-666.

13 Przybylski, A./Weinstein, N.: "Violent video game engagement is not associated with adolescents' aggressive behaviour: evidence from a registered report," in: *Royal Soci-*

To conclude this section on research from psychological studies, the data from nearly four decades worth of research is, on balance, not impressive for violent game effects. Nonetheless, it remains common to find a few scholars defending the potential for effects. These defenses are undoubtedly in good faith, but include critical errors in thought. Namely, these include the misuse of meta-analysis, as well as declining standards of evidence wherein ever smaller, close-to-zero "crud factor" effect sizes are considered "evidence" for effects, despite many reasons to suspect that such tiny effect sizes do not represent population level effects. It is to these issues I now turn.

ON THE MISUSE OF META-ANALYSES

It has become something of an unfortunate tradition in the social sciences that, when individual research studies disagree regarding support for a hypothesis, meta-analyses are summoned as a djinni to fix the problem via a magical wish. Unfortunately, meta-analyses only function well in this regard when considering a homogeneous pool of randomized controlled trials. For messy social science studies with unstandardized measures, poor control condition contrasts, researcher expectancy effects, and the like, we can be certain that the pooled average effect size is *not* a remotely precise measure of a population effect size. Put simply, meta-analyses can tell us which foibles of research methodology are associated with higher or lower effects, but they cannot tell us what the *true* effects are. Nonetheless, many scholars persist in such a belief.

As an example, the American Psychological Association relied on meta-analysis in its technical report on video game violence.[15] From a field that, during the time frame considered, likely included 60-70 empirical studies, the APA included only 18. Puzzlingly, 5 of these contained no data relevant to the question of whether violent games cause aggression, lacking either aggression

---

ety for Open Science 6, 2 (2019). https://royalsocietypublishing.org/doi/10.1098/rsos.171474

14 Ivory, AH/Ivory JD/Lanier M: "Video Game Use as Risk Exposure, Protective Incapacitation, or Inconsequential Activity among University Students: Comparing Approaches in a Unique Risk Environment," in: *Journal of Media Psychology* 29 (2018), pp. 42–53.

15 American Psychological Association: "APA review confirms link between playing violent video games and aggression" (2015). Apa.org https://www.apa.org/news/press/releases/2015/08/violent-video-games.aspx, retrieved April 16, 2019.

measures or contrasts between violent and non-violent games. Thus, it is unclear how the APA task force extracted effect sizes from these studies. But the task force's failure to consider the impact of the methodological issues discussed earlier, as well as their overreliance on spuriously high bivariate effects from correlational and longitudinal studies, result in pooled effect size estimates that assuredly bear little resemblance to population level effects.

At least for video game violence, and likely for many other research fields as well, it is likely time to abandon the belief that meta-analyses are debate enders, or that the pooled mean effect size is meaningful. Such pooled mean effect sizes, capitalizing on elevated power, are almost always "statistically significant," (which is to say they cross an arbitrary line that suggests results aren't due only to random chance in the selection of samples from a population) causing scholars to have overconfidence in the strength of evidence for effects, despite weak effect sizes (more on this in a moment). This is not to say meta-analyses are without value: as indicated above, they can actually be quite informative in understanding *why* effect sizes are elevated in some studies and lowered in others. But they seldom tell us what the *true* population effect size is.

PSYCHOLOGY'S CRUD FACTOR

The concept of "crud" factor was described by psychologist Paul Meehl to refer to the observation that almost everything correlates just a little bit with almost everything else, but that these tiny correlations should not be interpreted as meaningful.[16] Unfortunately, as sample sizes increase (normally a good thing), these tiny effect sizes can pop out as "statistically significant" even though they are crud. This is an easy issue for scholars to lose sight of, considering that many are inherently excited (or biased) to find "statistically significant" results and loathe to embrace the null. This crud factor can cause scholars to make bad decisions regarding the interpretation of crud-level findings as meaningful.

Orben and Przybylski recently demonstrated this with statistically significant (but trivial) relationships between screen use and mental health. The authors compared these to statistically significant effects of similar magnitude for obviously irrelevant factors such as eating potatoes or wearing eyeglasses on mental health. If the magnitude of screen use is similar to potatoes on mental health,

---

16 Meehl Paul: "Why summaries of research on psychological theories are often uninterpretable," in: R. E. Snow/D. E. Wiley (Eds.), *Improving inquiry in social science: A volume in honor of Lee J. Cronbach Hillsdale*, NJ: Erlbaum 1991, pp. 13–59.

such correlations should clearly be dismissed as nonsense even if "statistically significant."[17]

Most meta-analyses of video game effects find effect sizes in the range of $r = .04$ to $.08$, particularly for longitudinal studies.[18] But what are we to make of effect sizes in such a range even when "statistically significant"? Such effect sizes are no different in magnitude than the effect of potatoes on suicide. Thus, is the overinterpretation of such effect sizes and indication of the crud factor or what we might also call the "suicide potato effect"?

The naïve interpretation of such effects is demonstrated by one recent meta-analysis by Prescott and colleagues.[19] The meta-analysis found a best-controlled effect size estimate of $r = .078$ for longitudinal studies of video game violence. But is such an effect a reasonable indication of population effect sizes or consistency between studies as the authors claimed? It seems doubtable this is the case. First, given that such an effect size is near zero, it would best be interpreted that most studies find an effect size that is little different from zero. Second, this effect size is based on self-report surveys, many of which suffered from the methodological limitations indicated above. As such, there are good reasons to conclude that even this effect size is upwardly biased. Third, taken at face value, this effect size indicates that the ability of knowing a person's video game habits when predicting their aggression is 0.61 % shared variance, essentially only 0.61 % better than a coin toss. Fourth, at least two of the effect sizes calculated from my own studies in the Prescott meta-analysis appear to be upwardly biased miscalculations, thus raising the possibility that even this effect size estimate is too high. On balance, the Prescott meta-analysis is better evidence against violent video game effects than for it. Only a decision to ignore the crud factor leads one to suggest otherwise.

---

17 Orben, A/Przybylski, A: "The association between adolescent well-being and digital technology use," in: *Nature: Human Behavior* 3 (2019), pp. 173-182.

18 Ferguson, CJ.: "Do angry birds make for angry children? A meta-analysis of video game influences on children's and adolescents' aggression, mental health, prosocial behavior, and academic performance," in: *Perspectives on Psychological Science* 10 (2015), pp. 646-666. Furuya-Kanamori, L/Doi, Sohail: "Angry birds, angry children, and angry meta-analysts: A reanalysis," in: *Perspectives on Psychological Science* 11(2016), pp. 408-414. Prescott, AT/Sargent, JD/Hull, JG.: "Metaanalysis of the relationship between violent video game play and physical aggression over time," in: *PNAS Proceedings of the National Academy of Sciences of the United States of America* 115 (2018), pp. 9882-9888.

19 Ibid.

Relying on such miniscule effect sizes to support a hypothesis is a statistical grasping at straws. Over time, the standards of evidence for this field considered sufficient for scholars to claim that evidence supports effects has gradually diminished. Just over a decade ago, scholars assured us that the effects were similar in magnitude to smoking and lung cancer with perhaps 10-30 % of the variance on aggression and violence attributable to video game and other media violence.[20] Now, without the slightest hint of embarrassment, our field is reduced to arguing whether 0.61 % shared variance is enough to ring the clarion bells of alarm in the general public. If this is all our field has to show for itself, it is time to pack it in or settle for being "that nasty little subject"[21] William James once repudiated psychology for being.

CONCLUDING THOUGHTS

Considering all of the above, I argue that it is time to reframe the debate away from the notion of the effects games have on people—a line of research that has seldom borne fruit. Rather, it may be helpful to understand the interactions between games and players, their motivations for playing action-oriented games, and how such game play can be understood in the context of a greater milieu of a given individual's life. In essence, I argue for an abandonment of the entire moral enterprise of blaming games, violent or otherwise, for negative outcomes and, instead, treating them more or less like any other hobby or, alternatively, cultural experience. I note this also means that we ought to be cautious in exaggerating positive as much as the negative impacts. But I think that removing games research from negative effects and, quite frankly, cultural criticism, would be beneficial to the objectivity of games research.

To this end, I found reasons for optimism among the other sessions at the Young Academics Workshop. Many of these sessions demonstrated the potential for a sophisticated inquiry into games and player experiences that eschewed the easy moralization of the "blame games" movement. I think a fundamental aspect of this optimism came from a degree of respect shown to gamers themselves and gamer culture. Too often, gamer culture appears to be an easy target for stigmatization, whether through the earlier paradigm of social psychologists or more

---

20 Strasburger, Victor: "Go ahead punk, make my day: It's time for pediatricians to take action against media violence," in: *Pediatrics* 119 (2007), pp. e1398-e1399.
21 James H. (Ed.). *The letters of William James.* Boston, MA: Atlantic Monthly Press 1920.

recently through cultural criticism. Divorcing the science of games from moral posturing is essential to an objective science of game effects or game culture.

As some excellent examples of the research being done, here were some of the things discussed as the Young Academics Workshop. Derek Price discussed how violence is represented in games outside the United States. Less focus on the violent game debate has allowed for a greater interest in other issues such as economic deprivation or social strife. Frank Fetzer discussed how avatars act as moral shields between the player and their behavior in games. This line of research may help us to understand the gulf between what people do in games and what they don't do in real life. Along this thread Christian Roth examined how moral disengagement allows players to take on roles in games they would not take on in real life. Natali Panic-Cidic examined how violence in games can take on meaning that allows players to explore cognitive and emotional boundaries. Exploring violence in games can actually help us to understand empathy and compassion in real life. Cornelia Janina Schnaars explored the aesthetics of violence in games and how violence itself can be rendered unto art as is often done in other media. Rüdiger Brandis and Alexander Boccia examined how ceremony and ritual in violent games are used to give meaning to the player experience. Taken together, all of these papers take seriously the perspective of game play from the player's experience, something that has been fundamentally lacking in most of the social science research.

After four decades of research, it is likely time to admit that we have not amassed an evidence base that justifies warning the public about harmful effects of violent video games. I suspect that the reluctance among some to let it go stems from dedicating a life's work to a topic that, in the end, may have been a false path. Or perhaps a defensiveness of psychology itself and a hope to see magic in the wonder of statistics however small and subjective they may be. Worse, we seem to have learned very little about the lack of value in "statistical significance" and are repudiating any worth in the concept of effect size by defending any effect size that is not zero and manages to achieve "statistical significance" in large samples, including meta-analyses. There are, to be sure, some positive movements such as preregistration and an increasing awareness that tiny effect sizes may not matter after all. But until a greater intellectually honest culture takes root in our science, it will continue chasing its tail as a *nasty little subject*.

LITERATURE

Adachi, PJC/Willoughby, T.: "The effect of violent video games on aggression: Is it more than just the violence?" in: *Aggression and Violent Behavior* 16 (2011), pp. 55-62.

Elson, M/Mohseni, MR/Breuer, J.et al.: "Press CRTT to measure aggressive behavior: The unstandardized use of the competitive reaction time task in aggression research," in: *Psychological Assessment* 26 (2014), pp. 419-432.

Ferguson, CJ: "Do angry birds make for angry children? A meta-analysis of video game influences on children's and adolescents' aggression, mental health, prosocial behavior, and academic performance," in: *Perspectives on Psychological Science* 10(2015), pp. 646-666.

Ferguson, Christopher J: "Does Media Violence Predict Societal Violence? It Depends on What You Look at and When," in: *Journal of Communication* 65 (2015), pp. E1–E22.

Ferguson, CJ/Trigani, B/Pilato, S.et al.: "Violent video games don't increase hostility in teens, but they do stress girls out," in: *Psychiatric Quarterly* 87 (2016), pp. 49-56.

Furuya-Kanamori, L/Doi, Sohail: "Angry birds, angry children, and angry meta-analysts: A reanalysis," in: *Perspectives on Psychological Science* 11(2016), pp. 408-414.

Hilgard, J/Engelhardt, CR/Rouder, JN: "Overstated evidence for short-term effects of violent games on affect and behavior: A reanalysis of Anderson et al (2010)," in: *Psychological Bulletin* 143 (2017), pp. 757-774.

Ivory, AH/Ivory JD/Lanier M: "Video Game Use as Risk Exposure, Protective Incapacitation, or Inconsequential Activity among University Students: Comparing Approaches in a Unique Risk Environment," in: *Journal of Media Psychology* 29 (2018), pp. 42–53.

James H. (Ed.). *The letters of William James.* Boston, MA: Atlantic Monthly Press 1920.

Markey, Patrick M/Ferguson, Christopher J: *Moral Combat: Why the War on Violent Video Games is Wrong,* Dallas, TX: BenBella Books 2017.

Markey, Patrick M./Markey, Charlotte/French, Juliana: "Violent Video Games and Real-World Violence: Rhetoric versus Data," in: *Psychology of Popular Media Culture* 4 (2015), pp. 277–295.

McCaffry, Kevin/Proctor, Ryan: "Cocooned from Crime: The Relationship Between Video Games and Crime," in: *Social Science and Public Policy,* In Press.

McCarthy, RJ/Coley, SL/Wagner, MF/Zengel, B/ Basham, A: "Does playing video games with violent content temporarily increase aggressive inclinations? A pre-registered experimental study," in: *Journal of Experimental Social Psychology* 67 (2016), pp. 13-19.

Meehl Paul: "Why summaries of research on psychological theories are often uninterpretable," in: R. E. Snow/D. E. Wiley (Eds.), *Improving inquiry in social science: A volume in honor of Lee J. Cronbach Hillsdale*, NJ: Erlbaum 1991, pp. 13–59.

Orben, A/Przybylski, A: "The association between adolescent well-being and digital technology use," in: *Nature: Human Behavior* 3 (2019), pp. 173–182.

Prescott, AT/Sargent, JD/Hull, JG.: "Metaanalysis of the relationship between violent video game play and physical aggression over time," in: *PNAS Proceedings of the National Academy of Sciences of the United States of America* 115 (2018), pp. 9882-9888.

Przybylski, A/Weinstein, N: "Violent video game engagement is not associated with adolescents' aggressive behaviour: evidence from a registered report," in: *Royal Society for Open Science* 6, *2* (2019).

Schwartz, JA/Beaver KM: "Revisiting the association between television viewing in adolescence and contact with the criminal justice system in adulthood," in: *Journal of Interpersonal Violence* 31 (2016), pp. 2387-2411.

Strasburger, Victor: "Go ahead punk, make my day: It's time for pediatricians to take action against media violence," in: *Pediatrics* 119 (2007), pp. e1398-e1399.

ONLINE RESOURCES

American Psychological Association: "APA review confirms link between playing violent video games and aggression" (2015). https://www.apa.org/news/press/releases/2015/08/violent-video-games.aspx, retrieved April 16, 2019.

School Safety Commission: "Final Report of the Federal Commission on School Safety" (2018). https://www2.ed.gov/documents/school-safety/school-safety-report.pdf, retrieved April 16, 2019.

United States Secret Service and Department of Education: "The Final Report and Findings of the Safe School Initiative: Implications for the Prevention of School Attacks in the United States (July 2004). https://www2.ed.gov/admins/lead/safety/preventingattacksreport.pdf, retrieved April 16, 2019.

Avatars Don't Kill People, Players Do!
Actor-Network-Theory, Mediation, and Violence in Avatar-Based Videogames

FRANK FETZER

In this chapter, I will apply Bruno Latour's actor-network-theory to address how the avatar co-shapes the player's program of action, especially concerning violent acts. The avatar functions primarily as instrument that mediates how the player perceives and acts in the game world.[1] Nonetheless, this instrument often has strong narrative aspects, which make it difficult to grasp as a tool alone. The lines between instrument and protagonist are blurred, making the nature of the avatar-character ambiguous. Because these aspects are intertwined, both form the player's being-in-the-gameworld. Therefore, I cannot discuss the instrumental side of the avatar and ignore the narrative aspect. In this light, I will begin by focusing on the instrumental nature of the avatar, then I will move to its story component.

Because of the ambiguous character of the avatar as tool or object on the one hand and protagonist or subject on the other, the work of Bruno Latour provides a perfect starting point. One of the main characteristics of his work is his attempt to overcome the subject-object dichotomy that is prevalent in contemporary philosophy. Latour claims that it is not just the human subject that shapes the way actions unfold, but that things or technologies are equally important—at least when we enter the realm of engineers and craftsmen where no unmediated

---

1 Cf. Klevjer, Rune: "Enter the Avatar: The Phenomenology of Prosthetic Telepresence in Computer Games," in: John Sageng/Hallvard Fossheim/Tarjei Mandt Larsen (eds.), *The Philosophy of Computer Games,* New York, NY: Springer, 2012, pp. 17-38, here p. 17.

action is possible.² As French philosopher Bernard Stiegler has argued,³ this is an essential part of the human condition, which is even truer regarding video games.

To foreground the symmetry between human beings and objects, Latour introduces the term "actant," which is used equally to describe human agents and non-humans or instruments.⁴ For Latour, reality cannot be understood if humans and non-humans are treated "asymmetrically." The two are always bound up with each other in a network of relations. Only these relations make them what they are. Therefore, the two basic concepts of Latour's theory are "actors" and "networks." His universe consists of actors that are related to each other and interact via networks. Agency, he claims, cannot be restricted to human beings.⁵

In his essay "On technical mediation," Latour contrasts the well-known claims of gun-control advocates ("Guns kill people") with the NRA's stance ("People kill people, not guns") to reflect on the role of technical mediation. He asks: "What does the gun add to the shooting?"⁶ Regarding the gun-control position, Latour claims that "the gun acts by virtue of material components irreducible to the social qualities of the gunman."⁷ He calls this the materialistic position: it is based on the view that the carrier is changed by the affordances of the gun.

For the NRA, on the other hand, the gun does nothing in itself: "it is a tool, a medium, a neutral carrier of will."⁸ This is what Latour calls the sociological position, which is based on the view that the gunman is the one that acts while the gun plays a neutral role.

But neither the materialistic nor the sociological position are right. It would be absurd to attribute the action of shooting someone to the gunman alone. Equally absurd would it be to think of the gun as solely responsible for the act. Don Ihde, a philosopher of technology, has also dealt with the NRA slogan and arrives at a similar conclusion:

---

2   Cf. Latour, Bruno: "On Technical Mediation," in: *Common Knowledge* 3, 2 (1994), pp. 29-64, here p. 29.
3   Stiegler, Bernard: *Technics and Time: The Fault of Epimetheus*, Stanford, CA: Stanford University Press, 1998, p. 134.
4   Cf. B. Latour: "On Technical Mediation," p. 33.
5   Cf. ibid., p. 35.
6   Ibid., p. 31.
7   Ibid.
8   Ibid.

"The gun of the bumper sticker clearly, by itself, does nothing; but in a relativistic account where the primitive unit is the human-technology relation, it becomes immediately obvious that the relation of human-gun (a human with a gun) to another object or another human is very different from the human without a gun. The human-gun relation transforms the situation from any similar situation of a human without a gun."[9]

While researching that bumper sticker I came across another one that stated: "Guns don't kill people, they just make it easier" which sums up Ihde's claim quite nicely, I believe. The absurdity of those positions which ignore the part technology or technological artifacts play in human relations is emphasized by Latour here: "The bizarre idea that society might be made up of human relations is a mirror image of the other no less bizarre idea that techniques might be made up of nonhuman relations."[10]

THE FOUR MEANINGS OF TECHNICAL MEDIATION

Technology and the connection between instruments and human beings play an important part in shaping actions. But how can this technical mediation be understood more precisely?

Latour identifies four meanings of technical mediation: translation, composition, reversible blackboxing, and delegation. I will focus here mostly on translation, composition, and delegation. These three meanings seem to be most relevant in analyzing how technical mediation takes shape and how the responsibility for actions is distributed in the special case of the avatar.

When technology or an instrument is part of an action, it translates the program of action. Regarding the example of the gun-man, we can assume that a person (actant 1) is angry and wants to take revenge. The person is probably not strong enough to follow through with her intention, and so the program of action is blocked. However, this person can take on a relation with a gun (actant 2). The gun mediates the program of action of actant 1, via its own program: "shooting." Note how Latour does not differentiate between human and object. The program of action of both actants is transformed or translated into a new one. Both actants

---

9   Ihde, Don: *Technology and the Lifeworld: From Garden to Earth*, Bloomington, IN: Indiana University Press, 1990, p. 27.
10   Latour, Bruno: "Where Are the Missing Masses?" in: Deborah J. Johnson/Jameson M. Wetmore (eds.), *Technology and Society, Building Our Sociotechnical Future*, Cambridge, MA: MIT Press 2008, pp. 151-180, here p. 162.

are transformed in the relation to one another. A new actant comes about (actant 1+actant 2) with a new translated program: the killing of a person.[11]

Mediation always involves several actants that jointly perform an action. Responsibility for that action, therefore, is spread out over the ensemble of parts. Latour calls this complexity of agency composition. By composition, he means that action "is simply not a property of humans but of an association of actants."[12] It is not the person that shoots, but person + gun.

Mediation consists not only of the programs of action but simultaneously of the links between actants. Mediation, therefore, seems to be not a matter of persons and objects, but a matter of hybrids. These hybrids arise in the form of complexes of human and technology.[13] Latour further introduces the terms "substitution and association" or "replacement and linkage."[14] Association is the dimension in which the forming of compositions is localized; substitution is the dimension of the translation of possible programs for action. Each mediation takes part within these two dimensions.

Latour illustrates these dimensions with the bulky key ring that hotel managers often attach to room keys, meant to remind hotel guests to return them when they check out.[15] The role of the bulky key ring can be understood in terms of the mediation of programs of action. The hotel manager's program of action is: make the guests return their keys upon departure. This program of action might conflict with that of the guests, who are not necessarily inclined to return their keys. Latour describes some of the options the manager has to counter the "anti-program" of the guests. In the first situation, the manager merely wishes that the hotel guest might return the key. That program of action does not conflict with the anti-program of the guests, but is also not very successful. In the second situation, the manager adds an oral message to counter the guests' "anti-program" —which is, arguably, already a technological mediation. In the third and fourth situation, she forges a connection with another entity. She hangs up a sign and attaches a large, heavy object to the key. With each of these steps, the manager broadens her network in order to realize her program of action. At the same time these associations transform the behavior of the hotel guests.

The third meaning of mediation is reversible blackboxing. Briefly put, blackboxing is a process that makes the joint production of actors and artifacts

---

11 Cf. B. Latour: "On Technical Mediation," p. 32.
12 Ibid., p. 35.
13 Cf. Verbeek, Peter-Paul: *What Things Do: Philosophical Reflections on Technology, Agency, and Design*, University Park, PA: Penn State Press, 2005, p. 156.
14 Cf. B. Latour: "Where Are the Missing Masses?" p. 171.
15 Ibid., p. 175.

entirely opaque. We become aware of an instrument's existence and of the role it plays in the network of relations when it breaks down—Latour uses the example of an overhead projector failing during a lecture. To analyze mediation, we have to open the box deliberately and look into the parts the network consists of.[16]

Latour calls the fourth meaning of technical mediation "delegation," and considers it the most important of the four. A popular example is the speed bump on a university campus, which translates a driver's goal from "slow down so as not to endanger students" into "slow down in order to protect your car's suspension."[17] The driver then adapts her behavior due to the mediation of the speed bump. Humans have "inscribed" the program of action they desire (to make drivers slow down on campus) in concrete.[18] Inscribing a program of action in a lump of concrete delegates the task of a traffic sign or a policeman to the speed bump. "Delegation," Peter-Paul Verbeek observes, "makes possible a curious combination of presence and absence: an absent agent can have an effect on human behavior in the here and now."[19]

Another example to illustrate the process of inscription is that of a door-spring: Humans delegate to the door-spring the task of shutting the door after somebody opened it; they inscribe the program of action "close the door if it is open" in the spring. The door-spring in turn invites a particular kind of use (e.g. walk quickly through, do not swing the door too hard).[20]

Technologies co-shape the use that is made of them; they define actors and relations between actors, and share responsibilities and competencies between humans and things. Latour calls the behavior that a non-human delegate imposes on humans a "prescription."[21] He indicates such "built-in" prescriptions as the script of a technology. Consequently, a script is the program of actions or behavior invited by an artifact. The designer of an artifact works with an inscribed user in mind to whom she prescribes properties and behavior. This does not mean that the user acts exactly in the way the designer intended. They can refuse to use the artifact, or use it in a novel and unexpected way. But, by using it, they have to subscribe to the inscriptions.

These four meanings of mediation are closely intertwined. In the case of the speed bump, this interrelation can be formulated like this: The president of the

---

16 Cf. B. Latour: "On Technical Mediation," p. 37.
17 Cf. ibid., p. 36.
18 Ibid., p. 38.
19 Cf. P.-P. Verbeek: *What Things Do: Philosophical Reflections on Technology, Agency, and Design*, p. 159.
20 Ibid., p. 160.
21 Cf. B. Latour: "Where Are the Missing Masses?" p. 157.

university campus where the speed bump has been installed associates herself with a lump of concrete (composition), assigning to it what is necessary to realize her goal (delegation). The resulting speed bump does not need the president to fulfill its task (blackboxing) because its physical properties allow it to change a driver's program of action from "drive slowly to be responsible" to "drive slowly to protect my shock absorbers" (translation). Translation, composition, reverse-blackboxing and delegation each describe a different aspect of technical mediation.[22]

TECHNICAL MEDIATION AND THE AVATAR

Now I will try to apply those four meanings of mediation to the avatar. In light of Latour's theory, what can we say about the ways the avatar mediates action?

In entering the virtual world of the video game, the player enters a realm of engineers and craftsmen where no unmediated action is possible. Therefore, the player necessarily has to connect with technology to experience the game world. Teaming up with an avatar translates the player's program of action to a great extent. Being able to act within the game world is a much bigger step than being able to shoot somebody. Now the player can shoot somebody in a virtual world.

Here, a new actant emerges (Player+Avatar) who is able to do things that none of the elements of that network would be capable of alone. Mediation always involves several actants that jointly perform an action. The responsibility for that action, therefore, is spread out over the ensemble of parts. It is not the person that shoots, but person+gun. Mediation consists not only of the programs of action but also and simultaneously of the linkage of actants.

Here, I want to make a brief detour: Henrik Nielsen describes his experience of playing CALL OF DUTY 4, and claims that while playing as a soldier he is somehow shielded from the actions, being positioned in the gunship let him experience the war with his own eyes:

"Up until that point (playing COD4), the conventionalized 'being' and 'not-being there' of the first-person perspective had worked as a buffer, separating me from the actions in the game – giving me status as a quasi-I. But when positioned in the gunship, the alterity of the perspective disappeared and left me with my own eyes to experience the war."[23]

---

22 Cf. ibid.
23 Nielsen, Henrik Smed: *Playing Computer Games: Somatic Experience and Experience of the Somatic*, Aarhus: Digital Aesthetic Research Center 2012, p. 136.

This experience is based on the narrative existence of the avatar. It has a life of its own. While playing as another subject, the player can pretend that the actions are not completely her own. But from the perspective of the instrument there is no difference between piloting an avatar or piloting a vehicle. For this matter, the fourth means of mediation, delegation, is the most useful of the four. The relation of player and avatar is loaded with delegations and prescriptions for action.

I skipped the third meaning of mediation, "reversible blackboxing," but for analyzing the connections between avatar and player we have to open the blackbox and look into their relation. The avatar, just like the game as whole, is a designed object. Therefore, it is similar to the speed bump, albeit more complex. The difference is that a program of action is inscribed into the avatar. The designer of an artifact works with an inscribed user in mind, who might not do as the designer has intended. In contrast to the material artifact that only invites a certain behavior, the video game demands it. The player subjects herself to the rules. The game is designed with, as Espen Aarseth calls it, an "implied player"[24] in mind. While it is entirely possible to use a gun as a hammer in the physical world, to behave differently from the intended behavior in a video game demands more effort. This is what Aarseth refers to as the "transgressive player;"[25] a player who makes use of bugs and does unexpected things to rebel against the tyranny of the game and to preserve a sense of selfhood in a completely rule-based environment.[26]

The idea of symmetry between human actors and things is an important perspective in the field of human-technology relations. Consequently, so is the idea that responsibility for action is spread across the complete network of humans and non-humans. Still, we have to examine it very carefully: In most of Latour's examples we find an asymmetrical treatment of humans and nonhumans: house owners delegate the task of closing the door to the door spring; hotel managers transfer the task of making sure that guests return their keys to the bulky key ring; and engineers and university officials transfer the task of getting drivers to slow down to the speed bump. Can Latour really claim that all actants are equally responsible when we find a human being at both ends of the chain? I think not. Therefore, responsibility for violence in video games can only be taken by the humans on both sides of the game.

---

24 Cf. Aarseth, Espen: "I Fought the Law: Transgressive Play and the Implied Player," in: Naomi Segal/Daniela Koleva (eds.), *From Literature to Cultural Literacy*, London: Palgrave Macmillan 2014, pp. 180-88, here p. 184.
25 Cf. ibid.
26 Cf. ibid., p. 185.

The program of action a gun provides, (i.e. the program of action it is scripted with) differs from the program of action of a virtual gun. The virtual gun is a second order technological artifact. It cannot be isolated from the game world, as opposed to a real gun, which is a technological artifact in its own right. Thus, the artifact we need to address here first is the video game as such. The gun that provides the player with certain options is part of the game world through the will of the designers and it certainly provides the player with some lethal options within the game world. To claim that those options are the player's to decide would be wrong. The game world was designed in a certain way and the affordances of that game world are reflected in the gun. The designers seem to follow a maxim attributed to Chekhov: "If in the first act you have hung a pistol on the wall, then in the following act it should be fired. Otherwise don't put it there."[27] In other words: the player is provided with a gun, so the problems of the game world are designed to be solved with a gun. Of course, in some games (mostly role-playing games) the player has other options, as exemplified by the vegan runs in THE LEGEND OF ZELDA: BREATH OF THE WILD.[28,29] However, what Diane Carr has observed here is still correct:

"This kind of replay does not represent real options in terms of interactive intervention in narrative outcome: as a player, I can do, undo and redo until Lara has effectively performed the challenge presented to her by the game, but I can only proceed through the game, through the space itself, if I perform the task as the game demands. [...] Driving Lara means occupying a place shaped and then vacated by her designers."[30]

Looking into the relations between gun and gun-man in the material world might be an overwhelming experience. Here, there are many aspects to consider, including the gunman's personal history, education, and character, as well as the position her social environment takes on the matter of gun-use. In video games the matter is simpler. As the game is a technological artifact in itself, we can hold the creators of that game world responsible for designing situations in a

---

27 Rayfield, Donald: *Anton Chekhov: A Life*, New York, NY: Northwestern University Press, 2000, p. 203.
28 THE LEGEND OF ZELDA: BREATH OF THE WILD, (Nintendo 2017, O: Nintendo)
29 Westerlaken, Michelle: "Self-Fashioning in Action: Zelda's Breath of the Wild Vegan Run," *Philosophy of Computer Games Conference*, Krakow 2017. http://muep.mau.se/handle/2043/23973
30 Carr, Diane: "Playing with Lara," in: Geoff King/Tanya Krzywinska (eds.), *Screenplay: Cinema/Videogames/Interfaces*, London, New York:Wallflower Press, 2002, pp. 171-80, here p. 174.

way that they can only be solved through violent acts. Equally responsible is the player for placing herself in those situations. The avatar and the virtual gun are scripted to invite certain actions, but so is the game as such. Where would we start to differentiate between the two? Gameworld and avatar are two sides of the same coin. The avatar is part of the gameworld and the gameworld is designed in a way that situations can be solved with the limited skills of the avatar. Because the avatar forms a part of greater artifact, the video game, to hold it responsible for violent acts would be absurd.

LITERATURE

Aarseth, Espen: "I Fought the Law: Transgressive Play and the Implied Player," In: Naomi Segal/Daniela Koleva (eds.), *From Literature to Cultural Literacy*, London: Palgrave Macmillan 2014, pp. 180-88.

Carr, Diane: "Playing with Lara," in: Geoff King/Tanya Krzywinska (eds.), *Screenplay: Cinema/Videogames/Interfaces*, pp. 171-80. London, New York: Wallflower Press 2002.

Ihde, Don: *Technology and the Lifeworld: From Garden to Earth*, Bloomington, IN: Indiana University Press 1990.

Klevjer, Rune: "Enter the Avatar: The Phenomenology of Prosthetic Telepresence in Computer Games," in: John Sageng/Hallvard Fossheim/Tarjei Mandt Larsen (eds.), *The Philosophy of Computer Games,* New York, NY: Springer 2012, pp. 17-38.

Latour, Bruno: "On Technical Mediation", in: *Common knowledge* 3, 2 (1994), pp. 29-64.

Latour, Bruno: "Where Are the Missing Masses," in: Deborah J. Johnson /Jameson M. Wetmore (eds.), *Technology and Society, Building Our Sociotechnical Future*, Cambridge, MA: MIT Press 2008, pp. 151-180.

Nielsen, Henrik Smed: *Playing Computer Games: Somatic Experience and Experience of the Somatic*, Aarhus: Digital Aesthetic Research Center 2012.

Rayfield, Donald: *Anton Chekhov: A Life*, New York, NY: Northwestern University Press 2000.

Stiegler, Bernard: *Technics and Time: The Fault of Epimetheus*, Stanford, CA: Stanford University Press 1998.

Verbeek, Peter-Paul: *What Things Do: Philosophical Reflections on Technology, Agency, and Design*, University Park, PA: Penn State Press 2005.

Westerlaken, Michelle: "Self-Fashioning in Action: Zelda's Breath of the Wild Vegan Run," *Philosophy of Computer Games Conference*, Krakow 2017. http://muep.mau.se/handle/2043/23973

LUDOGRAPHY

THE LEGEND OF ZELDA: BREATH OF THE WILD, (Nintendo 2017, O: Nintendo)

The (American) Way of Experiencing Video Game Violence

NATALI PANIC-CIDIC

"THIS IS VIOLENT, ISN'T IT?"

In the US, video games are entitled to First Amendment protection, which protects their designer's right of free speech. Additionally, the artistic value of video games is recognized by the US National Endowment for the Arts (NEA).[1] This is a significant step towards mitigating the concerns that started around 1976 with games such as DEATH RACE (1976) and continued into the 90s with NIGHT TRAP (1992) or MORTAL COMBAT (1992) where people were afraid that graphic content and violence will be emulated in real life.

While the First Amendment protects video games, these concerns are still prevalent in American society. This faulty logic is built on a lack of knowledge about the medium and is fueled by powerful members of society such as the current president of the United States, Donald Trump. In March of 2018, he invited several video game industry representatives to discuss his belief that there is a causal link between video game violence and gun violence in the US. He even opened the meeting with a video reel of random violent acts in video games to prove his point.

According to the 2018 sales, demographics, and user data report by Electronic Software Association (ESA),[2] the top 20 selling games do not have any opposable content in them. Although there are some titles—that are not under the

---

[1] NEA is an American government agency that grants artistic projects.
[2] ESA, Entertainment Software Association: "Essential Facts About the Computer and Video Game Industry 2018," April 2018, pp. 12, http://www.theesa.com/wp-content/uploads/2018/05/EF2018_FINAL.pdf, retrieved 2019.

top selling games—which contain graphic violence, it is this minority that tends to feed negativity into the general public's perception of video games. It is safe to say that Trump's arguments are not only unjustified and based on superficial observations, but they also clearly show that there is a need for a better-informed discourse on video game violence.

This paper argues that video game violence, apart from being a form of entertainment, lets us explore and develop cognitive processes and offers the possibility to experience the sublime. Additionally, I will illustrate how American gun violence history correlates with Trump's claims on game violence and those of other American politicians before him. This step is vital to understand the role of violence in American culture, which in turn exposes the roots of the moral panic[3] towards video games.

In the following, I will first discuss Trump's fallacy in the light of American history and importance of gun violence for today's society. Then, the player's experience of violence in video games is assessed with three parameters that can be linked: cognitive, emotional, and aesthetic. This will reveal possible positive effects of violence exposure. Lastly, I will revise and summarize the results.

THE ROOTS OF AMERICAN VIOLENCE

American history began with the arrival of early European settlers seeking to sever their ties to European church and improving their life and fortune. This goal lead to repeated cycles of separation and regression (e.g. into the wilderness), and the so-called savage wars.[4]

The promised land of milk and honey overwhelmed the settlers with its unfamiliar natural wilderness and 'uncivilized savages,' the Native Americans. The only language the settlers used to address this threat was conflict.

Every step taken towards the West and any act of forming a community was achieved through violent actions. In a continent constantly trying to kill you—either with its landscape, weather, animals, or people—guns became a successful coping strategy. Settler's achieved goals through forming a unique American spirit by "playing through a scenario of separation [cultural heritage], temporary

---

3   Markey, Patrick M./Christopher J. Ferguson: *Moral Combat. Why the War on Violent Video Games is Wrong*, Dallas, TX: BenBella Books 2017, p. 29.

4   Slotkin, Richard: *Gunfighter Nation. The Myth of the Frontier in Twentieth-Century America*, Norman: University of Oklahoma Press 1942, pp. 11-14.

regression to a more primitive or "natural" state [taming the wilderness], and regeneration though violence [guns as a copying strategy]".[5]

What Richard Slotkin describes here is the famous *Frontier Thesis* as introduced by Frederick Jackson Turner on July 12, 1893 in his essay THE SIGNIFICANCE OF THE FRONTIER IN AMERICAN HISTORY. For Turner, the Frontier is characterized by two important intertwined steps. With the arrival of the Europeans, the Wilderness changes them. Then, the changed settlers change the Wilderness by the newly adapted characteristics of the Frontier: adaptability, perseverance, and self-reliance.[6] As Stephen McVeigh summarizes, this then produces individualism and democracy leaving the Frontier as a necessary ingredient to create the unique American character.[7]

Slotkin takes up Turner's Frontier Thesis and concludes that America is rooted in violence from its birth. The settlers find violent acts to be a successful coping strategy and integrate it into the American character, history, and society. Slotkin points to historical events where violence is used by the settlers to show that violence does not solve problems but, in fact, creates only more violence.[8]

If we look at current and historical events, this helps explain Trump's standpoint. For instance, the US prison system is built on violence as demonstrated by the way they are managed and by how they treat their inmates.[9] The most obvious example is the gun culture, which is deeply engrained in the American society, so that guns have become a necessity and 'human right' to the majority of Americans.[10] In addition, as Markey and Ferguson argue in *Moral Combat*, a large body of psychological and social scientific research shows that there is no causal link between acts of violence and video games.[11]

In summary, video games are not responsible for tragic events, such as school shooting or gun violence in general, but deeper historical reasons are to

---

5 Ibid.
6 Turner, Frederick Jackson: *The Frontier in American History*, New York: Dover Publications 1996, p. 4.
7 McVeigh, Stephen: *The American Western*, Edinburgh: Edinburgh University Press 2007, pp. 1-2.
8 R. Slotkin: *Gunfighter Nation. The Myth of the Frontier in Twentieth-Century America*, pp. 11-14.
9 Morgan Jr., W. J.: "The Major Causes of Institutional Violence," in: *American Jails* 23 (2009): pp. 63-68.
10 Cramer, Clayton E.: *Armed America: The Remarkable Story of How and Why Guns Became as American as Apple Pie*, Nashville: Nelson Current 2006.
11 P. M. Markey /C. J. Ferguson: *Moral Combat. Why the War on Violent Video Games is Wrong*.

blame. Markey and Ferguson call this phenomenon *moral panic* which they define as "a tendency for societies to develop overblown fears of an innocuous scapegoat or "folk devil", which is then blamed for a real (or often imagined) social problem".[12]

The next section presents three different approaches to show that exposure to video-game violence is not the cause of gun bloodshed in the US.

COGNITIVE PARAMETER: MIRROR NEURONS

Have you ever experienced that when you yawn next to someone, this person yawns as well? When this happens, we might be dealing with mirror neurons. Consider the following sentence:

> *I grasp a cup to **drink**.*

According to Giacomo Rizzolatti, the mirror neuron system is involved in understanding motor actions and their intention:

"*Motor action* describes a series of motor acts (e.g., reaching, grasping, bringing to the mouth) that allow individuals to fulfill their intention (e.g., eating). When an individual observes a motor act, he or she understands the *what* of the motor act (e.g., grasping an object) but typically is also able to make inferences about *why* the motor act is being performed (e.g., grasping for eating), that is, the intention behind the action of which that motor act is part."[13]

When you observe me reaching for the cup and bringing it to my mouth as in the "*I grasp a cup to drink"* example, you understand what the motor act of reaching means. It further makes inferences that *reaching for drinking* is the *why* I am performing that particular action. Therefore, the motor act is a part of the intention behind an action.

---

12 Ibid, p. 29.
13 Rizzolatti, Giacomo, Leonardo Fogassi, and Vittorio Gallese: "The Mirror Neuron System: A Motor-Based Mechanism for Action and Intention Understanding," in: Michael S. Gazzaniga (Ed.), *The Cognitive Neurosciences*, Cambridge, London: The MIT Press 2009, pp. 625-640, here p. 632.

Eysenck and Keane add that mirror neurons are necessary for empathy, a capacity that is vital to human beings.[14] Mirror neurons basically force us to imitate or simulate intentions of others, which is the foundation for empathy.

GRAND THEFT AUTO V[15] is the perfect example to illustrate how our mirror neurons work and influence players. There is a mission in GTV V called *By the book* that made many people uncomfortable.[16,17] In it, you play as Trevor Philips, a fictional character who is required to torture Ferdinand Kerimov by waterboarding him, beating him with a wrench, giving him electrical shocks, or extracting one of his teeth using pliers. To make things worse, you do not even know if that person is 'bad.'

When the game was released in 2013, it was clear that the events were a satire to the American society and government. This scene is supposed to visualize how "[t]orture's for the torturer or for the guy giving orders to the torturer. You torture for the good times – we should all admit that. It's useless as a means of getting information."[18] Mirror neurons can help players come to such a realization or to start questioning their in-game actions. You as a player probably do not have a problem killing 100 enemies in a game, but you will have issues performing torture on digital characters.[19]

The latter is being experienced by several players of GRAND THEFT AUTO V (2014) (GTA V). If you google "GTA V torture scene," almost every other result is on how to skip that scene. This highly questions causation between video game violence and gun violence as referred by Trump. If players feel uncomfortable torturing a digital character and are looking for a way to avoid it while still playing the game, then it seems unlikely that video games are motivating players with healthy neural systems to commit crimes on their pets, parents, or other humans. Even if a player does commit an act of violence, this does not imply

---

14 Eysenck, Michael W., and Mark T. Keane: *Cognitive Psychology. A Student's Handbook*. Hove, New York: Psychology Press 2010 (6. ed), here pp. 140-141.

15 GRAND THEFT AUTO V (Rockstar Games 2014, O: Leslie Benzies, and Imran Sarwar)

16 Bromwell, Tom: "Is the most disturbing scene in GTA 5 justified? Video and analysis of the scene everyone will talk about," in: *Eurogamer*, September 16, 2013, https://www.eurogamer.net/articles/2013-09-16-is-the-most-disturbing-scene-in-gta5-justified

17 Han: "How to skip the torture scene" [Online forum comment], April 25, 2015, message posted to https://steamcommunity.com/app/271590/discussions/0/61170473031 7 005301/?l=german

18 GRAND THEFT AUTO V (Rockstar Games 2014, O: Leslie Benzies, and Imran Sarwar)

19 Slater, Mel, et al.: "A Virtual Reprise of the Stanley Milgram Obedience Experiments," in: *PloS One* 1, *1* (2006), pp. 1-10.

that there is a causal link between playing video games and violence. Furthermore, studies by Barlett et al. on the effects of violent and non-violent computer games could not confirm any statistically significant results. Rather, playing video games generally increases cognitive performance in problem-solving and attention tasks.[20] Violent acts have only a transient and not a long-lasting effect on players in order for us to understand other's actions and emotions.

EMOTIONAL PARAMETER: VIOLENCE AND COMPASSION

From the perspective of mirror neurons, being exposed to video game violence can help increase a player's ability of understanding complex emotional states, as players can be confronted with hypothetical acts that challenge their worldview and alter their physical and emotional states. Mirror neurons can partially increase empathic abilities. Signals triggered by an expression or emotion are sent through the insula to the limbic system. The latter provides the feeling of the observed emotion.[21]

Telltale's THE WALKING DEAD[22] is constantly activating these emotional brain centers because of the amount of elicited emotions.[23] The game is set in a violent environment, but it is about people and their struggles to survive. Players can feel a character's despair, regret, anxiety, or guilt because of two corresponding narrative perspectives.

From the design perspective, the creative lead directors decided to tell their story through facial animations that convey those moods and emotions, as Jamie Madigan points out.[24] From the play perspective, these facial expressions are

---

20 Barlett, Christopher, et al: "The Effect of Violent and Non-violent Computer Games on Cognitive Performance," in: *Computers in Human Behavior* 25 (2009), pp. 96-102.
21 This is only a very basic explanation for a complex process. Please refer to Michael S. Gazzaniga's *The Cognitive Neurosciences* from 2009 for in-depth insights into neural mechanisms of empathy or neural processes in general. I recommend the chapter on "The Mirror Neuron System: A Motor-Based Mechanism for Action and Intention Understanding," pp. 625-640.
22 THE WALKING DEAD (Telltale Games 2012, O: Sean Vanaman)
23 Madigan, Jamie: "The Walking Dead, Mirror Neurons, and Empathy," in: *Psychology Today,* November 7, 2012, www.psychologytoday.com/us/blog/mind-games/201211/the-walking-dead-mirror-neurons-and-empathy.
24 Ibid.

perfectly integrated into the overall narrative, as scholars such as Madigan or Gerald Farca[25] highlight.

Based on the presented arguments and seen from the context of this paper, understanding other people's emotions, whether simulated or real, helps us (on a global scale) advance our ability for compassion.[26] To avoid any confusion, compassion in this section is not equal to empathy, but it is the next step in processing emotional stimuli. While empathy lets us feel the pain or joy of others, we are not able to resist or control our empathetic abilities. As Tara Well summarizes, too much empathy has negative effects on our well-being, but not compassion.[27] Compassion is a controlled awareness of empathy. We simulate so many emotions through games such as THE WALKING DEAD, THIS WAR OF MINE[28] or DETROIT: BECOME HUMAN[29] that we might actually be expanding our emotional responses.

AESTHETIC PARAMETER: THE SUBLIME

Finally, the perspective on violence in video games presented through Edmund Burke's philosophical concept of the sublime—that takes up the idea of violent acts in video games – might expand the players' emotional responses as introduced in the previous paragraph:

"[W]hatever is in any sort terrible, or is conversant about terrible objects, or operates in a manner analogous to terror, is a source of the sublime. [...] [P]ain is stronger in its operation than pleasure, so death is in general a much more affecting idea than pain. [...] [T]error is a passion which always produces delight when it does not press too close, and

---

25 Farca, Gerald: "Agency and Personal Responsibility in The Walking Dead," in: *Making Games Magazin* 1 (2014), pp. 444-449.
26 Mercadillo, Robert, and Arias Nallely: "Violence and Compassion. A Bioethical Insight into their Cognitive Bases and Social Manifestations," in: *International Social Science* 61 (2010), pp. 221-232.
27 Well, Tara: "Compassion Is Better than Empathy. Neuroscience explains why," in: *Psychology Today*, March 4, 2017, www.psychologytoday.com/intl/blog/the-clarity/201703/compassion-is-better-empathy
28 THIS WAR OF MINE (11 bit studios 2014, O: 11 bit studios)
29 DETROIT: BECOME HUMAN (Sony 2018, O: Quantic Dream)

pity is a passion accompanied with pleasure, because it arises from love and social affection."[30]

According to Burke, there is a threshold between beauty and terror that evokes overwhelming aesthetic responses. A sublime experience is so strong that it can have the power to affect us on many levels because "it anticipates our reasonings and hurries us on by an irresistible force."[31]

The sublime is characterized by being vast, gloomy, dark, threatening, or terrifying. Figure 1 is a screenshot from UNCHARTED 4 (2016) where the protagonist, Drake, for the first time, sees the cave where the treasure he seeks is hidden. He is surrounded by vast and magnificent cliffs that amaze him, but also represent an obstacle. Furthermore, the mist and the blue color give this scene a pinch of beauty and a pinch of a threat to form a sublime setting. This reveals a further characterization of the sublime being at the same time delightful and beautiful. Figure 2 and 3 are taken from THE LAST OF US (2012) and, while the world in this game is mainly occupied by violence, the power of nature can create such a strong feeling of pleasure that might astonish anyone who plays that game. But how is violence in these two examples connected to the sublime?

UNCHARTED 4 and THE LAST OF US are two good examples of games that implement the sublime violence deliberately to remind us about our small size in relation to nature, while using violence to create pleasurable experiences. The sublime violence in UNCHARTED 4 is experienced through its landscape. The violence is motivated by the landscape because the character Nathan journeys to different places. Without landscapes, Nathans' story does not exist and the violent acts he commits are not necessary. While playing UNCHARTED 4,[32] the player is constantly being reminded of nature's strength in comparison to Nathan, e.g. Nathan has to endure violent storms or travel through huge mountains. As Shinkle points out, the "sublime sensation [...] also involves an awareness of the limits of the self."[33] The "terrifying" scenography in Uncharted 4 is an active agent that stands it Nathan's way.

---

30 Burke, Edmund: *A Philosophical Enquiry into the Sublime and Beautiful*, New York: Oxford University Press 2015, here pp. 33-34, 39.
31 Ibid. p. 47.
32 Ibid.
33 Shinkle, Eugénie: "Videogames and the Digital Sublime," in: Athina Karatzogianni and Adi Kuntsman (Eds .), *Digital Cultures and the Politics of Emotion*, London: Palgrave Macmillan, 2012, pp. 94-108.

Figure 1: A sublime perspective of the Libertalia island.

Source: UNCHARTED 4. A THIEF'S END (Sony 2016, O: Neil Druckman, Bruce Straley/ Naughty Dog).

Figure 2: Ellie and players finding beauty in a violent world.

Source: THE LAST OF US (Sony 2012, O: Neil Druckman, Bruce Straley/Naughty Dog).

Figure 3: Nature taking over.

Source: THE LAST OF US (Sony 2012, O: Neil Druckman, Bruce Straley/Naughty Dog).

On the other hand, THE LAST OF US has nature as primarily source of sublime violence. In this game's world, there are non-human enemies created from nature. Also, the human opponents are the product of their, what has become, violent environment. Even the two protagonists are motivated by nature's powers, e.g. the main protagonist Ellie is infected by nature's own virus. Her being infected is what eventually drives the game.

Violence and (sublime) nature are linked in both instances. Acts of violence come from the sublime landscapes and nature. Taking sublime elements of nature and nature from these titles, would dilute them to having no goal, aesthetic, or affective power. The product could not be called a finished game or game at all.

Furthermore, following Kant, Shinkle defines the sublime affect as "a means of testing subjective boundaries of exploring and affirming the limits of the human self and its relationship to nature."[34] Both games have that sublime affect, which one is more affective is a topic for another paper. What still needs to be answered is how the violent sublime is expanding emotional responses?

Sublime experiences create pleasure, as Burke,[35] Kant,[36] or Shinkle[37] argue, and there is a high chance that pleasurable experiences move us emotionally.

---

34   E. Shinkle: "Videogames and the Digital Sublime," p.96.
35   E. Burke: *A Philosophical Enquiry into the Sublime and Beautiful*.

This is because other people's emotions need to be processed by our brain in order to be fully understood. Violent content as presented in THE LAST OF US can be sublime. Its affective power can be used to criticize a society, challenge our worldviews, or simply exist as a pleasurable piece of art that will still change us emotionally or at least expand emotional responses. Even if a sublime encounter does not lead to an immediate response, it will still affect us on some level which sometimes cannot be expressed through words.

Lastly, what connects sublime experiences to the first cognitive parameter is that they move us emotionally and emotions need to be activated cognitively.

Conclusion

We have seen that violence in American society is a social problem and that it dates to the early settlers. Instead of scheduling a meeting with a few representatives from the game industry and making some uneducated guesses, Trump should tackle the violence issue at its core: society and gun law.

This paper argues that video game violence can have positive effects on players, and I presented three ways to support this view.

The example of GTA V and the science behind mirror neurons show that video game violence has only transient effects on players. This is necessary and possible through mirror neurons. Mirror neurons are vital for our understanding of other people's intentions, actions, and emotions.

Digital violence in THE WALKING DEAD (2012) has the beauty of constantly tapping into our emotional systems because it requires interpretation of evoked emotional responses. We can learn to be more compassionate.

Lastly, THE LAST OF US and UNCHARTED show how violent content can engage players on many levels which can expand emotional responses.

Nonetheless, it should be noted that mirror neurons are still highly debated among neuroscientist because some studies tend to exaggerate what their discovery explains about our human nature.[38] Furthermore, the presented parameters

---

36 Kant, Immanuel: *Critique of Judgement*, trans. Werner S. Pluhar, Indianapolis: Hackett Publishing Company 1987.
37 E. Shinkle: "Videogames and the Digital Sublime."
38 Jarrett, Jamie: "Mirror Neurons: The Most Hyped Concept in Neuroscience?" in: Psychology Today, December 10, 2012, www.psychologytoday.com/us/blog/brain-myths/201212/mirror-neurons-the-most-hyped-concept-in-neuroscience, retrieved 2019.

offer starting points for further research that relies on data from longitudinal studies.

Literature

Barlett, Christopher, et al: "The Effect of Violent and Non-violent Computer-Games on Cognitive Performance," in: *Computers in Human Behavior* 25, *1* (2009), pp. 96-102.

Burke, Edmund: *A Philosophical Enquiry into the Sublime and Beautiful*, New York: Oxford University Press 2015.

Cramer, Clayton E.: *Armed America: The Remarkable Story of How and Why Guns Became as American as Apple Pie*, Nashville: Nelson Current 2006.

Eysenck, Michael W., and Mark T. Keane: *Cognitive Psychology. A Student's Handbook*. Hove, New York: Psychology Press 2010 (6. ed).

Farca, Gerald: "Agency and Personal Responsibility in The Walking Dead," in: *Making Games Magazin* 1 (2014), pp. 444-449.

Hartmann, Tilo: "The 'Moral Disengagement in Violent Videogames' Model," in: *Game Studies* 17, *2* (2017).

Iacoboni, Marco: *Mirroring People*, New York: Farrar, Straus and Giroux 2008.

Kant, Immanuel: *Critique of Judgement*, trans. Werner S. Pluhar, Indianapolis: Hackett Publishing Company 1987.

Kocurek, Carly A: "The Agony and the Exidy: A History of Video Game Violence and the Legacy of Death Race," in: *Game Studies* 12, *1* (2002).

Markey, Patrick M./Christopher J. Ferguson: *Moral Combat. Why the War on Violent Video Games is Wrong*, Dallas, TX: BenBella Books 2017.

McVeigh, Stephen: *The American Western*, Edinburgh: Edinburgh University Press 2007.

Mercadillo, Robert, and Arias Nallely: "Violence and Compassion: A Bioethical Insight into their Cognitive Bases and Social Manifestations," in: *International Social Science* 61, *200-201* (2010), pp. 221- 232.

Morgan Jr., W. J.: "The Major Causes of Institutional Violence," in: *American Jails* 23, *5* (2009): pp. 63-68.

Raine, Adrian: *The Anatomy of Violence: The Biological Roots of Crime*. New York: Vintage Books, 2013.

Rizzolatti, Giacomo, Leonardo Fogassi, and Vittorio Gallese: "The Mirror Neuron System: A Motor-Based Mechanism for Action and Intention Understanding," in: Michael S. Gazzaniga (Ed.), *The Cognitive Neurosciences*, Cambridge, London: The MIT Press 2009, pp. 625-640.

Slater, Mel, et al.: "A Virtual Reprise of the Stanley Milgram Obedience Experiments," in: *PloS One* 1, *1* (2006), pp. 1-10.
Shinkle, Eugénie: "Videogames and the Digital Sublime," in: Athina Karatzogianni and Adi Kuntsman (Eds.), *Digital Cultures and the Politics of Emotion*, London: Palgrave Macmillan, 2012, pp. 94-108.
Slotkin, Richard: *Gunfighter Nation. The Myth of the Frontier in Twentieth Century America*, Norman: University of Oklahoma Press 1942.
Turner, Frederick Jackson: *The Frontier in American History*, New York: Dover Publications 1996.

LUDOGRAPHY

DEATH RACE (Exidy 1976, O: Exidy)
DETROIT: BECOME HUMAN (Sony 2018, O: Quantic Dream)
GRAND THEFT AUTO V (ROCKSTAR GAMES 2014, O: LESLIE BENZIES, AND IMRAN SARWAR)
MORTAL COMBAT (Midway 1992, O: Ed Boon, and John Tobias)
NIGHT TRAP (Sega 1992, O: Digital Pictures)
THE LAST OF US (Sony 2012, O: Neil Druckman, Bruce Straley/Naughty Dog)
THE WALKING DEAD (Telltale Games 2012, O: Sean Vanaman)
THIS WAR OF MINE (11 bit studios 2014, O: 11 bit studios)
UNCHARTED 4. A THIEF'S END (Sony 2016, O: Neil Druckman, Bruce Straley/Naughty Dog)

ONLINE MEDIA

Bromwell, Tom: "Is the most disturbing scene in GTA 5 justified? Video and analysis of the scene everyone will talk about", in: *Eurogamer*, September 16, 2013; https://www.eurogamer.net/articles/2013-09-16-is-the-most disturbing-scene-in-gta5-justified, retrieved 2019.
ESA, Entertainment Software Association: "Essential Facts About the Computer and Video Game Industry 2018", April 2018; http://www.theesa.com/wp-content/uploads/2018/05/EF2018_FINAL.pdf, retrieved 2019.
Han: "How to skip the torture scene" [Online forum comment], April 25, 2015; https://steamcommunity.com/app/271590/discussions/0/611704730317005301/?l=german, retrieved 2019.

Jarrett, Jamie: "Mirror Neurons: The Most Hyped Concept in Neuroscience?," in: *Psychology Today*, December 10, 2012, www.psychologytoday.com/us/blog/brain-myths/201212/mirror-neurons-the-most-hyped-concept-in-neuroscience

Madigan, Jamie: "The Walking Dead, Mirror Neurons, and Empathy," in: *Psychology Today,* November 7, 2012; www.psychologytoday.com/us/blog/mind-games/201211/the-walking-dead-mirror-neurons-and-empathy, retrieved 2019.

Well, Tara: "Compassion Is Better than Empathy. Neuroscience explains why," in: *Psychology Today*, March 4, 2017; www.psychologytoday.com/intl/blog/the-clarity/201703/compassion-is-better-empathy, retrieved 2019.

Video Game Violence from the Perspective of Cognitive Psychology
Role Identification and Role Distancing in A WAY OUT

CHRISTIAN ROTH

INTRODUCTION

The connection between the performance of violence in video games and violence in the real world is still a topic of much debate. Despite the maturing of the field, the majority of mainstream video games are still built on the premise of violence. This ranges from mowing down dozens of virtual passersby with a car in open world games such as the GRAND THEFT AUTO series, to the virtual killing of other (non-)player figures in first-person shooters such as CALL OF DUTY: WWII (2017) or DOOM (2016). Watching young adults interacting with highly violent content can easily be disturbing, as graphics, animations, and sound improved tremendously over the last two decades, creating scenes with strong emotional impact. The depiction of video game violence seems to become more and more realistic, and thus ever more disturbing when perceived by non-gamers.

Assuming, interpreting and judging the experience of players by merely watching them is easily misleading, as each player perceives the game based on their individual involvement. Their mental processing is mostly focused on the interpretation of a game situation in relation to its in-game meaning. Thus, the player's mind is presumably busy with decision-making, resulting in adequate reactions and promising strategies. For a player, game mechanics involving violent behavior give immediate feedback on in-game performance and competence: *Did my shot hit the target? Am I actually doing damage? How should I adapt my strategy in case of failure?*

Non-gamers observing the same violent content are likely to find other aspects prevalent: Why are they killing each other? This is gruesome, this can't be healthy entertainment! What if virtual violence influences real-world behavior?

While this difference in perception between player and observer might be true for action-oriented, competitive games, how do players perceive violence in games that give their characters more depth and meaning? Games that entice players to identify with a given or chosen character allow for emotional experiences that are driven by gameplay in a narrative context. Does this change their perception of virtual violence?

This paper aims to shed light on the meaning-making processes of players through the concepts of ludonarrative hermeneutics, role identification, and role distancing. Role identification, which allows the player to inhabit the character, contributes to the immersive experience and player engagement. Role distancing, on the other hand, enables the player to remain detached from a given or chosen role and thus any related atrocities committed while in it. An example of this would be moral disengagement, which suppresses feelings of guilt or remorse, which would otherwise hamper enjoyment.[1] In theory, video games allow players to take on the role of characters that are distinct from themselves, and supply a premise that justifies the actions that must be performed—including violence —without impacting the world outside of the game.

Adept game designers create character motivations that blend with those of the player's, blurring the distinction between what is play and what is real. However, this balance between identification and distance is maintained only for as long as players understand on a cognitive level that they are operating within a simulated environment. Within this environment the rules inherent to the simulation apply and interaction with the system triggers a process of meaning-making that includes understanding a character's motives, objectives and levels of agency. In the narrative action game, A WAY OUT (2018), players are confronted with a moral dilemma of killing, or being killed by, their in-game partner and real-life co-player. This situation forces them to question their understanding of their characters' motives and their agency as players.

In a recent study, Van Nuenen, Koenitz, and I analyzed the A WAY OUT dilemma and players' reactions to it from the perspective of ludonarrative meaning-making.[2] Ludonarrative meaning-making as a cognitive psychological ap-

---

1   Hartman, Tilo/Vorderer, Peter: "It's Okay to Shoot a Character: Moral Disengagement," in: *Violent Video Games Journal of Communication* 60, *1* (2010), pp.94 -119.
2   Roth, Christian/Van Nuenen, Tom/Koenitz, Hartmut: "Ludonarrative Hermeneutics: A Way Out and the Narrative Paradox," in: Rebecca Rouse/Hartmut Koenitz/Mads

proach offers a promising framework for further discussion and analysis of video game violence and player perception.

LUDONARRATIVE MEANING-MAKING

When playing a video game, players are engaged in a constant meaning-making process. This happens on two levels 1) when players interact with the game system and derive meaning purely based on a mechanical level and 2) when they interpret the resulting narrative meaning of game events and their actions.[3]

In many violent video games, killing another character does not change the game's narrative. Killing player avatars in a competitive multiplayer game such as CALL OF DUTY: WWII, DOOM or MORTAL KOMBAT (1992), results in the temporary death of that play figure. Following a penalty time or at the beginning of a new round, players are back in the game; their characters are revived without any narrative explanation. This underlines the fictitious nature of such games. The meaning that can be derived is therefore: violence and death are different in this virtual environment and have only temporal consequences. The fatalities in MORTAL KOMBAT are gruesome but, with the press of a button, the player character that was torn to pieces is alive again, ready for another fight. Players reflect what the system allows them to do and what narrative they can extract from their actions. The reading of such rules and mechanics make it clear that the simulated game environment does not follow the rules of the real world, where violence is felt as physical pain and where gunshots can be lethal.

While interacting with a game system, players are continuously extracting information to understand past and present events and to plan their actions. A game designer creates meaning through the use of signifiers and feedback clues to help players understand what is happening. Players in return make sense of the given information, based on previous experiences, for instance, with similar games, their intentions, expectations, beliefs, and morals (Figure 1).

Haahr (eds.), *Proceedings of the 11th International Conference on Interactive Digital Storytelling*, Springer 2018.

[3] Ibid.

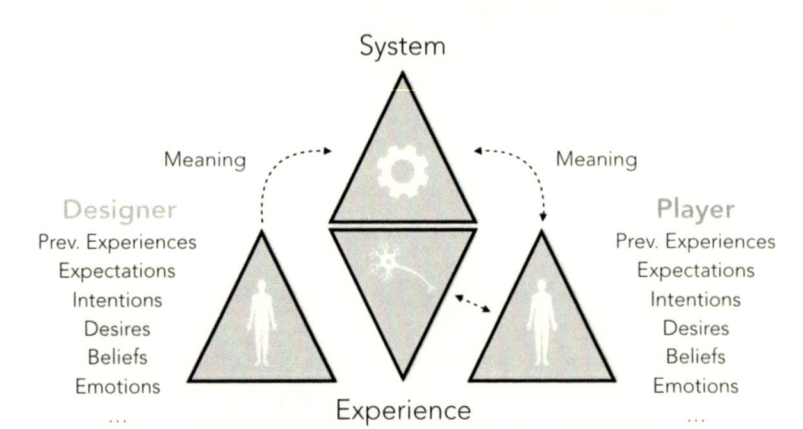

Figure 1: Factors influencing the player's ludonarrative meaning-making.

This meaning-making process can be understood from a cognitive perspective on narrative. Following cognitive narratologists Herman[4] and Bordwell,[5] narrative meaning is a cognitive construct, or mental image, built by the interpreter in response to the narrative construct. Intuitively, we might understand narrative as located within a narrative product like a printed book or a movie. However, the cognitive perspective stresses the point that narrative resides within the human mind as a mental construct. Through interaction with a game such as A WAY OUT, players create mental narratives in an effort to make sense of the simulated environment and constantly check if their assumptions are consistent. New information leads to an updated projection and conflicting information can lead to perceived dissonance. Thus, video games can be understood to have two types of narrative agents: on the one hand what is conveyed, implied as intended by the designer on a system level, and on the other hand what is performed, interpreted, assumed, expected, speculated and planned by the player. Within the following case study, we will look at potential dissonance players experience during the closing sequences of A WAY OUT.

---

4 Herman, David: *Story Logic*. Lincoln, NV: U of Nebraska Press 2002.
5 Bordwell, David: *Poetics of Cinema*. New York, NY: Routledge 2007.

CASE STUDY: A WAY OUT

A WAY OUT is a game about the prison break of Leo and Vincent, two inmates who meet in jail and become unlikely partners in planning a daring escape. Leo is an experienced gangster, convicted of a number of violent crimes. He is impulsive and brutish. Vincent, on the other hand, is a banker. He is freshly convicted of embezzlement and murder. He is smart, calm and looks for rational solutions to problems. This uneven pair is united not just by their goal to escape from jail, but by their wish for revenge on Harvey, who framed Leo and killed Vincent's brother. The two have to cooperate to achieve a number of tasks, both during their escape and after. This cooperation shows in the gameplay itself. Teamwork is at the core of A WAY OUT's design. It is played in split screen, with each player seeing both character perspectives. This setup shows the dependency of both characters (and players) on each other. Only at crucial points of interaction do both screens merge, emphasizing shared experiences. This underlines the gradual development of friendship while juxtaposing dichotomic choices, which contrast Leo's violent tendencies with Vincent's careful approach. Competitive elements are present but typically make way for a cooperative approach that leads to success. This changes radically once the pair has killed Harvey. Vincent turns out to be an undercover cop, who used Leo to get to Harvey. Now the gameplay turns combative, culminating in a showdown where both characters fight over a single gun. Once a player character reaches the gun, the game leaves no choice but to execute the other, leaving out alternative actions or the option of non-participation (see Figure 2).

Figure 2: Character Vincent is about to kill Leo.

Source: Screenshot of A WAY OUT.

Method

The study[6] uses Let's Play (LP) videos as samples for the evaluation of player responses to A Way Out's mechanical and narrative twist. Let's Play is a style of videos documenting the playthrough of a video game, usually including commentary by the gamer. The first selective step consisted of watching a number of popular Let's Play videos (N = 40), showing up under the search query "A Way Out Let's Play"[7] on the popular video platform YouTube. The selection was then narrowed to 20 videos for the conversational analysis as some responses to the telling moment seemed not to yield any new insights. To transcribe the findings of the selected LP sessions we turned to Conversation Analysis (CA)[8] which attempts to discover and describe the structure of interactions produced through successive turns.

For the purpose of this analysis we focus on two important scenes at the end of the game, when the narrative twist takes place. In the first scene, Vincent reveals that he is an undercover cop and Leo becomes aware of his betrayal. The second scene is the showdown in which Leo and Vincent fight each other, ending with one of them dead. We decided to exclude heavily edited Let's Play videos as we were interested in a recording situation that resembles an unedited think-aloud protocol. While the kinds of performative behavior that Let's Players demonstrate are likely not the same kinds of behavior found in everyday, unrecorded home scenarios, we found that the performativity allows us more insight, not less, into the ways in which players respond to the tensions arising out of the particular combination of gameplay and narrative. YouTubers *act out* their responses, often using performative aspects of mass media, namely hyper-ritualizations and dramatic scriptings, in the Goffman's sense.[9] We view the videos we analyze as "over-performed" interactive narrative user experiences, telling of the ways in which games produce affective responses in their players.

---

6   Roth, Christian/Van Nuenen, Tom/Koenitz, Hartmut: "Ludonarrative Hermeneutics: A Way Out and the Narrative Paradox," in: *ICIDS conference proceedings* 2018.
7   Example videos can be found here: https://kotaku.com/watching-people-react-to-a-way-outs-ending-is-too-good-1824119464, retrieved 2019.
8   Wooffitt, Robin: *Conversation Analysis and Discourse Analysis*. London, Thousand Oaks, New Delhi: SAGE Publications 2005.
9   Goffman, Erving: Frame analysis: *An essay on the organization of experience*. Boston, MA: Northeastern University Press 1974.

ANALYSIS

As the final confrontation between the characters commences, all of the players remain highly motivated to continue, as this event at first seems in line with the gradual escalation of the competitive elements that it has included from the beginning. Then, after a long fight scene between the characters, Leo and Vincent (both badly wounded) stumble onto a gun at the edge of a building's rooftop. Still enthralled by the game's ludonarrative harmony, players shout and curse at each other as their movements bring them closer to the gun. Then, as one player reaches the gun, they are confronted with the results: the camera pans behind the winning character, and all they can do is to pull the trigger. In all of the analyzed LPs in which Vincent was the victor, players did not want to shoot the other, trying out a myriad of ways to avoid the outcome. Some temporarily put down the controller in refusal; others started playing meta-games with the mechanism of pointing the gun at the player; yet others simply waited for a long time. A closer look at a particular response[10] demonstrates the disbelief of players as the game forces their hand and negates the ludonarrative harmony of comradery that has characterized the majority of the playthrough. The following conversations are transcribed using the Jefferson system,[11] showing the timing of utterances and between turns (in tenths of a second). It also captures features of the production of talk, such as emphasis (underlined), intonational shift (up ↑, down ↓), speaker in-breath (h) and out-breath (.h), and stretching of the preceding sound (:). The amount of 'h's and colons denote the length.

```
P Vincent:   wha- aim, i don't wanna shoot. (.5)
P Leo:       oh::: my god (.4)
P Vincent:   i don't gonna i'm not gonna shoot (.) are you kidding
             me? {switches between pointing and pointing away at Leo}
             (.3) do I have to? (.3) no, what if i don't. (.6) i don't wanna
             d(h)o this (.h) ↑ it's gonna f(h)orce me ↑
P Leo:       (h) (.h) you don't have an option. (.3)
P Vincent:   (h) i don't wanna do this (.3) I really don't wanna do this (.2)
P Vincent    [holy shit]
P Leo:       [ahh:: this is so] (.hh)
P Vincent:   {shoots} ohh:: ↓ my god. ↓ why? (..) ohh:: come o::n
P Leo:       (.hhh) (hhh)
```

---

10 T&J Nexus: *A Way Out, Vincent Reaction*. YouTube Video has been deleted.
11 Wooffitt, Robin: *Conversation Analysis and Discourse Analysis*. London, Thousand Oaks, New Delhi: SAGE Publications 2005.

P Vincent: fuck this ga::me. No:: i didn't w(h)ant it to e(h)nd like this

What we see here is a familiar mapping of players onto their characters, despite the fact they have played a round character for the entirety of the game. Players refer to their characters in the first person yet simultaneously reflect on their own position as players. Additionally, they use the subject pronoun "it" to refer to the agency of the game itself, clearly no longer a game in the sense of free movement within a more rigid structure,[12] but a system of predetermined choices instead. We also see players rationalizing the choices made by their characters and, instead of resisting, "playing along" and roleplaying as the idiosyncratic character they are controlling. One player who gets to shoot while playing the cop, Vincent, rationalizes by saying "Well, it's my job" and "there's no honor among thieves" to his co-player. At the same time, players who control the character who shoots the other discursively, distance themselves from the act they engage in. One player, while having used first and second person pronouns throughout the scene, slips into third person directly after his avatar shot the other:

P Vincent: ↑ why did he ↑ shoot him? (.) i mean i guess he-
P Leo: leo definitely was gonna kill him
P Vincent: ↑ yeah i mean ↑ he (.) had (..) all the right to

The player demonstrates what Goffman calls "role distancing"[13] which pertains to the act of presenting one's 'self' as being removed or at a distance from the role one is being required to play. Role distancing is a strategy that allows the individual to play the role but to resist it. For example, by keeping your eyes open when asked to pray or say grace, you communicate to the group by role distancing that you are making no commitment to the role. As such, people get to deny "the virtual self that is implied in the role for the allocating performers."[14] While role distancing is a well-known trait from everyday life, it has not yet been connected to the complex performances of streamed video game play.

Let's Players have to negotiate the space between themselves as performers vis-a-vis both the game (which fixes them into certain roles) and their potential audience (which may expect certain roles to be played). In this particular case,

---

12 Salen, Katie/Zimmerman, Eric: *Rules of Play: Game Design Fundamentals*, Cambridge, MA.: MIT Press 2004.
13 Goffman, Erving: *Frame analysis: An Essay on the Organization of Experience*. Boston, MA: Northeastern University Press 1974.
14 Ibid., p. 108.

their linguistic behavior signals a dissonance not between their play and the narrative, but between their prior investment in their role and the new one they are forced to take. The re-evaluation of that *self* occurs the moment the players are forced to perform an action to which they do not subscribe.

Let's Play videos construct a broader narrative of demonstrative play. In this context, the use of role distancing shows the subtle ways in which players claim authorship over parts of the game experience they cannot control. It also demonstrates that the ludonarrative dissonance,[15] here, is not primarily one between mechanics and narrative. The dissonance is not necessarily created by a tension between the story of the betrayed partner and the mechanical consequences that flow from that. Instead, the dissonance is caused by the different hermeneutics of the designer and that of the player—the meaning as it is intended by the designer versus the meaning as it is interpreted by each player.

CONCLUSION

A WAY OUT creates a collaborative experience while highlighting the friction between collaboration and competition, which characterizes many friendships. Each player is capable of relating this social model to their own life.

Thus, the violent act becomes a moral decision, game narrative and personal narrative mix and conflict. Killing the former partner feels like a betrayal to many players, especially to those in the role of undercover cop Vincent. Here the act of the execution violates the player's assumptions and expectations of what the game should be like and how their character should behave. The permanent death of their co-op player's character is something that crosses the boundaries of the game world as it taps into the moral understanding of the real world, thus creating a dissonance that breaks the game flow. This forced break allows for even more reflection on the unwanted action. Role distancing is a method to clearly differentiate between the game character and real-world feelings. Future research on violence in video games needs to further investigate how the identification of the player with their character and their actions in-game, both freely decided and enforced by the game's system, influence their meaning-making processes in the real world.

---

15 Hocking, Clint: Ludonarrative Dissonance in Bioshock: "The problem of what the game is about," in: *Click Nothing*, October 7, 2007; http://clicknothing.typepad.com/click_nothing/ 2007/10/ludonarrative-d.html, retrieved 2019.

LITERATURE

Goffman, Erving: *Frame analysis: An Essay on the Organization of Experience*. Boston, Massachusetts: Northeastern University Press 1974.

Hartman, Tilo/Vorderer, Peter: "It's Okay to Shoot a Character: Moral Disengagement in Violent Video Games," in *Journal of Communication* 60, *1* (2010), pp.94 – 119.

Herman, David: *Story Logic*. Lincoln, Nevada: U of Nebraska Press 2002

Bordwell, David: *Poetics of Cinema*. New York: Routledge 2007

Roth, Christian/Van Nuenen, Tom/Koenitz, Hartmut: "Ludonarrative Hermeneutics: A Way Out and the Narrative Paradox," in: Rebecca Rouse/Hartmut Koenitz/Mads Haahr (eds.) *Proceedings of the 11th International Conference on Interactive Digital Storytelling*, Dublin, Ireland: , Springer 2018, pp. 93-106.

Salen, Katie/Zimmerman, Eric: *Rules of Play: Game Design Fundamentals*, Cambridge, Massachusetts: MIT Press 2004.

Wooffitt, Robin: *Conversation Analysis and Discourse Analysis*. London, Thousand Oaks, New Delhi: SAGE publications 2005.

LUDOGRAPHY

A WAY OUT (Electronic Arts 2018, O: Hazelight Studios)
CALL OF DUTY: WWII (Activision 2017, O: Sledgehammer Games)
DOOM (Bethesda Softworks 2016, O: id Software)
GRAND THEFT AUTO V (Rockstar Games 2013, O: Rockstar North)
MORTAL KOMBAT (Midway 1992, O: Midway)

ONLINE MEDIA

Hocking, Clint: Ludonarrative Dissonance in Bioshock: "The problem of what the game is about," in: *Click Nothing*, 2007; http://clicknothing.typepad.com/click_nothing/2007/10/ludonarrative-d.html, retrieved 2019.

The Playing Voyeur
Voyeurism and Affect in the Age of Video Games

ANH-THU NGUYEN

INTRODUCTION

Public opinion on the relationship between video games and violence remains a point of controversy. In an interview from 2016, anti-gaming activist and attorney Jack Thompson sees a clear connection between violence in video games and the Columbine High School shooting from 1999, pointing out the shooters' DOOM (1993) references in their suicide video.[1] The World Health Organization further solidified non-compliant behavior associated with video games in 2018 when video games addiction was included in its catalogue of mental health conditions.[2] Yet, in a recently published study by the Oxford Institute, video games were not found to be the reason for aggressive behavior.[3] Despite scientific evidence of the contrary then, the negative effects often associated with video games remain a point of interest in the media. Looking at similar past discourses of other media formats, it is worth recalling the debate on *Lesesucht* or reading addiction in the 18th century in Germany, in which excessive reading was said to

---

1 Wilbur, Brock: "Attorney Jack Thompson And His Personal Vendetta Against Video Games," in: *Inverse*, April 7, 2016 http://www.inverse.com/article/12633-attorney-jack-thompson-and-his-personal-vendetta-against-video-games, retrieved 2019
2 WHO, World Health Organization: http://www.who.int/features/qa/gaming-disorder/en/, retrieved 2018.
3 Przybylski, Andrew K/Weinstein, Netta: "Violent video game engagement is not associated with adolescents' aggressive behavior: evidence from a registered report," in: *Royal Society open science* 6, 2 (2019), pp. 1-16.

have caused sickness and memory loss.[4] Shortly before the popularization of video games, a nearly identical debate on the dangers of television consumption took place. Perhaps the debate and fear surrounding video games is a repetition of past discourses, occurring whenever a new medium takes its place culturally and socially.

Thus, rather than describing video games merely as violent, this paper is a transdisciplinary approach aimed at widening the vocabulary that seeks to describe the relationship of the consumer to its medium. The terms violence and addiction are too imprecise to meaningfully describe the effects of either television or video games. Without disregarding those terms entirely, the description of violence or addiction in games will be closely interlinked with voyeurism and affect borrowed from (reality) television studies. The game in question throughout this paper will be the life-simulation game THE SIMS 4 (2014).

VOYEURISM

In an essay written in 1993, David Foster Wallace writes: "Sorry to sound judgmental, but there it is: six hours a day [of television] is not good."[5] The concern is usually that spending 'too much' time watching television or playing video games could lead to losing the sense of what 'really' matters and, in the worst-case scenario, to forgetting about reality entirely. In another instance, the aforementioned activist Jack Thompson even draws a direct comparison between GRAND THEFT AUTO: SAN ANDREAS (2004) and THE SIMS 2 (2004) in relation to nude content. Nudity or pornographic content often falls together with violence in critique formulated against games. In an open letter to Leland Yee, a Democratic Senator in California at the time, Thompson urged Yee to conduct hearings on what he calls an "even worse abuse [than GRAND THEFT AUTO: SAN ANDREAS] by the video game industry":

"It turns out that Electronic Arts [...] has allowed the player, with a simple cheat code that even the New York Times is distributing, to remove a 'censor flag' in the game in order to make the players nude, including the Sims children. [...] This is not artistic license, in my

---

4   Von König, Dominik: "Lesesucht und Lesewut," in: Herbert G. Göpfert (Ed.), *Buch und Leser*, Hamburg: Hauswedell 1977, pp. 89-124.

5   Wallace, Foster: "E Unibus Pluram: Television and U.S. Fiction," in: *Review of Contemporary Fiction* 13 (1993), pp. 151-194, here p. 163.

opinion. It is conspiracy to violate the law at the expense of vulnerable children, behind their parents' backs."[6]

To a certain extent, Thompson is correct to draw the connection between these two games. His primary concern is the consumption of these revealing images and in the further discussion, the allegedly nude content will be taken as a formal quality of video games and analyzed. The risks, to which Thompson refers as abuse, will be commented on in detail later. To address the media-specific formality, the capacity of each medium to capture their audience, the first central term will be introduced here: voyeurism.

Originally coined by Sigmund Freud in an essay on sexual aberrations, the fourth edition of the DIAGNOSTIC AND STATISTICAL MANUAL OF MENTAL DISORDERS describes voyeurism as a psychologically-assessed disorder: "a sexual disorder or form of sexual deviance," "[t]he act of looking ('peeping') is for the purpose of achieving sexual excitement, and generally no sexual activity with the observed person is sought."[7] However, in his book VOYEUR NATION, Clay Calvert correctly assesses that sexual voyeurism is "inapplicable for much of the mediated voyeurism on television newsmagazines and reality-based shows."[8] Calvert borrows Peter Keough's definition of voyeurism in relationship to violent and sexually explicit movies as an "urge to gaze at the alien and the intimate"[9] and transforms the term into mediated voyeurism to describe the general practice of looking and watching in media. The term refers to the "consumption of revealing images of and information about others' apparently real and unguarded lives, often yet not always for purposes of entertainment but frequently at the expense of privacy and discourse, through the means of the mass media and the internet."[10] Calvert also observes that the history of mediated voyeurism is rooted long before television had become popularized and refers to year 1050 when the legend of Lady Godiva emerged, one of the oldest legends of voyeur-

---

6   N.N.: "Video Game Cases – The Sims 2," http://www.jackthompson.org/video_game_cases/the_sims_2.htm, retrieved 2019
7   APA, American Psychiatric Association: *Diagnosis and Statistical Manual for Mental Disorders. Fourth Edition*, Washington DC: American Psychiatric Association 1994, p. 532.
8   Calvert, Clay: *Voyeur Nation. Media, privacy and peering in modern culture*, Boulder, Colorado: Westview Press 2000, here p. 49.
9   Keough, Peter: *Flesh and Blood: The National Society of Film Critics on Sex, Violence, and Censorship*, San Francisco: Mercury House 1995, p. 2.
10 C. Calvert: *Voyeur Nation. Media, privacy and peering in modern culture*, p. 23.

ism.[11] In what Calvert describes as the step to electronic voyeurism, the history of mediated voyeurism moved beyond legends, folklore, and literature when photography became a common practice in journalism at the beginning of the 20th century.[12] From here, it would not take many decades until television combined the voyeuristic practices long rooted in Western history to embed them in the cinema screen, for instance in Alfred Hitchcock's REAR WINDOW (1954) and reality television formats such as BIG BROTHER (1999).

With regards to reality television, the immediate connection with voyeurism is made rather clear, but less so with video games. After all, as video games require player input to be played, they are inherently interactive: "[...] if someone does not act on it, they are not playing a video game, they are doing something else."[13] Whilst this is a key difference to a rather passive consumption of images on the television screen, the terms "voyeurism" and "interactivity" should not be seen as mutually exclusive. Rather, they should be seen as different modi operandi utilized by video game designers to produce immersion.

Here, immersion is understood in its broadest sense as "the sensation of being surrounded by a completely other reality, [...] that takes over all of our attention, our whole apparatus."[14] There is, however, some criticism regarding this definition, as it is too one-sided and ringing close with the fear surrounding video game addiction, the complete loss of reality. In contrast, Britta Neitzel stresses that immersion or submersion into new worlds always requires knowledge of both realities, of here and there, and immersion is therefore an ambivalent experience, rather than a one-way journey.[15] Taking this definition of immersion then, players need to be aware of all the worlds they immerse themselves into, both the virtual and the real world.

---

11 Ibid., here p. 36. The legend of Lady Godiva is also linked with the emergence of Peeping Tom: "According to some versions of the tale, when Lady Godiva rode naked on a horse [...] a young man named Tom – known today as the Tom behind the moniker Peeping Tom – dared to gaze at Godiva. For this, he was, depending on the particular account or version of the retelling, killed or blinded." (p. 36)

12 Ibid., pp. 38-40.

13 Landay, Lori: "Interactivity," in: Mark J. P. Wolf/Bernard Perron (eds.), *The Routledge Companion to Video Game Studies*, New York: Taylor & Francis 2014, pp. 173-184, here p. 181.

14 Murray, Janet H.: *Hamlet on the Holodeck. The Future of Narrative in Cyberspace*, New York: Free Press 1997, pp. 98-99.

15 Neitzel, Britta: "Involvierungsstrategien des Computerspiels," in: Michael Hagner (ed.), *Theorien des Computerspiels*, Hamburg: Junius Verlag GmbH 2012, pp. 75-103, here p. 79.

The game THE SIMS 4 should illustrate that both voyeurism and interactivity may enter a symbiotic relationship, rather than separate modes of experiencing media. The premise of the fourth installation of the franchise remains the same as its predecessors as a life-simulation game with open-ended gameplay and an absence of a prescribed narrative. Instead, the player is usually tasked with building a (happy) life surrounding their character, also called "sim," which often requires finding a job, making money, and building up a fortune in order to improve the sim's lifestyle.

In its premise alone, to simulate reality, a quick connection to reality television can be made in the sense of a highly constructed space: "[...] reality television is a distinctive cultural form wherein the tensions between fact and fiction create a space within which producers and audiences 'round out' reality."[16] The same aesthetic, fact and fiction, is the main appeal of THE SIMS 4, to 'play' a realistic world. The intersection of reality television and THE SIMS 4 will be discussed in a later section in detail. For now, it should be noted that the player may design a specific cast of characters and set them out to simulate a scripted life, all of which is controlled by the player in place of a producer. In fact, the player, who has the same control over the game as a producer has over a television show, incorporates a voyeuristic gaze into its gameplay. The game strongly resembles a BIG BROTHER (1999) set-up in which the player can look at their sim at any given time, from almost any perspective. Typically, the player will overlook the entire household from a bird's-eye perspective. This permanent visibility is a vital game mechanic that also bestows the player with full control. In addition to permanent visibility, the player is also given the option to freeze, slow, or speed up time. These tasks are interactive and require active input from the player.

Despite the extent of control, THE SIMS 4 is insofar remarkable as it invites the player to do nothing at all to play the game. On top of the voyeuristic gaze, the player may choose to completely remove themselves from the position of the player and become a voyeur instead. As each sim can act of its own free will,[17] they are able to make decisions autonomously. Although THE SIMS 4 is a rather ideal case to demonstrate the integrity of voyeurism in gameplay, it is not the only game to capitalize on it. For instance, another game to consider in the con-

---

16 Hill, Annette: "Reality TV Experiences: Audiences, Fact and Fiction," in: Laurie Ouellette (ed.) *A Companion to Reality Television*, Chichester: John Wiley/Sons, Inc. 2014, pp. 116-133, here p. 116.
17 Free will is an option in the settings of the game that determines how autonomous sims may be. If set on high, they will go after their basic needs and entertain themselves. If set on low, they will do nothing unless the player commands them do so.

text of voyeurism is WATCH DOGS (2014), in which the player is often tasked with hacking into surveillance cameras in order to grasp the outline of the level they must overcome. Given that the setting of WATCH DOGS is a surveillance society, voyeurism is closely linked to surveillance, as players can exert influence over their enemies by hacking into surveillance cameras but may also watch and observe passersby in the city and hack into their private messages, learning about their profession and bank details. In the sense of mediated voyeurism, the WATCH DOGS player is similar to a player of THE SIMS 4, who might observe a sim taking a bath, having sex, and doing other seemingly mundane but intimate things in private spaces. Whilst voyeurism and surveillance are closely linked, particularly with games that draw heavily on surveillance technology, THE SIMS 4 will serve as the primary example of voyeurism in games.

Stealth gameplay mechanics require the player to use the voyeuristic gaze to gain information and knowledge, even beyond games like THE SIMS 4 and WATCH DOGS. As an action survival game, THE LAST OF US (2013) has multiple ways of conquering enemies and levels but stealth gameplay promises to be the most sufficient and economical way in terms of the player's resources. Stealth gameplay requires information and knowledge of the level, including close observation of enemies, and almost always halts the player for a short moment to study the surroundings with care. With THE SIMS 4 as the ideal example, it is vital to note that the capacity to change between the voyeur and the player fluidly is not only a gameplay mechanic embodied in this game, but already integrated in countless others. With reference to Thompson's critique on THE SIMS 2, the voyeuristic practices in games are deeply linked to inherent formal qualities of games as an interactive medium, rather than specifically tied to violent or nude images in video games.

AFFECT

The concern that violence or nudity in video games translate into abnormal real-life behavior grounds itself in the effect of media consumption in general. With the preceding discussion on voyeurism, the precise question then should be: What kind of effect does voyeurism have on the voyeur or the player?

The term introduced here to tackle this question is affect. In the introduction of THE AFFECT THEORY READER, Gregory J. Seigworth and Melissa Gregg define affect as the following: "Affect arises in the midst of in-between-ness: in the capacities to act and be acted upon. Affect is an impingement or extrusion of a momentary or sometimes more sustained state of relation as well as the passage (and the duration of passage) of forces or intensities."[18] This transdisciplinary term is rather loose and broad in its definition. Discourse on affect had initially begun to circulate in feminist and queer theory to investigate the body, power, and emotions.[19] More recently, affect has also become of interest in (reality) television studies. Misha Kavka writes on her experiences as a voyeur of American reality television formats such as WIPEOUT (2008) or FEAR FACTOR (2001), in which candidates are faced with extreme bodily tasks to test their limits in somewhat extreme versions of the cult show TAKESHI'S CASTLE (1986): "Every now and again I have had to look away, literally averting my eyes when an expectant face crumpled or a vulnerable joint popped and my own body became tremulous, queasy."[20] Kavka calls these forces materialized affectivity due to the greater focus of "kinetic operations of the human body in relation to its physical environment."[21] Slow-motion, repetitions of scenes, close-ups of the candidate's pained face, or disgusting challenges involving insects or other animals are ways of production to capitalize on the pain that candidates have to go through in order to immerse their audience. Reality television production consciously works with these materialized affects to provoke these forces even across the television screen. It is therefore evident that affected bodies do not have to be physically close to other bodies to transmit these forces; the screen alone suffices to do the same, as it is a "necessary part of this situatedness."[22] An analysis of affective forces requires the identification of these bodies first. Whilst in reality television it is the candidates and the voyeur on both sides of the screen, where are those bodies situated in video games?

To answer this question, it is necessary to introduce the term avatar in its most generic sense: "the user's representative in the virtual universe."[23] The definition of avatar may be contested,[24] they may vary in degrees of visual repre-

---

18 Seigworth, Gregory J/Melissa Gregg: *The Affect Theory Reader*, Durham North Carolina: Duke University Press 2009, here p.1.
19 Clough, Patricia Ticineto: *The Affective Turn. Theorizing the Social*, London, Durham: Duke University Press 2007, here p. 9.
20 Kavka, Misha: "A Matter of Feeling. Mediated Affect in Reality Television," in: Laurie Oullette (ed.), *A Companion to Reality Television*, John Wiley / Sons, Inc. 2014, pp. 459-477, here p. 459.
21 Ibid., p. 464.
22 Ibid., here p. 461.
23 Filiciak, Miroslaw: "Hyperidentities. Postmodern identity patterns in massively multiplayer online role-playing games", in: Mark J.P. Wolf/Berhard Perron (eds.), *The Video Game Theory Reader*, New York: Routledge 2003, pp. 87-102, here p. 89.
24 For a further discussion of the avatar, see MY AVATAR, MY SELF (Waggoner, 2009).

sentation or how they are controlled by the player and other games may operate perfectly fine without one. This is not to say that affect does not work in games without an avatar or that the various types of avatar are irrelevant, yet the avatar remains the most interesting subject when looking at affected bodies in video games. This is because the avatar is the body of the player in the virtual game, the body on the other side of the screen, just as Kavka's clashing bodies. Unlike Kavka's real physical bodies, however, the virtual body is linked to the player through a real-time feedback loop. They are the means to experience and, most importantly, to interact with the virtual world. For video game designers and players alike, an avatar is the greatest tool for immersion. In its visual representation, the avatar may be a speck of pixels in PONG (1972), a round character with their own narrative storyline such as Joel from THE LAST OF US, or a self-drafted but flat character, like in MONSTER HUNTER: WORLD (2018). In a study conducted by Casey Hart with the role-playing game SKYRIM (2011), results showed that players do indeed project their personality onto the avatar to a certain extent.[25] Furthermore, the player is also subjected to different kinds of virtual affect through game mechanisms when the avatar gets hurt, suffers, or feels pain. Games utilize their affective tools efficiently and consciously to achieve the desired affect from avatar to player, maybe in even better ways than television.

Affect theory usually concerns itself with bodily genres, i.e. horror films or pornographic content that can evoke strong bodily reactions from their audience. THE SIMS 4 is therefore a rather unlikely candidate for an affective video game, as many horror games naturally capitalize on these affective forces as an immersive strategy. Whilst not purely a horror game, THE LAST OF US has its moments of horror given its apocalyptic setting and infected humans as enemies. The game features particularly gruesome death scenes of Joel, the player's avatar. When dying in the hands of a special type of monster called 'clicker,' which the player frequently encounters, the player loses all control of their avatar and is forced to watch as the creature bites into Joel's neck, tearing it apart while he screams in agony. These violent and perhaps disturbing scenes act as a warning

---

25 Hart, Casey: "Getting Into the Game: An Examination of Player Personality Projection in Videogame Avatars", in: *Game Studies*17, 2017: http://gamestudies.org/1702/articles/hart. The study investigated several dimensions of projection onto the avatar, which resulted in players not necessarily projecting their entire self onto the avatar but use the avatar as "facilitators for experimentation [with alternative self-concepts] than for vehicles for direct projection." One dimension that was consistent was that of "openness to experience", a "desire to seek out opportunities and an inclination toward growth and self-actualization." (n.p.)

to let the player feel something has gone awfully wrong. Ultimately, these moments of materialized affect are meant to provoke unsettling physical reactions from the player and create the tension necessary for the survival gameplay in THE LAST OF US.

Of course, THE SIMS 4 is neither a survival nor a horror game. Yet, it is possible to evoke affective forces by pushing the sim to its physical limit, at times resulting in death. There are many ways a sim can die, including natural causes such as old age, being tasked to do chores outside of their skill level, or simple neglect. However, given the free will setting, death is unlikely to actually happen. Rather than unintentionally, players seek the death of their sim quite consciously. In PLAYERS UNLEASHED!, Tanja Sihvonen writes:

"I still remember the day I learned how to kill my Sims. [...] So I set off to build pools, directed my Sim kids to take a dip and then I removed the ladder, watching the little children exhaust themselves to death in the water. [...] Some starved to death or were abducted by aliens. And for some I bought a cute little pet – with the result of them getting ill and even dying from the 'Guinea Pig Disease' that was raising havoc among THE SIMS players in the early 2001."[26]

As far as affect is concerned, it is crucial to observe that all the above descriptions are physical in nature; they convey the avatar's bodily sufferings. As a life-simulation, it is necessary for these sufferings to be visible to the player to react accordingly: the sims are quite expressive avatars, emotionally, vocally (despite speaking a pseudo-language), and physically. It requires a conscious effort and a player's active input for these deaths to occur, which are often orchestrated by the player. Much like the production of a reality television show, the player acts as the producer and voyeur who consumes the images they have set up to happen. Horror is not needed to provoke intensities of affect. THE SIMS 4 may be subtle in its affect, yet players can actively seek and amplify it.

---

26 Sihvonen, Tanja: *Players Unleashed! Modding* The Sims *and the Culture of Gaming*, Amsterdam: Amsterdam University Press 2011, here p.7.

Addressing the Debate

Returning to Thompson's critique of THE SIMS 2, the terms of voyeurism and affect are perhaps different ways of exploring the relationship of the player to the game and its impact on them. With regards to the preceding discussion, voyeurism is an omni-present practice, and to refer to Keogh's definition again, the urge to look at the alien and intimate did not come with video games, or even television. Calvert's mediated voyeurism should then be understood in the context of the rising intensity of voyeuristic practices in an age coined by mass media and internet technology. As far as THE SIMS 2 or THE SIMS 4 is concerned, they are games that actively interlace moments of playing and watching with varying degrees of affect. Even if nude contents may have higher affective forces in a sexual context, they are primarily moments in interlacing modes of game experience, rather than, in Thompson's words, a conspiracy by the video game industry. Thus, while his connection between THE SIMS 2 and GRAND THEFT AUTO: SAN ANDREAS was perhaps not too far-fetched, he not only ignores the formal qualities of video games as a medium but also ignores the cultural practice of gazing and looking that goes beyond media.

In Thompson's same letter to Leland Yee, he also criticizes the game's potential to be modded, i.e. to be altered by the player community, possibly adding explicitly pornographic content to the game: "Electronic Arts has encouraged the 'mod community,' [...] to create 'skins' for the nude figures that are explicit in nature as they depict genitalia, with some specific mods appealing to 'fetishists' as well. The unlocked nudity dovetails nicely into this modding."[27] Despite the existence of these explicit pornographic mods, they are not to be mistaken as symptoms of fetishists, an abnormal player base, or even a threat to young consumers. Without dwelling on the extensive modding culture surrounding the franchise, sexual mods only make up a small percentage of those available online. Many of these are simple cosmetic additions, whilst others improve the user interface or even offer additional and detailed career paths for the player to choose from. Tanja Sihvonen's first encounters with mods were indeed of sexual nature; these would allow her characters to have uncensored sex and to engage in intercourse beyond the parameters of the bed, as usually restricted by the game.[28] However, rather than a place that facilitates fetishism or sexual satisfaction, these are ways of experimenting with the game and pushing its limits. In terms

---

[27] N.N.: "Video Game Cases – The Sims 2," http://www.jackthompson.org/video_game_cases/the_sims_2.htm, retrieved 2019

[28] T. Sihvonen: *Players Unleashed! Modding* The Sims *and the Culture of Gaming*, p.7.

of affect, modding may also be considered a way to amplify affective forces by going beyond what the gamer offers. For Sihvonen, it created a new experience of play: "[…] I also learned to utilize all kinds of cheats, tricks and hacks so I could create interesting scenarios in the game to amuse myself (and not all were that morbid)."[29]

While video games are in need of critique as much as any other media, Thompson fails to do so in a productive manner. Video games play with voyeuristic practices already prevalent in culture, not to mention in mediated spaces. Affect may be the result of these practices but to what extent and in what manner they take place may be as varied as the term itself. This paper offers an insight of how critique could be formulated, rather than jumping to quick conclusions without addressing the specific formal aspects of video games. Future research could thus address what exactly these affective forces are and how they influence the player and gaming experience.

CONCLUSION

This paper is an approach to reshape the way to speak of violence in video games and has made clear that the term violence is often too imprecise for a nuanced discussion of the video game medium. Drawing on the terms voyeurism and affect from television studies and expanding on how techniques of voyeurism and affect are already present in media consumption, this study demonstrates basic principles of video games and how these are already well integrated in the way games are designed. THE SIMS 4 was taken as an ideal game to bridge (reality) television and video games. The fast pace at which video games and game design change requires a better vocabulary to debate and formulate game critique. A sensible discourse can thus only be achieved if all parties involved share the interest of understanding each media platform and their specific constitution. Should the relationship between violence and media continue to be of interest, the discourse needs to foster an understanding of various media forms and the corresponding terms to comprehend their relationship to its consumers in a mediated space.

---

29 Ibid.

Literature

Calvert, Clay: *Voyeur Nation. Media, Privacy and Peering in Modern Culture*, Boulder, Colorado: Westview Press 2000.

Clough, Patricia Ticineto: *The Affective Turn. Theorizing the Social*, London, Durham: Duke University Press 2007.

Filiciak, Miroslaw: "Hyperidentities. Postmodern Identity Patterns in Massively Multiplayer Online Role-Playing Games," in: Mark J.P. Wolf/Berhard Perron (eds.), *The Video Game Theory Reader*, New York: Routledge 2003, pp. 87-102.

Hart, Casey: "Getting into the Game: An Examination of Player Personality Projection in Videogame Avatars," in: *Game Studies* 17, 2 2017; http://gamestudies.org/1702/articles/hart, retrieved 2019

Hill, Annette: "Reality TV Experiences: Audiences, Fact and Fiction," in: Laurie Ouellette (ed.) *A Companion to Reality Television*, John Wiley / Sons, Inc. 2014, pp. 116-133.

Kavka, Misha: "A Matter of Feeling. Mediated Affect in Reality Television," in: Laurie Oullette (ed.), *A Companion to Reality Television*, John Wiley / Sons, Inc. 2014, pp. 459-477.

Keough, Peter: *Flesh and Blood: The National Society of Film Critics on Sex, Violence, and Censorship*, San Francisco: Mercury House 1995.

Landay, Lori: "Interactivity," in: Mark J. P. Wolf/Bernard Perron (eds.), *The Routledge Companion to Video Game Studies*, New York: Taylor & Francis 2014, pp. 173-184.

Murray, Janet H.: *Hamlet on the Holodeck. The Future of Narrative in Cyberspace*, New York: Free Press 1997.

Neitzel, Britta: "Involvierungsstrategien des Computerspiels," in: Michael Hagner (ed.), *Theorien des Computerspiels*, Hamburg: Junius Verlag GmbH 2012, pp. 75-103.

Seigworth, Gregory J/Melissa Gregg: *The Affect Theory Reader*, Durham North Carolina: Duke University Press 2009.

Sihvonen, Tanja: *Players Unleashed! Modding* The Sims *and the Culture of Gaming*, Amsterdam: Amsterdam University Press 2011.

Von König, Dominik: "Lesesucht und Lesewut," in: Herbert G. Göpfert (Ed.), *Buch und Leser*, Hamburg: Hauswedell 1977, pp. 89-124.

Przybylski, Andrew K/Weinstein, Netta: "Violent video game engagement is not associated with adolescents' aggressive behavior: evidence from a registered report," in: *Royal Society Open Science* 6, 2 (2019), pp. 1-16.

Waggoner, Zach: *My Avatar, My Self*, Jefferson, North Carolina: McFarland & Company, Inc., 2009.

Wallace, Foster. "E Unibus Pluram: Television and U.S. Fiction," in: *Review of Contemporary Fiction* 13, 2 (1993), pp. 151-194.

LUDOGRAPHY

DOOM (id Software 1993, O: id Software)
GRAND THEFT AUTO: SAN ANDREAS (Rockstar Games 2004, O: Rockstar North)
GRAND THEFT AUTO V (Rockstar Games 2013, O: Rockstar North)
MONSTER HUNTER: WORLD (Capcom 2018, O: Capcom)
PONG (Atari 1972, O: Atari)
THE LAST OF US (Sony Computer Entertainment 2013, O: Naughty Dog)
THE SIMS 2 (EA Games 2004, O: Maxis)
THE SIMS 4 (EA Games 2014, O: The Sims Studio)
SKYRIM (Bethesda 2011, O: Bethesda Game Studios)
WATCH DOGS (Ubisoft 2014, O: Ubisoft Montreal)

FILMOGRAPHY

BIG BROTHER (NL 1999)
FEAR FACTOR (USA 2001)
REAR WINDOW (USA 1954, D: Alfred Hitchcock)
TAKESHI'S CASTLE (JP 1986)
WIPEOUT (USA 2008)

ONLINE MEDIA

N.N.: "Video Game Cases – The Sims 2," http://www.jackthompson.org/video_game_cases/the_sims_2.htm, retrieved 2019.

WHO, World Health Organization: http://www.who.int/features/qa/gaming-disorder/en/ from September 2018.

Wilbur, Brock: "Attorney Jack Thompson And His Personal Vendetta Against Video Games," in: *Inverse*, April 7, 2016; http://www.inverse.com/article/12633-attorney-jack-thompson-and-his-personal-vendetta-against-video-games, retrieved 2019.

The Spectacle of Murder

Over-Aestheticized Depiction of Death in Horror Video Games

CORNELIA J. SCHNAARS

INTRODUCTION

The implementation of game mechanics that depict violent acts, whether abstract and playful or explicit and brutal, has been prevalent in video games since the medium's advent. However, there appears to be a significant disparity across genre boundaries concerning respective design strategies; one need only compare the elimination of enemies in family-friendly platform games like SUPER MARIO (1983–) and shooter games with explicit depictions of violence, not to mention franchises like MORTAL KOMBAT (1992–), which seem to celebrate the act of violence per se. As Gareth Schott states: "[v]iolence has the capacity to be expressed in a number of different ways, both within and across game genres."[1] In order to limit the vast field of violence in video games, violence will be understood here mainly as a deliberate, physical act of one person (or rather, character) harming another, not taking into consideration psychological violence and self-harm. In addition, the focus will be on the act of violence marked by the most destructive nature: murder. Across media boundaries, the horror milieu seems to be predestined to feature death and murder, in particular, because "[h]orror offers death as spectacle and actively promises transgression; it has the power to promote physical sensation."[2]

---

1   Schott, Gareth: *Violent Games. Rules, Realism and Effect (Approaches to Digital Game Studies* 3), New York: Bloomsbury Academic 2016, here p. 176.
2   Krzywinska, Tanya: "Hands-On Horror," in: *Spectator: The University of Southern California Journal of Film & Television* 22 (2002), pp. 12–23, https://cinema.usc.edu/assets/098/15877.pdf, here p.13.

Today, the horror film genre is strongly associated with splatter, gore, and torture porn—such as in the SAW (2004) series. Some video game adaptations of horror films reflect this tendency, like the multiplayer game FRIDAY THE 13TH: THE GAME (2017) with its portrayal of horrific murder scenes which have been 'transferred' into the game in order to depict as much brutality as possible.[3] Yet, such transposing is not typical in most horror-based games. Even within horror games,[4] there is a substantial diversity in terms of how violence is represented. Depictions of violence do not simply follow an unwritten guideline to be as horrifying and gory as possible.

In a narrative sense, killing in horror games is usually enacted as a means of self-defense (sometimes as the only way to survive against monstrous threats).[5] Enemies are seldom human beings like the player-character but are either overtly evil or already dead and/or monsters of some kind (for example, the ubiquitous zombie). Regardless, enemies are not on the same level as the player-character, who often has access to limited resources in the face of manifold threats. If this stark contrast to the evil- or monstrousness of enemies is not maintained, the player might be confronted with sheer moments of astonishment or even shock.

The SILENT HILL-series (1992–2014) is known to feature player-characters who have no particular fighting skills. Yet they have to escape the titular town's forces of evil as well as the character's own specters that haunt them from the past. Just a few minutes into SILENT HILL: DOWNPOUR (2012), the protagonist is locked in with a fellow inmate, whom he has to eliminate. While this sequence serves as a tutorial for the player in terms of combat mechanics, it also evokes emotions in them quite contrary to the will to survive they might anticipate from a (survival) horror game. Having to kill a human being—crouching in front of you, dressed only in a towel around the hips, defenseless and vulnerable—is something entirely different from shooting monsters or zombies who are threat-

---

3   See Bloody Disgusting: "Friday the 13th: The Game—Motion Capture Shoot," YouTube Video, 3:41, February 25, 2016, https://www.youtube.com/watch?v=i4Tx7RsUT9Y

4   Horror, in this paper, is not understood as a distinct genre. Rather as atmospheric aesthetics, a milieu (see King, Geoff/Krzywinska, Tanya (eds.): *Screenplay. Cinema/Videogames/Interfaces*, London: Wallflower 2002, p. 27). By contrast, survival horror is regarded as a genre as it establishes various mechanical, representational, and narrative design choices that, taken together, constitute a survival horror experience.

5   This essence has been distorted in some horror shooters in which the elimination of zombie hordes might evoke a sensation of (racist) power rather than mere a survival instinct and relief when the imminent danger is averted.

ening your life.[6] The power constellation between the inmates is clearly asymmetrical in terms of weaponry and physique. The non-player character tries to escape, and the player has to press a button to attack him. The player's genre-based expectation of fighting inhumane monsters—which can sometimes be evaded—is subverted right at the beginning of the game. While nudging the player into beating and stabbing an unarmed, human character, the game removes the player's possibility to think of this act as necessary to survive. Instead, the inevitable act of murder induces a feeling of horror. Violence, in this case, becomes an "offensive obstacle that the player is required to manage."[7]

Rune Klevjer notes that there is a tendency in academia to analyze violence in video games merely on a representational plain, which is—so to say—laid on top of the mechanical system as to make gameplay plausible.[8] For instance, the splatter of blood indicates that the target has been hit, and thus the shot successful. In the review of Gareth Schott's publication VIOLENT GAMES, Klevjer summarizes that Schott sees "[v]iolence as an added theme, a visual spectacle, a mode of representation rather than a mode of action,"[9] which Klevjer regards as "unnecessarily restrictive in the context of a public debate on the role of violence in games."[10] Klevjer is right that such a generalized claim is too limited to account for all kinds of video game violence. However, there might be examples of aestheticized violence that, in their explicitness, have no narrative nor mechanical function and primarily contribute to the sensationalism of violence.

THE EVIL WITHIN 2

Recurring, only slightly modified, scenes in THE EVIL WITHIN 2 (2017) stage homicides as thought-provoking art installations. The very moment of death has been conserved in time and place, emphasizing the representational reiteration of

---

6   With regard to the narrative, the scene is just a dream and the other inmate is a criminal, a child molester, and a murderer, which is only revealed much later in the game. However, in this initial scene, the player not only has to witness but to actively engage in an act that—without the necessary context—might be perceived as utterly baseless and vile.

7   G. Schott: *Violent Games*, p. 167.

8   Klevjer, Rune: "It's Not the Violence, Stupid," in: *Game Studies* 18 (2018). http://gamestudies.org/1801/articles/review_klevjer.

9   Ibid.

10 Ibid.

ephemeral brutality for the sake of pleasure. Apart from vague narrative clues and the creation of suspense regarding the threat of a serial killer that is roaming the game world, this explicit installation of violence seems to have no significance in terms of gameplay.

With his concept of "wound culture," Mark Seltzer exposes a collective fascination with violence in American society. The conflation of private and public spheres engenders a pathological communality characterized by taking pleasure in witnessing violence.[11] For Seltzer, the serial killer is a symptom of this society and not necessarily a pathological individual, not an insane deviant of society's sanity. Instead, the culture itself is the pathological subject in a way, producing serial killers as a result of its obsession with bodies being harmed. In such a setting, violated and wounded human bodies become a spectacle most people—secretly or otherwise—like to watch:

> "One discovers again and again the excitations in the opening of private and bodily and psychic interiors: the exhibition and witnessing, the endlessly reproducible display, of wounded bodies and wounded minds in public. In wound culture, the very notion of sociality is bound to the excitations of the torn and opened body, the torn and exposed individual, as public spectacle."[12]

---

11 "[T]he very idea of 'the public' has become inseparable from spectacles of bodily and mass violence. The spectacular public representation of violated bodies, [...] these 'atrocity exhibitions' indicate something more than a taste for senseless violence. They have come to function as a way of imagining the relations of private bodies and private persons to public spaces. These exhibitions make up the contemporary pathological public sphere, our wound culture" (Seltzer, Mark: *Serial Killers. Death and Life in America's Wound Culture*, New York: Routledge 1998, here p. 21).

12 M. Seltzer: *Serial Killers*. p. 21.

Figure 1: Framing of murder within a photoshoot setting.

Source: Screenshot by author.

Figure 2: View through camera.

Source: Screenshot by author.

Twenty years after its publication, Seltzer's point continues to resonate. The spectacle of violence seems to satisfy an inherent human curiosity. For instance, people gather around crash sites, take pictures and videos of the carnage without helping the victims; also alarming trends like *happy slapping* spread among teenagers,[13] and the interest in TV series that revolve around the solving of (fictional or real) crime continues.[14] Sensationalism and voyeurism are thus closely linked to the *spectacleness* of violence and body horror. Murder as one particularly extreme form of violence can be linked even more closely to the notion of spectacle, because death and murder are ever-recurring motifs in fiction and art. This might be best explained with Edmund Burke's notion of the sublime:

"The ideas of pain, sickness, and death, fill the mind with strong emotions of horror [...] Whatever is fitted in any sort to excite the ideas of pain, and danger, that is to say, whatever is in any sort terrible, or is conversant about terrible objects, or operates in a manner analogous to terror, is a source of the sublime; that is, it is productive of the strongest emotion which the mind is capable of feeling."[15]

He refers to elements of nature that—in their concurrent beauty and menace—induce an overwhelming sensation in the viewer. This can be transferred to mediated (inter)human acts of committing violence and murder in particular. "(If) any human act evokes the aesthetic experience of the sublime, certainly it is the act of murder."[16] Like natural threats, we seem to be likewise fearful of and fascinated by murderers, as long as we are safe to experience them at a distance.

---

13 For further analysis of this phenomenon and others see Hilgers, Judith: *Inszenierte und Dokumentierte Gewalt Jugendlicher: Eine Qualitative Untersuchung von 'Happy Slapping'-Phänomenen*, Wiesbaden: VS Verlag 2011.

14 Seltzer identifies series such as ER (1994–2009) as paradigmatic of wound culture. (M. Seltzer: *Serial Killers*. p. 22) By extension, this also applies to crime series such as CRIMINAL MINDS (2005–) as they too deal with ever new wounds and "torn and opened bodies." (Ibid.) Real-life murder cases and serial killers seem to get exploited increasingly with particular focus on the murderer's motives, for example in the recent Netflix series' KILLER WOMEN WITH PIERS MORGAN (2016–2017), I AM A KILLER (2018), and CONVERSATIONS WITH A KILLER: THE TED BUNDY TAPES (2019).

15 Burke, Edmund: *A Philosophical Enquiry into the Origin of our Ideas of the Sublime and Beautiful; With an Introductory Discourse Concerning Taste*, New York: Harper & Brothers 1844 [1757], here p. 51.

16 Black, Joel: *The Aesthetics of Murder. A Study in Romantic Literature and Contemporary Culture*, Baltimore: Johns Hopkins University Press 1991, here p. 14.

THE EVIL WITHIN 2 portrays murder in the moment of the bullet piercing the victim's head: blood sprays into the air, forming an arch over the floating corpse as cerebral matter emerges from the shattered skull in slow-motion. The display repeats itself every few seconds in an infinite loop, accompanied by classical music. Moreover, the player has the option to frame the carnage through the lens of the camera, exposing a voyeuristic gaze as if secretly looking into a private room. Here, murder is framed as a work of art. This strange relation between violence and art can be perceived on an affective level, as Joel Black points out:

"Violent acts compel an aesthetic response in the viewer of awe, admiration, or bafflement. If an action evokes an aesthetic response, then it is logical to assume that this action—even if it is a murder—must have been the work of an artist."[17]

AESTHETICIZATION OF VIOLENCE

With regard to the overall spatial representation in THE EVIL WITHIN 2, it can be noted that the entire city hall is set as an art gallery. The entrance hall, for instance, is decorated with red curtains up to the high ceiling, creating a scenery reminiscent of an empty theatre, a stage respectively. The heterotopian setting is continued in the narrow hallways with an abundance of framed photographs adorning the walls, further functioning as exhibition space. Most of them show individual human body parts. At the crime scene, the murder victim is hovering in the air. The transparent cube around the body appears like a sort of gas-like or liquid display case. Once this case is entered, the classical music, which has been playing inside the room all along, becomes louder and a choir joins the instruments. The most salient feature of this crime scene tableau might be the over-aestheticized framing of the blood emanating from the victim's wounded head.

For Margaret Bruder, the depiction of violence is aestheticized if it is "stylistically excessive in a significant and sustained way."[18] The blood in THE EVIL WITHIN 2 seems exaggerated in color, volume, and consistency. This aestheticization and excess can be accounted for with respect to the player's possible reaction, as "the mode of representation is instrumental to the creation of af-

---

17 Ibid., p. 39.
18 Bruder, Margaret E.: *Aestheticizing Violence, or How to Do Things with Style*, Bloomington, Indiana University 1998, http://www.gradnet.de/papers/pomo98.papers/mtbruder98.htm.

fect."[19] Thus, there appears to be a thin line between a powerful depiction of violence and one that could come across as too realistic and hence revolting. As Stan Beeler states with regard to the TV-series Dexter (2006–2013), which also features copious amounts of blood: "[T]he use of color—especially blood red—is hyper-real. [...] The brightly, highly saturated primary color, comicbook visual aspects of the series provide a counterpoint to the ethical distortion."[20] To some extent, meaning seems to become irrelevant in such depictions. The intensity, beauty, or simple artfulness one might experience is the essential takeaway. As Roland Barthes' punctum cannot be explained rationally, such an aestheticization affect is observed on a more visceral level.[21]

Furthermore, stylistic devices, such as slow-motion, enhance the effect of aestheticized blood on screen: by decelerating the representation, the transition of bodily states can become comprehensible in its continuity and inevitability, which is only reinforced by the bright signaling effect of the color red.[22] In reference to bullet time, coined by THE MATRIX (1999) franchise to convey that time has become slowed down, so that bullets are distinctly visible in their trajectories, some games even implement this bullet time feature as a central gameplay mechanic (for example, MAX PAYNE's (2001) famous shootdodge mechanic). However,

"[i]n MAX PAYNE 3 (2012) employing bullet time or shootdodge does not necessarily heighten the effect or outcome of simulated violence [...] the game's appropriation of temporal manipulation is primarily ludic and therefore quite distinct from the relationship

---

19 Krzywinska, Tanya: "Gaming Horror's Horror: Representation, Regulation, and Affect in Survival Horror Videogames," in: *Journal of Visual Culture* 14 (2015), pp. 293-297, https://doi.org/10.1177/1470412915607924, here p. 295.

20 Beeler, Stan: "From Silver Bullets to Duct Tape: Dexter versus the Traditional Vigilante Hero," In: Douglas L. Howard (ed.), *Dexter. Investigating Cutting Edge Television*, London: Tauris 2010, p. 221-230, here p. 228.

21 The "punctum is that accident, which pricks me (but also bruises me, is poignant to me)." (Barthes, Roland: *Camera Lucida. Reflections on Photography*. Translated by Richard Howard. New York: Hill and Wang 1981 [1980], p. 27; orig. emphasis) *Punctum* is that essence in a work of art that engages the spectator's or reader's subconscious mind and produces subjective bliss or pain in a way that cannot be rationalized.

22 Peschke, André: "Gewalt kann schön sein – schön brutal," *Gamestar*, July 13, 2013, https://www.gamestar.de/artikel/gewalt-kann-schoen-sein-schoen-brutal,3025598 .html

that has been formed between slow motion and the aestheticization of violence within film."[23]

The murder displays in THE EVIL WITHIN 2 are reminiscent of yet another quite popular form of slow-motion, the so-called kill-cams or bullet-cams, which are especially common in action games, for instance in RED DEAD REDEMPTION 2 (2018). Whereas the shootdodge mechanic in MAX PAYNE has a clear function within gameplay, kill-cams and the slow-motion display in THE EVIL WITHIN 2 primarily serve the sensationalism and voyeurism of the spectator in contemporary wound culture. Slow-motion, in these cases, allows for the more conscious perception of bodily harm, since the mutilation of the human body can be watched in close detail and does not seem to serve another purpose. Gareth Schott emphasizes the *spectacleness* of this form of slow-motion:

"[u]nlike bullet time, the effect of bullet cam is an elaboration, exaggeration, and aestheticization of an action that is otherwise performed many times within active play in order to create a conscious spectacle."[24]

Therefore, the repetitiveness of enemy elimination as a mandatory part of the game's mechanic, is counterposed with the unique modality of each murder. In slow-motion, the shooting of a non-player character is aestheticized in detailed imagery, revealing the projectile's as well as the blood's trajectories.

PHOTOGRAPHY AND THE MAD ARTIST

In THE EVIL WITHIN 2, the temporal loop creates a spectacle in eternal repetition, to be celebrated again and again. This aspect is emphasized by the camera and the reflector umbrella which blatantly give the scene the setup of a photo-shoot. By spatially integrating the camera into the artistic arrangement and also by making it available for interaction with the player, photography reflects the person behind the camera, not only the 'object' in front of it. Apart from the aestheticized depiction of violence as a spectacle itself, THE EVIL WITHIN 2 thus involves a concomitant reminder of the act of inspection itself. Art cannot be perceived without the human senses; it always already contains statements about the spectator—emphasizing the act of seeing as central to the notion of spectacle.

---

23 G. Schott: *Violent Games*, p. 183.
24 Ibid., p. 186.

Photography adds to this another layer of inspection insofar as the camera contains implications of voyeurism: looking through the viewfinder is like looking through a peephole, rendering the space inside the frame more private than it might seem without the intimate framing. Conversely, the setup discloses the murder as an act that has happened in private surroundings but has been transferred into public space, an exhibition piece to be gazed at. Photography is also the medium of remembrance; it freezes moments in time and space and is always already linked to death as "the inventory of mortality."[25] Photos make us realize our own mortality and always include the notion of the ultimate *punctum* being one's impending death.

Photography, then, is a medium well-chosen for a serial killer-artist such as Stefano Valentini in THE EVIL WITHIN 2, who employs it to create his art in multiple ways. He is fascinated by the destruction of human bodies, transforming them into art installations and also capturing them on film. Coming back to Seltzer's concept of wound culture, one could argue that Stefano is indeed just an individual, acting out collective cultural fantasies and affirming the "continuing fascination with the motif of the murderer as artist."[26] This is based on the narrative trope of the mad artist, arguably engendered by contemporary (western) society and its public sensationalism, and, by extension, anchored in particular design strategies of aestheticized representations of violence in various media. In reference to the medium of film, horror film producer and scholar Steven Jay Schneider contends that there are:

"two major trends in the artistic (re-)presentation of murder: on the one hand are those horror films which showcase murder as an artistic product, and on the other are those which showcase it as an artistic performance. With respect to the former trend, what matters most from an aesthetic point of view is the scene of the crime and/or whatever remains of the victim(s), rather than the motive, the modus operandi or even the presence of the murderer. With respect to the latter trend, what matters most aesthetically is precise-

---

25 Sontag, Susan: *On Photography*, New York: RosettaBooks LLC 2005 [1973], p. 54. Further: "Photographs state the innocence, the vulnerability of lives heading toward their own destruction, and this link between photography and death haunts all photographs of people." (Ibid., p. 55)

26 Black, Joel: *The Reality Effect. Film Culture and the Graphic Imperative*, New York: Routledge 2002, p. 113.

ly the contrary of this, namely the way in which the murderer goes about committing his crime."[27]

For Stefano, both apply to some extent. He actually creates two pieces of art meant for eternity: the installation at the crime scene and the photograph of it. Both of them "show murder as an artistic product,"[28] emphasizing the crime scene's layout. With the art installation Stefano is reiterating the moment of death in its "beauty of destruction" as he calls it,[29] rendering himself a murder-artist: "[I]f murder can be experienced aesthetically, the murderer can in turn be regarded as a kind of artist—a performance artist or anti-artist whose specialty is not creation but destruction."[30] With the photograph he tries to eternalize the very moment of death once more, just in a different way. Instead of a strangely dynamic reiteration, he uses fixation by precisely capturing the second of death on film. Beyond that, THE EVIL WITHIN 2 has players witness Stefano when committing one of his crimes. Thus, his modus operandi is revealed and "murder as an artistic performance" celebrated.[31]

---

27 Schneider, Steven J.: "Murder as Art/The Art of Murder: Aestheticising Violence in Modern Cinematic Horror," December 2012, https://intensitiescultmedia.files.wordpress.com/2012/12/schneider-murder-as-art.pdf, here p. 4.
28 Ibid.
29 GameNewsOfficial: "The Evil Within 2 Stefano The Deadly Photographer Trailer (2017)," YouTube Video, 2:04, August 16, 2017, https://www.youtube.com/watch?v=YYdhD_fEWog, TC: 00:30.
30 J. Black: *The Aesthetics of Murder*, p. 14.
31 St. J. Schneider: "Murder as Art/The Art of Murder," p. 4. The cutscene reveals Stefano's way of killing: first he inflicts the lethal wound to the victim and then he takes a photograph of them. At this very moment, the camera seems to generate the transparent cube around the crime scene. When the player is not careful enough in the stealth sequence ensuing the cutscene, Stefano murders the protagonist Sebastian, however, he does so in reversed order. He takes a picture of Sebastian, which immobilizes him. Stefano then slits his throat, blood is gushing out of the wound. A few seconds later, Sebastian falls to the ground and the player is presented with an increasingly red and then black screen. Interestingly enough, Stefano seems to consider Sebastian not worthy as object of art.

Conclusion

This cursory study has indicated that violence in video games is multifarious and that Klevjer's stance remains relevant: "Violence is important to the DNA of gaming. The idea that it is simply a matter of visual representation is misleading because it implies a concept of action in games that is cleansed of the violent."[32] And even after the debate around the correlation of playing (violent) video games and committing violent acts in real life has cooled down, there must be means of "seeking positive articulations of what violence means in different types and genres of gaming, to different kinds of players in different situations."[33]

With regard to THE EVIL WITHIN 2, it can be said that the aestheticized depiction of murder in the case of Stefano's art is a mere visual spectacle. It bears no significance in terms of interacting with the game world and little direct relevance in terms of the game's narrative. Rather, it satisfies a need in wound culture, insofar as a violent human act is displayed as a spectacle—an object of art for the public to examine. In doing so, THE EVIL WITHIN 2's representation of violence walks a fine line between trivializing violence (alienating players) and displaying it as art (fascinating players). Emphasizing visual elements of violence can thus either be perceived as appropriate or crude representation.

THE EVIL WITHIN 2 exposes contemporary western culture's fascination with violence in displaying murder as an object of art—murder for the sake of art. The setup reminiscent of a photographer's studio with the camera through which the player can gaze at the scene of the crime, frames the observation of violence, not violence per se. Different stylistic devices, such as the visual aestheticization of blood and slow-motion, highlight the purely aesthetic experience. Similarly, kill-cam shots in other action games, for instance in RED DEAD REDEMPTION 2, work as a playful examination of the viewer's sadistic gaze by translating violence into artful imagery that has no further relevance than bizarre visual appeal. These forms of representing violence in video games stand in contrast to aestheticized gameplay elements that serve a helpful function for the players, for example in MAX PAYNE. Violence in THE EVIL WITHIN 2 does not refer to specific game mechanics that indicate violence, but to a broader cultural approach to violence with a predisposition to be exhibited as visual spectacle. This particular example can be seen as a critique of violence as cultural spectacle in that the display of violence is cleverly subverted by its constant reference to the back of

---

32 R. Klevjer: "It's Not the Violence, Stupid."
33 Ibid.

the camera. Fatally wounded bodies, here, are exposed as objects of art, readily exhibited to be taken in by a culture that is inherently fascinated with violence.

Literature

Barthes, Roland: *Camera Lucida. Reflections on Photography*. Translated by Richard Howard, New York: Hill and Wang 1981 [1980].

Beeler, Stan: "From Silver Bullets to Duct Tape: Dexter versus the Traditional Vigilante Hero," in: Douglas L. Howard (ed.), *Dexter. Investigating Cutting Edge Television*, London: Tauris 2010, p. 221-230.

Black, Joel: *The Aesthetics of Murder. A Study in Romantic Literature and Contemporary Culture,* Baltimore: Johns Hopkins University Press 1991.

Black, Joel: *The Reality Effect. Film Culture and the Graphic Imperative*, New York: Routledge 2002.

Bruder, Margaret E.: *Aestheticizing Violence, or How to Do Things with Style*, Bloomington, Indiana University 1998, http://www.gradnet.de/papers/pomo 98.papers/mtbruder98.htm

Burke, Edmund: *A Philosophical Enquiry into the Origin of our Ideas of the Sublime and Beautiful; With an Introductory Discourse Concerning Taste*, New York: Harper & Brothers 1844 [1757].

Hilgers, Judith: *Inszenierte und Dokumentierte Gewalt Jugendlicher: Eine Qualitative Untersuchung von ‚Happy Slapping'-Phänomenen*, Wiesbaden: VS Verlag 2011.

King, Geoff/Krzywinska, Tanya (eds.): *Screenplay. Cinema/Videogames/ Interfaces*, London: Wallflower 2002.

Klevjer, Rune: "It's Not the Violence, Stupid," in: *Game Studies* 18 (2018). http://gamestudies.org/1801/articles/review_klevjer.

Krzywinska, Tanya: "Hands-On Horror," in: *Spectator: The University of Southern California Journal of Film & Television* 22 (2002), pp. 12–23, https://cinema.usc.edu/assets/098/15877.pdf.

Krzywinska, Tanya: "Gaming Horror's Horror: Representation, Regulation, and Affect in Survival Horror Videogames," in: *Journal of Visual Culture* 14 (2015), pp. 293-297, https://doi.org/10.1177/1470412915607924

Peschke, André: "Gewalt kann schön sein – schön brutal," *Gamestar*, July 13, 2013, https://www.gamestar.de/artikel/gewalt-kann-schoen-sein-schoen-bru tal,3025598.html

Schneider, Steven J.: "Murder as Art/The Art of Murder: Aestheticising Violence in Modern Cinematic Horror," December 2012, https://intensities cultmedia.files.wordpress.com/2012/12/schneider-murder-as-art.pdf.

Schott, Gareth: *Violent Games. Rules, Realism and Effect (Approaches to Digital Game Studies* 3), New York: Bloomsbury Academic 2016.

Seltzer, Mark: *Serial Killers. Death and Life in America's Wound Culture*, New York: Routledge 1998.

Sontag, Susan: *On Photography*, New York: RosettaBooks LLC 2005 [1973].

LUDOGRAPHY

FRIDAY THE 13TH: THE GAME (Gun Media 2017, O: Illfonic & Black Tower Studios)
MAX PAYNE (Rockstar Games 2001, O: Remedy Entertainment)
MAX PAYNE 3 (Rockstar Games 2012, O: Rockstar Studios)
MORTAL KOMBAT Series (Midway Games 1992-, O: Midway Games/ Netherrealm Studios)
RED DEAD REDEMPTION 2 (Rockstar Games 2018, O: Rockstar Games)
SILENT HILL: DOWNPOUR (Konami 2012, O: Vatra Games)
SILENT HILL Series (Konami 1999-2014, O: Konami)
SUPER MARIO Series (Nintendo 1983-, O: Nintendo)
THE EVIL WITHIN 2 (Bethesda Softworks 2017, O: Tango Gameworks)

FILMOGRAPHY

CRIMINAL MINDS (USA 2005- , P: JEFF DAVIS)
CONVERSATIONS WITH A KILLER: THE TED BUNDY TAPES (USA 2019- , P: Joe Berlinger)
DEXTER (USA 2006-2013, P: James Manos Jr.)
ER (USA 1994-2009, P: Michael Crichton)
I AM A KILLER (UK 2018, P: Tom Adams/Ned Parker/Danny Tipping)
KILLER WOMEN WITH PIERS MORGAN (UK 2016-2017, P: Piers Morgan/Will Daws)
MATRIX (USA 1999, D: Lana Wachowski/Lilly Wachowski)
SAW (USA 2004, D: James Wan)

ONLINE MEDIA

GameNewsOfficial: "THE EVIL WITHIN 2 Stefano The Deadly Photographer Trailer (2017)," *YouTube* Video, 2:04, August 16, 2017, https://www.youtube.com/watch?v=YYdhD_fEWog.

Bloody Disgusting: "FRIDAY THE 13TH: THE GAME - Motion Capture Shoot," *YouTube* Video, 3:41, February 25, 2016, https://www.youtube.com/watch?v=i4Tx7RsUT9Y.

Designing Rituals Instead of Ceremonies
The Meaningful Performance of Violence in Video Games

RÜDIGER BRANDIS & ALEX BOCCIA

INTRODUCTION

The research of violence in video games has been mainly centered around the question of whether or not playing video games makes players more aggressive. Within this question, two major approaches remain the most prominent: on the one hand, the focus on the content of media itself and on the other hand, the user as the constitutive agent.[1] Instead, we propose a perspective on violence in video games as a series of interactive processes, in which both the player and the game system are actively involved as part of a performance through which meaning is created.[2]

We will argue that these processes can either be designed as ceremonies or rituals. While a ceremony indicates a status, a ritual transforms an agent from one state into another by passing through a liminal phase.[3] Using these classifications enables us to distinguish those mechanics which utilize violence to signify the status of a player and their skills (ceremony) from those which use a system to tell the player something about the significance and meaning of the action while also offering a choice (ritual). Both approaches have merit depending on

---

1 Egenfeldt Nielsen, Simon/Heide Smith, Jonas/Tosca, Susana Pajares: *Understanding Video Games*, New York, NY: Routledge 2008, p. 224.
2 Bell, Catherine: *Ritual Theory, Ritual Practice*, Oxford: Oxford University Press 2009, p. 37-38.
3 Turner, Victor: "Social Dramas and Stories About Them," in: Victor Turner (Ed.): *From Ritual to Theatre. The Human Seriousness of Play*, Baltimore, MD: The John Hopkins University Press 1992, pp. 61-88, here p. 80.

what a designer wants to achieve. However, we will argue that ritualistic systems actively draw the player's attention to the meaning of a violent action opposed to ceremonial systems which mainly create an enjoyable experience.

As game genres and their mechanics are manifold, we will focus our analysis on close quarters combat in Action-Adventures/RPGs, namely: GOTHIC (2001) and DARK SOULS (2011). Our analyses will focus less on the actual fighting and instead more on the approaches and choices these games offer to players within close quarter combat situations.

RITES OF PASSAGE

In 1909, cultural anthropologist Arnold van Gennep wrote THE RITES OF PASSAGE, an attempt to understand people's relationship to society by studying their transformation through the performance of and traversal through rituals. Van Gennep postulates that rites of passage surround the necessary events which occur throughout the lifespan of an individual, and serve as an essential connection between them and the societies in which they belong. These fundamental events and related ceremonies determine the path and structure of one's life and, though they may vary from culture to culture, they also maintain an overall similarity to one another. Such special acts can include, but are not limited to, festivals surrounding a seasonal solstice or a change in the phase of the moon, certain birthday celebrations, and even apprenticeships.[4]

Rites of passage, as described by Van Gennep, can be classified into three primary forms: rites of separation, transition, and incorporation. The rite of separation marks the beginning of a transition from one social world into the next. It is the detachment from one's former self before being suspended in a transitory phase during the rite of transition. For example, such a separation occurs in the development from infant to child, from child to adolescent, and, finally, from adolescent to adult. Here, the individual's social slate is wiped clean, opening the door for the codification of a new status during the transition. A rite of transition occurs at points where one has made the major leap from one social stage of life to another and is now caught between the separation and incorporation phase. This transitory phase allows the individual to temporarily exit the mundanity of the everyday and enter the sacred realm, where one glimpses briefly the structural trappings of their culture. Finally, the aggregation phase, or rite of incorpora-

---

4 Van Gennep, Arnold: *The Rites of Passage*, Chicago, Illinois: University of Chicago Press 1960, pp. 2-4.

tion, creates a sum of the former self in conjunction with the experience gained during the rite of transition, where one re-enters society, not entirely new, but with altered status and responsibility.[5] The rites of passges' different stages can have different levels of importance depending on the situation, such as the rite of aggregation in weddings, or the rite of separation in funerals.[6]

Above examples might seem a strange starting point for the analysis of design principles of digital games, but Van Gennep's approach to describing rituals shares a common detail with games: clearly defined systems which result in modifiable processes through interaction. Contemporary ritual studies tend to focus more on everyday actions and habits of people and no longer define rituals in such a systemic way. We aim to instead harness the notion of more essential symbolic actions delineating the relationship between individuals and the societies they find themselves a part of, which can be used to improve readability in the design of video game mechanics.

CEREMONIES VS. RITUALS

For our analysis, it is essential to understand how these two concepts differ. While Van Gennep defines the term "ceremony" as an event which often occurs or is used to mark the different rites of passage, we will follow Victor Turner's definition, who expanded on Van Gennep's work in the 1960s and 1970s. Turner focuses less on the actual structure of a ceremony but more on what is conveyed through its performance. While the ritual process is about transformation, ceremony is about celebrating the already known. Through form and formality, it celebrates man-made meaning, the culturally determinate, the regulated, the named, and the explained. Turner refers here to Moore and Myerhoff's definition: "[...] ceremony is a declaration [of form] against indeterminacy."[7]

Therefore, ceremonies are often set up as a performance to illustrate a dualistic struggle between order and chaos. A ritual does not portray this. "Rather it is a transformative self-immolation of order as presently constituted [...] in the

---

5 Bachmann-Medick, Doris: *Cultural Turns. New Orientations in the Study of Culture*, Berlin/Boston: Walter De Gruyter 2016, pp. 81.
6 A. van Gennep: *The Rites of Passage*, pp. 10-11.
7 Moore, Sally F./Myerhoff, Barbara: "Introduction: Secular Ritual. Forms and Meanings," in: Sally F. Moore / Barbara Myerhoff (Ed.): *Secular Ritual*, Amsterdam: Van Corcum, Assen 1977, p. 16.

subjunctive depths of liminality."[8] Marriage is a good (although less romantic) example to show the difference between the two. The whole process of marriage from engagement to consummation consists of all rites of passage. The proposition is the rite of separation from the unmarried life, the time between the proposition and the marriage ceremony is the rite of transition, or what Turner calls the phase of liminality, and the consummation marks the end of the rite of incorporation into married life. The ceremony is only the spectacle, which announces the marriage to the public. It only states what has already been decided on in the liminal phase before.

What Turner calls liminality is comparable to Van Gennep's rites of transition, but in Turner's analysis it takes a more essential role in the process than the stages of separation and aggregation. Liminality describes the space and time in between those two, in which the old order has already been destroyed, but the new has not yet formed. It is a space of possibility, chaos, and uncertainty. Ceremonies do not have this phase. Even though it is technically there, it does not possess the possibility for active change, because its outcome has been already determined beforehand. Rituals, on the other hand, are defined by their liminal phase. This is what Turner means when he uses the linguistic term subjunctive: "The subjunctive [...] is always concerned with 'wish, desire, possibility, or hypothesis'; it is a world of 'as if,' ranging from scientific hypothesis to festive fantasy. It is 'if it were so,' not 'it is so.'"[9] For video games, this notion is especially interesting, as it caters to the players' ability to actively influence the game systems they are interacting with.

The core difference between ceremony and ritual is, therefore, that "ceremony indicates, ritual transforms," with the concept of a liminal space full of uncertain possibilities marking this difference. For Turner, "Without taking liminality into account, ritual becomes indistinguishable from 'ceremony,' or 'formality' [...]."[10]

To illustrate how the difference between ritual and ceremony becomes essential for the design of meaningful combat systems, we will investigate two games, GOTHIC and DARK SOULS.

---

8   V. Turner: "Social Dramas and Stories About Them," p. 83.
9   Ibid.
10 Ibid., p. 80.

THE ROLE OF LIMINALITY IN COMBAT SYSTEMS

GOTHIC (2001) is an action role playing game developed by the German studio Piranha Bytes. It is set in a gritty fantasy world and takes place in a giant prison, which was originally used to force convicted criminals to mine for a magical ore needed to craft powerful weapons. After a plan to secure the prison with a magical barrier goes wrong, the inmates riot against their guards and seize power. The protagonist is thrust into this situation and has to learn to survive. However, the setting and story of GOTHIC is of subordinate importance. This section will focus completely on the mechanics surrounding the game's combat system. We will distinguish between fighting against beasts and human opponents as there is a very essential difference between the two, highlighting the possibilities of using rituals as a model.

In GOTHIC, fighting is a staged process, with players being offered different approaches to engage an opponent. The following analysis uses a fight with two mole rats as an example.

Figure 1: Phases of monster behavior (GOTHIC).

When players enter a monster's aggression radius, they begin the encounter by stopping their patrol routine and fixating their gaze on the player character. When players move even closer, the enemy will show warning signals. Most enemies in GOTHIC will do this three times, but in rare cases the stage is skipped completely. For instance, an especially powerful enemy might attack immediately. After performing these signals, the enemy will start to attack the player character. Players do not have to draw their weapon to anger monster enemies, something human opponents will react towards differently.

Figure 2: Fighting a monster (GOTHIC).

The fight itself is an open stage for several decisions to be made. The most common is to fight the monsters, which can either result in the death of the monster or the player. However, if enemies are too powerful or players decide not to fight, they can simply run away. The monster will give chase for some time but will eventually perform a final scare animation and return to its place of origin.

Figure 3: Monster return to routine (GOTHIC).

In this example, we managed to kill one of the two enemies we attracted, but would have been overpowered by the second, as indicated by the nearly depleted health bar in the lower left corner of the screen. We decided to flee the combat and the remaining enemy is now returning back to its original place after chasing us away.

This fight resembles the ritualistic structure of separation, transition, and aggregation, with the actual fight taking place in the transitional phase. Approaching the enemy starts the separation of players from a non-combat status, but does not immediately drop them into combat. Options to act remain, giving the transition phase a ritualistic sub-structure with a liminal phase of its own, during which neither the old status (non-combat) nor the new status (combat) is true. Players have the option to withdraw or remain in this uncertain period for as long as they wish, provided no other agent enters the situation. In this case, we decided to trigger the fight and enter the transitional phase. Although we are now engaged in the combat, the outcome is still unclear, as it does not have to end in either our death or success in overpowering our enemies. Finally, withdrawal is the last phase of aggregation: By removing ourselves from the fight prematurely, we decided to change our status to one in which we achieved only half of our potential goal: killing both enemies. The ritual process is complete and can start anew.

Of course, the number of options players have is limited by GOTHIC's system design. But GOTHIC also offers variations of the above described system throughout the game. This becomes most apparent in the way human opponents react towards players. In opposition to monsters, humans are generally peaceful and will not attack players, although there are a few exceptions. Human NPCs (non-player characters) will react angrily towards players breaching one of the social rules in the world of GOTHIC, such as entering someone's home without permission or drawing weapons in a residential area. Even in the wilderness, some NPCs react with hostility towards a drawn weapon.

Similar to monsters, NPCs will warn players three times before attacking and NPCs witnessing a fight might join in to defend another (unjustly) attacked NPC. If players defeat NPCs, however, they will not be instantly killed (again, there are a few exceptions in the later part of the game). Instead, they will fall to the ground unconscious, a time period players can use to rob them of weapons and other belongings. Soon after, the NPCs will regain composure, make a snarky comment and continue with what they were doing before the fight. So the primary difference compared to fighting monsters is that human NPCs do not die automatically when defeated. This leads to one of the most interesting features of GOTHIC's fighting system: To kill a human, one must stab the opponent as they lie defenseless on the ground.

Figure 4: Defeated human opponents laying on the ground (GOTHIC).

This conscious decision of killing draws the players' attention toward the violent act they are performing. By leaving the choice to players and making the systems surrounding the actual fight more complex, killing another human is not just the act of using a predetermined and necessary mechanic (as is the case in many games). Instead, the game offers players a moment for possible reflection on their actions. It is also possible to kill NPCs who are important for quests. The main quest line is protected from player sabotage, but side quest chains can be broken by a random killing.

Figure 5: Killing a human NPC (GOTHIC).

Therefore, human fights expand on the combat mechanic by extending the liminal phase to delay the decision of killing to the last possible moment. This makes the violent act a particularly gruesome form of aggression. Such a liminal phase imbues the act of violence with meaning and significance beyond its function as a central mechanic of player progress. Turner describes this potential when he identifies ritual as part of a social drama in general: "Ritual is [...] a synchronization of many performantice genres, and is often ordered by a dramatic structure [...], which energizes and gives emotional coloring to the interdepending communicative codes which expess in manifold ways the meaning inherent in the dramatic leitmotiv."[11]

In contrast to GOTHIC, many games do not use this staged approach to fighting. The creator's systems do not offer the possibility to negotiate an outcome. Uncertainty is never really given, as the only two possibilities of ending the fight are often only the death of the opponent or the player character's death. Through this design, these games offer a stage to perform predefined meaning, which is reminiscent of ceremonies as we described above. A good example of this is DARK SOULS (2011).[12]

DARK SOULS is an action role-playing game set in dark fantasy world released in Japan in 2011 and it is infamous for its unforgiving difficulty curve. The game's story is very ambiguous, with few non-aggressive NPCs spread through a world mainly populated by seemingly insane and deformed undead and other monsters. The fighting mechanic is the central element of the game.

Figure 6: An opponent attacks (DARK SOULS).

---

11 V. Turner: "Social Dramas and Stories About Them," p. 81.
12 To clarify: We do not want to say that a ritualistic fighting system is better than a ceremonial one. It depends on what the intention and targeted experience of a game is. DARK SOULS would probably not become a better game by making the approach to fighting more complex. It would just become different. We choose it as an example, because it enables us to show the difference between ceremony and ritual.

While there are a variety of enemies with very different and complex behaviors, they all share one common behavior. They attack players as soon as they enter their aggression radius.

Once engaged in the fight, it is nearly impossible to flee, which makes fighting the only viable option in the game. Nothing except the players' or opponents' death is being negotiated. If players die, they will respawn at one of the many bonfires spread through the game world, which function as save points and subsequently travel hubs. All enemies will respawn after players die, making it necessary to have a strategy to progress from one bonfire to the next. New players are not aware of the bonfire locations, resulting in many deaths and retries.

Figure 7: "You Died" message in DARK SOULS.

The repetitive nature of dying, retrying, dying, and eventual success starts anew with every encounter in DARK SOULS. These stages might seem similar to a ritualistic process. But their lack of a liminal phase does not permit any decision outside of the players' tactics and positioning in the inevitable fight. The effect of this ceremonial approach to fighting is twofold: The fighting system encourages mastery, not reflection on the system itself; which means this game is not about fighting, but rather about the *act* of fighting itself. This is the major difference distinguishing the design approaches between GOTHIC and DARK SOULS.

CONCLUSION

Game design is primarily concerned with the creation of engaging experiences. In many cases, these experiences incorporate violent actions which even today attract the attention of concerned criticism about the content of certain digital games. This is where rituals and ceremonies become interesting. Following Turner's simple definition "ceremony indicates, ritual transforms,"[13] we suggest employing ritual systems as a framework to analyze and design the creation of meaning by players.

Integral for this approach is what Turner calls the liminal phase—the uncertain period after a ritual has been initiated but not yet completed. Its main property is that it offers a possibility for the negotiation of norms, rules, and the perception of reality in general. For games this would mean that a liminal phase simply offers ambiguous choices to the player, forcing them to think about what path they want to take. Ambiguity requires thought and this directly results in the creation of a meaningful discourse, even if it just happens between the player and the game's system. This is especially important for violence in video games, as it forces the player to reflect on the actions they are about to perform or have performed already.

Liminality presents designers with the possibility of creating dynamic and thoughtful gameplay imperatives, bringing more intention and meaning to their games through repetitive yet engaging actions decided upon by players. The perspectives of designers must change not to simply cast out the ceremonial model, but to study and include ritualistic systems where applicable, and use their knowledge of the differences between these two processes to define the core loop in games. Especially in those cases in which designers strive to create a self-reflective system and a meaningful performance of violence in video games.

LITERATURE

Bachmann-Medick, Doris: *Cultural Turns. New Orientations in the Study of Culture*, Berlin/Boston: Walter De Gruyter 2016.
Bell, Catherine: *Ritual Theory, Ritual Practice*, Oxford et al.: Oxford University Press 2009.

---

13 V. Turner: Social Dramas and Stories About Them, p. 80.

Egenfeldt Nielsen, Simon/Heide Smith, Jonas/Tosca, Susana Pajares: *Understanding Video Games*, New York, NY: Routledge 2008.

Moore, Sally F./Myerhoff, Barbara: "Introduction: Secular Ritual. Forms and Meanings," in: Sally F. Moore / Barbara Myerhoff (Ed.): *Secular Ritual*, Amsterdam: Van Corcum, Assen, 1977, pp. 3-24.

Turner, Victor: *From Ritual to Theatre. The Human Seriousness of Play*, Baltimore, MD: The John Hopkins University Press 1992.

Turner, Victor: "Social Dramas and Stories About Them," in: Victor Turner (Ed.): *From Ritual to Theatre. The Human Seriousness of Play*, Baltimore, MD: The John Hopkins University Press 1992, pp. 61-88, here p. 80.

Van Gennep, Arnold: *The Rites of Passage*, Chicago, Illinois: University of Chicago Press 1960.

LUDOGRAPHY

DARK SOULS (Namco Bandai Games 2011, O: From Software)
GOTHIC (Shoebox 2001, O: Piranha Bytes)

Damage over Time

Structural Violence and Climate Change in Video Games

DEREK PRICE

In October 2018, the Intergovernmental Panel on Climate Change released a new report which offered revised predictions about current trends in global greenhouse gas emissions.[1] According to that report, if emissions continue at the current rate, the global temperature will increase by 1.5 degrees Celsius as early as 2040, creating unlivable temperatures around the equator, food and water shortages, and mass extinctions.[2] Even the most conservative estimates in the report imply not only serious social and political crises, but also a fundamental restructuring of the world as we know it. In many ways, the analyses and conclusions from the report resonate with historian Dipesh Chakrabarty's observation that we have entered a new global era that he and others call "the Anthropocene," an age in which humans have become "geological agents" capable of altering the planetary ecosystem in previously unthinkable and violent ways.[3] While this new agency is not equally distributed across the global population, the consequences of living in the Anthropocene will be felt by nearly everyone.[4] With little more than a decade to make the drastic economic, political, and social changes that would avoid the 1.5 degrees Celsius threshold, the question of how to mobilize

---

1 Intergovernmental Panel on Climate Change (IPCC): "Global Warming of 1.5°C," 2018, https://www.ipcc.ch/sr15/, retrieved 2019.
2 Ibid. pp. 9 – 12.
3 Chakrabarty, Dipesh: "The Climate of History: Four Theses," in: *Critical Inquiry* (2009), p. 207.
4 As the CDP Carbon Majors Report 2017 shows, just 100 state and corporate producers "account for 71 % of global industrial GHG [greenhouse gas] emissions," (Griffin, Paul: "The Carbon Majors Database," in: *CDP Carbon Majors Report*, 2017, p. 8.).

to stop climate change is urgent. But mobilization against climate change requires some knowledge of the problem and its sources, which means that we also must ask: by what means can we come to terms with our new geological agency?

Here, I will argue that video games that thematically, narratively, and systemically engage with ecological and "structural" violence can help us understand what it means to live in the Anthropocene. The term structural violence was made popular by sociologist Johan Galtung, who defines it as any form of action or inaction that causes harm by depriving people of "fundamental human needs,"[5] and is often carried out indirectly and collectively against vulnerable social, cultural, or political groups. Although many people associate video games with direct, immediate, or interpersonal violence, the games that will be analyzed here largely eschew these forms of violence and engage instead with the moments of production, management, and policy-making in which many forms of structural violence, including climate change, can begin. By allowing players to act systemically and collectively, these games offer a shift in perspective which can serve as a starting point for understanding the relationship between climate change and economic, colonial, and bureaucratic forms of structural violence.

In order to test the idea that video games can contribute to a better understanding of climate change, this paper will analyze how four different games engage with structural violence and climate change in very different ways. The first two games, ANNO 2205 (2015) and IMAGINE EARTH (2014), are economy-simulation city-builder games that approach the problem of climate change from very different angles.[6,7] The second two games, FATE OF THE WORLD (2011) and THUNDERBIRD STRIKE (2017), imagine, respectively, policy-driven and activist-driven solutions to the political obstacles that prevent action on climate change. Taken together, educators can use these games as starting points for critical discussions about the nature of and remedies for climate change.

ANNO 2205 was developed by Ubisoft Blue Byte and released in 2015. It is the most recent iteration in the ANNO series, which began in 1998 when developer Max Design released ANNO 1602: CREATION OF A NEW WORLD (1998). As the first game's title suggests, the ANNO series is predicated on the fantasy of colonization, of "discovering" a new world and snapping up every resource around you to expand as far as you possibly can, and this remains largely true in ANNO 2205. The game is set on Earth in a distant, post-global-warming future in which all recognizable nations and institutions have dissolved, leaving only the

---

5   Galtung, Johan: "Kulturelle Gewalt," in: *Der Bürger im Staat*, Vol. 43 (1993), p. 106.

6   Anno 2205 (Ubisoft 2015, O: Ubisoft Blue Byte)

7   Imagine Earth (2014, O: Serious Brothers)

"Global Union," a sort of world-government, and several mega-corporations as the major political players. In the game's campaign, the player assumes the role of the CEO of a new corporation, which has been tasked by the Global Union to build a power-plant on the moon and to transfer energy back to earth to solve an "impending energy crisis." The player works toward that goal by founding corporate towns on earth in various regions, growing them to increase revenue, supplying goods for the workers' increasingly complex needs, and establishing trade routes between cities in different regions.

While building a moon base colony to save the world might sound stressful and complex, ANNO 2205 is designed to make this task as calming, simple, and frictionless as possible. Questions about land rights, use, or urban planning take a backseat to the singular challenge of the game: regulating supply and demand within and between cities. After the player learns how to satisfy their growing population's needs, they can simply slip into the cycle of expanding, acquiring and processing natural resources, producing more goods, promoting workers, and then expanding again. Though there are unlockable "extreme weather" modes and optional military scenarios, players are always given the choice to ignore any instances of direct violence or struggle in which their agency could be challenged, thereby keeping the focus of play on the peaceful "flow" of city-building.

Historically, of course, colonial and economic expansion has always been bound up with violence, and it is worth thinking about what ANNO 2205 has to leave out in order to generate and maintain its frictionless fantasy of colonization. One important design choice which allows this fantasy to function is that there are no conflicts with indigenous people in any of the city-building regions. In fact, based on the maps where the player builds their cities, one might conclude that no one and nothing *ever* lived on Earth. The closest approximations of indigenous culture in the game are the "Arctic Custodians" in the polar region,[8] who only exist in cutscenes and interfaces to remind the player that they must "abide by and respect the Arctic Custodians' rules" while building in their region. However, what these "rules" might be remains unarticulated, as well as how those rules might impact how and where players are allowed to build and expand.

ANNO 2205 also removes the negative effects of construction and expansion. Players do not have to think about construction (or human) waste, nor about the impact of construction on soil or water. All options for generating power are

---

8   Within the fiction of the Anno series, the Arctic Custodians seem to be a continuation of the "Eden Initiative," a faction in ANNO 2070 (Ubisoft 2011, O: Related Designs/Blue Byte).

"renewable" or "sustainable," though it is unclear how a few wind turbines are capable of powering a city that can add ten new apartment buildings in a few seconds. But more importantly, there seems to be no connection between the player's nearly-infinite industrial and economic expansion and the production and release of greenhouse gases. Even though the game is set on an Earth which has been fundamentally altered by climate change, nothing in the game suggests that human activity had anything to do with creating the disaster which resulted in the empty, human-free islands in which most of the action of the game occurs.

ANNO 2205's refusal to include any form of tension or friction reveals that its fantasy of violence-free and unlimited economic and colonialist expansion is made possible only by using the violence of those activities as a "structuring absence." Popularized by Richard Dyer, the term "structuring absence" refers to a set of facts or arguments that an artwork carefully avoids engaging with and structures itself around, giving the appearance of an "organic whole."[9] However, once we become aware of this absence, the artwork feels, inevitably, "misshapen" or incomplete.[10] In order to achieve its design goal of conflict-free and pleasurable city-building, ANNO 2205 must omit, both ideologically and systemically, the political clashes and environmental costs that are always part of construction and unlimited economic expansion. But it is precisely these absences which open up ANNO 2205's value in pedagogical and political contexts: by drawing attention to this structuring absence, educators can use ANNO 2205 as a starting point for critical discussions about colonialism and "green capitalism."

In contrast to ANNO 2205, a game like IMAGINE EARTH is much more interested in foregrounding the consequences of economic growth and expansion. Developer Serious Brothers (an indie studio founded by Martin Wahnschaffe and Jens Isensee) has been developing the game since 2014, and it is clear that they want to create a city-builder that engages with and pushes back against the genre's typical political and ecological ideology. One major difference between ANNO 2205 and IMAGINE EARTH is that the latter not only refers to climate change thematically, but also simulates how city-building can negatively impact

---

9 Dyer, Richard: *The Matter of Images: Essays on Representations*, London and New York: Routledge 1993, p. 83.

10 Here, I prefer Dyer's idea of a "structuring absence" to Clint Hocking's idea of "ludonarrative dissonance" which is more common in game studies, as Dyer's term draws attention to how moments of absence or dissonance in artworks are not only aesthetically, but also politically and materially constituted. For more on "ludonarrative dissonance," see Hawking, Clint: "Ludonarrative dissonance in Bioshock: The problem of what the game is about," 2007, https://clicknothing.typepad.com/click_nothing/2007/10/ludonarrative-d.html, retrieved 2019.

the environment. For example, oil platforms in oceans will slowly pollute the water and must be cleaned up, and they always reduce fish stock in the surrounding area, reducing the efficiency of fisheries placed nearby. In a similar fashion, industrial farms and other production facilities will slowly exhaust the land tile they are built on and turn it into a desert, meaning that tile can no longer be used for food production.

Another way in which IMAGINE EARTH differs from many games in the city-builder genre is by refusing to give players total control over what happens in and to their cities. Natural disasters and destructive weather are common, and buildings are never totally safe from wildfires, tornadoes, and falling meteors. And, perhaps most importantly, every building that players create and every tile of vegetation that they cut down affects the planet's overall "emissions balance," which is represented by a positive or negative number. If a planet has too many buildings on it and not enough plant-life and empty space to process emissions, then the climate begins to "collapse." This leads to melting polar ice caps, mass "desertification," and intensified weather conditions which can easily end the game.

By merging strategic, rule-based decisions (how do I win?) with moral and political ones, IMAGINE EARTH forces players to think about and negotiate a balance between growth and sustainability as they play. As Hans-Joachim Backe writes in his article about "greenshifting" game studies, both ecological and digital game systems are characterized by "a fragile equilibrium on the constant verge of radical changes."[11] IMAGINE EARTH creates that feeling of fragility procedurally through unpredictable events that players can never totally predict or control and through the inclusion of climate change as a game mechanic. And even in the more player-centered actions of city-building, IMAGINE EARTH troubles the ideology of unlimited growth in the "city builder" genre by reminding players that every new building, source of power, and industrial practice has costs and consequences which can easily spin out of control into violence and destruction.

If ANNO 2205 and IMAGINE EARTH are most useful for understanding the economic and colonial violence of climate change, then FATE OF THE WORLD and THUNDERBIRD STRIKE go one step further and ask players to think about how they might *stop* climate change. FATE OF THE WORLD, developed by studio Red Redemption and released in 2011, is a digital card game about using policy to stop climate change. Players act as a fictional international organization (the Global Environment Organization), which has the power to implement welfare,

---

11 Backe, Hans-Joachim: "Greenshifting Game Studies: Arguments for an Ecocritical Approach to Digital Games", in: *First Person Scholar* (2014), n.p.

political, technological, environmental, and energy policies around the globe. Over the course of several "scenarios," players play out different policy-driven approaches to addressing global warming—from "using the profits of oil production to offset the effects of global warming" to "prioritizing CO2 emissions reduction" to "totally ignoring climate change," players learn how different policy approaches, implemented on a global scale, might affect climate change.

In many of the scenarios, the difficulty of the game comes from trying to balance policy that decreases CO2 emissions with policy that promotes well-being and social stability in the member states. For example, implementing "organic" farming techniques also lowers crop yields, and in countries with a low food supply, this can lead to civil discontent, protests, or even the expulsion of the regional GEO office. However, players are not obligated to give the public what they want, and are free to simply hire police to tamp down protests, fund Black Ops to disseminate disinformation or overthrow regimes, or even unleash a plague in a region to "reduce the population." Whether players choose to be a benevolent, enlightened, planetary monarch or a cold-hearted, calculating eco-fascist, FATE OF THE WORLD suggests that there is no solution to climate change that does not involve some form of violence, either structural, political, or interpersonal, and that even the best approaches will require human suffering. Perhaps one reason that violence seems inevitable in FATE OF THE WORLD is because the game focuses on combating climate change "from above."[12] The people who live in the countries that players manage are not seen as agents who can act to help stop climate change, but are rather obstacles that players must overcome in order to implement the perfect combination of policies to save the day. While the policy-driven approach of FATE OF THE WORLD is undoubtedly a necessary part of the solution to climate change, the game suggests that only policy-making bureaucrats have the necessary knowledge and authority to determine "the fate of the world," a position which can easily be used to justify and rationalize violence against "ignorant" masses. For a perspective "from below" which gives masses agency in the fight against climate change, we need a game like THUNDERBIRD STRIKE.

THUNDERBIRD STRIKE, released in 2017, is a 2D side-scrolling game developed by artist, developer, and writer Dr. Elizabeth LaPensée. As with many

---

12 Here, I borrow the language of "from above" and "from below" from Jamie Woodcock and Mark R. Johnson's article on gamification (Woodcock, Jamie, and Mark R. Johnson: "Gamification: What It Is, and How to Fight It", in: *The Sociological Review* 66, *3* (2018), pp. 1 – 17), who in turn borrowed it from Hal Draper's essay THE TWO SOULS OF SOCIALISM (Draper, Hal: "The Two Souls of Socialism," in: *New Politics* 5, *1* (1966), pp. 57 – 84).

artistic and collective interventions "from below," the game has clear references to local events and communities, in this case to the protest movements around the construction of the Dakota Access Pipeline in 2016 and 2017 at the Standing Rock Indian Reservation. In the game, players control a thunderbird, an important symbol in many indigenous cultures, and protect wildlife and protestors while destroying trucks and machinery used for oil extraction and transportation. While cheesy voice-overs and an over-the-top boss battle against a hydra-like monster made out of industrial oil pipes give the game a light-hearted tone, THUNDERBIRD STRIKE does pose challenging questions about the legitimate uses of violence in the fight *against* climate change. But the game seems less interested in endorsing particular tactics for fighting climate change and more interested in reminding players of the material impact of climate change on local communities and inspiring communities to organize and take local action against a global problem.

Though it is difficult to predict what the effects of climate change might be, research by climate scientists suggests that poorer regions around the equator and near oceans will be hit first and hardest.[13] The games presented here offer opportunities to reframe climate change as a form of structural violence that intersects with other forms of material deprivation and oppression. Games like IMAGINE EARTH and FATE OF THE WORLD allow players to act at planetary and transnational scales and give a sense of how vast the problem of climate change is and how it intersects with social, political, and economic forces. ANNO 2205, with its fantasy of nonviolent, infinite expansion, can serve as an excellent pedagogical opportunity for discussing the blind spots of "green capitalism" which seeks to erase the tensions between the pursuit of profit and more sustainable forms of production and consumption. And THUNDERBIRD STRIKE serves as a reminder that the violence of climate change has local and material consequences and that fighting climate change takes many forms. By using these games to help reframe climate change as structural violence, we can better understand what it means to live in the Anthropocene and begin to imagine how we can build a more just and sustainable future.

---

13 Schiermeier, Quirin: "Clear Signs of Global Warming Will Hit Poorer Countries First", in: Nature 556 (Apr. 2018), p. 415.

LITERATURE

Backe, Hans-Joachim: "Greenshifting Game Studies: Arguments for an Ecocritical Approach to Digital Games," in: *First Person Scholar* (2014), n.p.
Chakrabarty, Dipesh: "The Climate of History: Four Theses," in: *Critical Inquiry* (2009), pp. 197-222.
Draper, Hal: "The Two Souls of Socialism," in: *New Politics* 5 (1966), pp. 57 – 84.
Dyer, Richard: *The Matter of Images: Essays on Representations*, London and New York: Routledge 1993.
Galtung, Johan: "Kulturelle Gewalt," in: *Der Bürger im Staat*, Vol. 43 (1993), p. 106.
Griffin, Paul: *The Carbon Majors Database. CDP Carbon Majors Report 2017*, 2017, pp. 1 – 16.
Schiermeier, Quirin: "Clear Signs of Global Warming Will Hit Poorer Countries First," in: *Nature* 556 (Apr. 2018), p. 415.
Woodcock, Jamie, and Mark R. Johnson: "Gamification: What It Is, and How to Fight It," in: *The Sociological Review* (2017), pp. 1 – 17.

ONLINE MEDIA

Hawking, Clint: "Ludonarrative dissonance in Bioshock: The problem of what the game is about," 2007, https://clicknothing.typepad.com/click_nothing/2007/10/ludonarrative-d.html, retrieved 2019.
Intergovernmental Panel on Climate Change (IPCC): "Global Warming of 1.5°C," 2018, https://www.ipcc.ch/sr15/, retrieved 2019.

LUDOGRAPHY

ANNO 1602: CREATION OF A NEW WORLD (Sunflowers Interactive 1998, O: Max Design)
ANNO 2070 (Ubisoft 2011, O: Related Designs/Blue Byte)
ANNO 2205 (Ubisoft 2015, O: Ubisoft Blue Byte)
FATE OF THE WORLD (2011, O: Red Redemption)
IMAGINE EARTH (2014, O: Serious Brothers)
THUNDERBIRD STRIKE (2017, O: Elizabeth LaPensée)

Perceiving Video Games

A Cyborg, If You Like

Technological Intentionality in Avatar-Based Single Player Video Games

FRANK FETZER

It is not an entirely new concept that the video game is a bodily experience. In this chapter, I will discuss how to apply the phenomenological concept of the lived body to the video game and how we can understand the player as cyborg. Starting with Merleau-Ponty's PHENOMENOLOGY OF PERCEPTION,[1] I demonstrate how our body provides us with an experience of the world. After that is established, I address how the player's being-in-the-world, the player's existence, is transduced into the virtual. Here, we can spot a major complication. The gameworld exists on a different plane from the physical body. This leads to the question: Can the player traverse this "material gap"?

The bridging of this gap includes the use of physical interfaces like the controller, mouse, or keyboard that transform the player's motor intentionality into the gameworld, as well as the screen, which provides the player with a notion of the content of these worlds. While those interfaces are vital for the video game experience, I will focus here on the avatar as extension of the player's physical body, on its materiality or "thingness," as well as on its capabilities for action and perception.

---

1   Merleau-Ponty, Maurice: *Phenomenology of Perception*, New York, NY: Routledge 2012.

THE BODY

Our body is the most fundamental element for experiencing a world. For Merleau-Ponty, "[t]he body is our general means of having a world."[2] "It is "[…] the vehicle of being in the world[…]."[3] With this, Merleau-Ponty aims at the old topos of mind-body-split that we encounter for example in the prominent Cartesian "ego cogito, ergo sum." Without a body, he argues, there is no world to experience. The body provides us with access to the world, with means for perceiving the objects of the world and for acting within it. Body and world are inextricably intertwined; the world provides background and context for action and perception. Being in the world means to have, or better to be, a body and it is this composite of body and world that provides the subject with means for potential actions. The body can be conceived as an instrument, which, unlike every other instrument, is irreducible. The physical body cannot be separated from the human subject. "I am my body," as Merleau-Ponty puts it.[4]

Our notion of the world is not given a priori as Descartes conceived it, instead it is experienced only through our incarnate existence. Therefore, it is not easy to grasp the body as a fundamental instrument, as a tool that you cannot put away. Jack Loomis states: "The perceptual world created by our senses and nervous system is so functional a representation of the physical world that most people live out their lives without ever suspecting that contact with the physical world is mediate [!]; […]."[5]

This instrument—the body—is, like every other tool, not neutral. It mediates our relations with the world. It is only through the body that the world is disclosed to us. Therefore, the body's capabilities for action and perception as well as its spatial extension shape our experience of the world.

INTENTIONALITY

This relationship between body and world is called intentionality. Basically, intentionality is just another word for the primordial connection between human subject and world. It is the fundamental structure of our relationship with the

---

2 Ibid., p. 147.
3 Ibid., p. 84.
4 Ibid., p. 187.
5 Loomis, Jack. M.: "Distal Attribution and Presence," in: *Presence* 1, *1* (1992), pp., 113-19, here p. 113.

world, the function of human existence itself. World and human subject are forever intertwined. Human beings experience themselves only as part of and in relation to the world. There is no consciousness without content. There is no action without context. The philosopher Peter-Paul Verbeek claims: "They [human beings] cannot simply 'think,' but they always think something; they cannot simply 'see,' but they always see something; they cannot simply "feel" but always feel something."[6]

Intentionality is a pre-reflective process "that silently and spontaneously organizes our world of perception."[7] It is the expression of existence, of our incarnate being in the world. Merleau-Ponty conceives motricity or motor action as original intentionality. "Consciousness," he states, "is originally not an 'I think that,' but rather an 'I can.'"[8] On this account, we can understand intentionality as pre-reflective function that provides us with possibilities for action. Actions are only meaningful in the context of the world, and it is perception that provides us with that context. For this reason, motor action and perception cannot be regarded separately from one another. Merleau-Ponty argues: "Vision and movement are specific ways of relating to objects and, if a single function is expressed throughout all of these experiences, then it is the movement of existence […]."[9] We are in the world not as objects, but as sentient beings. It is the ability to act and perceive that enables us to experience the world and ourselves as part of the world.

TECHNOLOGICAL INTENTIONALITY

Before we enter the realm of the virtual, I want to address how the use of technological artifacts, of instruments, co-shapes our relationship with the world. To engage with the world through instruments makes us subject to the latent amplification/reduction structure of instruments. For example, using a dentist's probe you get a better sense of the structure of the tooth than with your fingers. You

---

6 Verbeek, Peter-Paul: "Cyborg Intentionality: Rethinking the Phenomenology of Human–Technology Relations," in: *Phenomenology and the Cognitive Sciences* 7, 3 (2008), pp. 387-395, here p. 288.
7 Shusterman, Richard: "The Silent, Limping Body of Philosophy," in: Taylor Carman/Mark B.N.Hansen (eds.), *The Cambridge Companion to Merleau-Ponty*, Cambridge: Cambridge University Press 2005, pp. 151-180, here p. 161.
8 Merleau-Ponty: *Phenomenology of Perception*, p. 139.
9 Ibid.

feel the hardness and softness of the tooth, the cracks and holes far better than you would using your fingers. The probe extends or amplifies your tactile intentionality,[10] but you will not sense the wetness or warmth of the tooth that you would experience with your finger. The use of the instrument therefore reduces and amplifies your tactile intentionality at the same time. The philosopher Don Ihde claims:

> "The difference [between body and technological artifact] is that all instruments have differently shaped 'intentionalities' which expose precisely those aspects of the world which have hitherto either been overlooked, taken as unimportant, not known at all, or even totally unsuspected."[11]

The technological intentionality of an instrument is narrower than the general intentionality of the body. Ihde, who came up with the concept of technological intentionality in the first place, is reluctant to call the *amplification/reduction structure* of the probe "technological intentionality." He reserves that term for instruments that do not provide the user with direct access to the world, but let her experience only the result of the instrument's engagement with the world, e.g. radiotelescopy or infrared photography.[12] These instruments, as Peter-Paul Verbeek claims, "do not represent a phenomenon of the world but construct a new reality."[13] They reveal a reality that is inaccessible by human intentionality alone. Verbeek speaks of a double intentionality that is involved here: "[...] one of technology toward 'its' world, and one of human beings toward the result of this technological intentionality."[14]

I will argue, following Peter-Paul Verbeek, that the intentionality involved in embodied relations, like using a probe, is not completely human either. The specific ways of experiencing the world through the probe can only exist because of an intimate relation between human and technology. All instrumental use co-shapes our experience of the world. While we are able to experience the world with or without the probe, the instrumentally constructed reality of the video game is exclusively accessible to us via instruments. Therefore, to experience that reality, the use of instruments is indispensable.

---

10 Ihde, Don: *Technics and Praxis*, Dordrecht: Reidel 1979, p. 18.
11 Ibid., p. 78.
12 Ibid.
13 Verbeek, "Cyborg Intentionality: Rethinking the Phenomenology of Human–Technology Relations," p. 393.
14 Ibid.

The body is our only means to access the world. Only through our body are we able to experience the world. In a similar fashion, it is only through teaming up with technology that we are able to experience the gameworld. It is for this reason, that it is impossible to untangle human intentionality and technological intentionality from the gameplay experience, as Olli Leino points out here:

"it is impossible to atomize phenomenon of gameplay to separate the influences of the player and FAR CRY in the player-game relationship like I can separate the influences of myself and my eyeglasses by simply taking them off and seeing what the world looks like without them."[15]

THE "MATERIAL GAP"

The requirement for instrumental mediation to experience the video game arises from the material gap between the physical world and the gameworld. The gameworld is an environment that "consists of pure information" and "the player is a carbon-based lifeform having no apparent way out from meatspace in the near future."[16] How can we transform the objective properties of the body as well as its capacities for motricity and perception into the virtual world? In other words: how can the body stretch into the virtual?

That gap is a complication, but probably not a major one.[17] It can easily be overcome, as every gamer knows. The body is not unchangeable but will adapt to its tasks. We do not perceive our body as limited to its physical properties. Instead, we conceive it in terms of possibilities for action. Merleau-Ponty states:

"What counts for the orientation of the spectacle is not my body, such as it in fact exists, as a thing in objective space, but rather my body as a system of possible actions, a virtual

---

15 Leino, Olli Tapio: "Untangling Gameplay: An Account of Experience, Activity and Materiality within Computer Game Play," in: John Sageng/ Hallvard Fossheim/Tarjei Mandt Larsen (eds.), *The Philosophy of Computer Games,* New York, NY: Springer 2012, pp. 57-75, here p. 72.

16 Wirman, Hannah and Olli Tapio Leino: "For Interface, against Regression!: An Exploratory Surgery of the Transhuman Umbilical Cord," *Proceedings of ISEA 2008: The 14th International Symposium on Electronic Art,* 2008, pp. 461-463, here p. 461.

17 Klevjer, Rune: "Enter the Avatar: The Phenomenology of Prosthetic Telepresence in Computer Games," in: John Sageng/Hallvard Fossheim/Tarjei Mandt Larsen (eds.), *The Philosophy of Computer Games,* New York: Springer 2012, pp. 17-38, here p. 36.

body whose phenomenal 'place' is defined by its task and by its situation. My body is wherever it has something to do."[18]

Still, to perceive the world and to interact with objects of the world, the subject has to be part of the world. To bridge this material gap, to inhabit the gameworld, the player-subject has to extend the subjective and objective dimensions of her body across the ontological border between materiality and virtuality. That is, the lived body of the player has to become part of the virtual world. Merleau-Ponty states: "Visible and mobile, my body is a thing among things, it is one of them. […]. The world is made of the very stuff of the body."[19] To extend the player's embodied existence into the gameworld, the capabilities of the body for movement and perception have to be transformed into the virtual: "[…] to inhabit a computer game the player has to be able to perform her embodied intentionality, or, motility, in the game."[20] To perform meaningful movement or motor intentionality, the player has to be provided with context. This goes for the physical world but applies to the gameworld as well, as Wirman and Leino make clear: "If the player is not given the possibility to sense what there is in the environment, it is impossible to offer him abilities to act within the environment."[21] Perception and movement are deeply interconnected, they form our relationship with the world. Without perception, all movement would be without meaning. There would be no context, no world to move within. Without movement, on the other hand, how would we be able choose what to perceive? And how would the perceived world make sense if we cannot relate to it through our actions? Merleau-Ponty makes clear that action and perception are two sides of the same coin: "We only see what we look at. What would vision be without eye movement?"[22]

---

18 Merleau-Ponty: *Phenomenology of Perception*, p. 260.
19 Merleau-Ponty, Maurice: "Eye and Mind," in: James Edie (ed.), *The Primacy of Perception: And Other Essays on Phenomenological Psychology, the Philosophy of Art, History and Politics,* Evanston, IL: Northwestern University Press 1964, pp. 121-149, here p. 124.
20 Wirman and Leino: "For Interface, against Regression!: An Exploratory Surgery of the Transhuman Umbilical Cord," p. 461.
21 Ibid., p. 463.
22 Merleau-Ponty: "Eye and Mind," p. 162.

THE AVATAR

The video game experience is based on instrumental mediation. The avatar transforms the player's bodily existence into the virtual, control interfaces mediate her motor intentionality, and the screen enables her to sense the virtual environment. While there is a complex gameplay apparatus at work to provide us with the gameplay experience, I will focus on the avatar, the player's virtual body.

This virtual entity enables us to experience the gameworld from within. It is the avatar that re-locates the player's existence into the virtual. To actually be in the gameworld, the player needs a vicarious body that transforms her physical properties into the virtual. This virtual body extends the materiality or "thingness" of the body into the virtual. Like our physical body, it can be described as a vehicle, or, as James Newman puts it, as "a set of available techniques and capabilities."[23] It is "a suite of capabilities for action"[24] and like our physical body it determines our relation to the (virtual) world. As the intentionality that organizes our existence in the material world, the technological intentionality of the avatar organizes our virtual existence. The intentionality that is involved here is not the narrow "instrumental intentionality" Don Ihde had in mind, but a broader, more complex intentionality—not unlike human intentionality.

To be clear: the avatar is not a subject in a phenomenological sense. As extension of the player's lived body, as instrument, the avatar is hollow. It is a tool, to be filled with the player's subjectivity. But the relation between player and avatar is different from those instrumental relations. The avatar is rarely a mere tool. The ultimate manifestation of technological intentionality we encounter in the video game is the fact that the avatar has a life of its own. This phenomenon is obvious in cut-scenes, but the use in role-playing games is more compelling. For example, if you walk around with your party, you will discover the entrance of a cave only if the perception-skill of one of your characters is high enough. Even if you as player know the cave is there, you as player cannot discover it, only the avatar can. Or, when you want to talk to someone and persuade her of something: This only works if the avatar's talking or charming skill is high enough. No matter how eloquent the player might be, it is only the skill of the avatar that is relevant in this situation.

---

23 Newman, James: "The Myth of the Ergodic Videogame. Some Thoughts on Player-Character Relationships in Videogames," in: *Game Studies* 2, *1* (2002), http://gamestudies.org/0102/newman

24 Clark, Andy: "Re-Inventing Ourselves: The Plasticity of Embodiment, Sensing, and Mind," in: *Journal of Medicine and Philosophy* 32, *3* (2007), pp. 263-82, here p. 272.

Another, less obvious example I found in GRAND THEFT AUTO: SAN ANDREAS (2004) while riding around the eponymous city on a bicycle.[25] Riding a bicycle in this game was a slightly annoying and difficult activity (and I am not sure why I even bothered). Still, over time it became easier and easier. After a while, I wondered if it was just me who was getting better at this activity. As it turns out, it was not. Our skill sets melded and together we became an experienced (virtual) biker in the process.

CONCLUSION

To become part of the gameworld, to be relocated into it, the human player needs to merge to a certain degree with the technological artifact that is the avatar. It is in light of this connection that we can speak of a cyborg relation between player and technology. Here, human and technology form a new experiencing (and acting) entity. This relationship is an extreme form of embodiment relation where no distinction is possible between player and avatar in the process of playing. In teaming up with technology, this new entity is able to experience (or even to create) a new reality, a reality that can only exist for human intentionality if it is complemented with technological intentionality.[26]

The connection between player and avatar is not limited to the cyborg relation, though. There is also a relationship between the instrumentally extended or even relocated player and the avatar as technological other. I would argue that it is not at all contradictory to combine the cyborg relation between player and avatar with an alterity relation. Take, for instance, Ihde's "spirited horse" example, which he uses to illustrate the alterity relation.[27] While Ihde focuses on the animal subject as quasi-subject, the relation with the horse is also an embodiment relation. The rider uses aids to give cues to the horse and ideally the horse responds so swiftly, that we could speak of a technologically extended rider-subject. Still, the horse is an animated being, a quasi- or animal-subject. It has certain capabilities that might evolve over time. Also, like the avatar, it might disobey occasionally. The main difference between horse and avatar is that we

---

25 GRAND THEFT AUTO: SAN ANDREAS, (Rockstar Games 2004, O: Rockstar North)
26 Cf. P.-P. Verbeek: "Cyborg Intentionality: Rethinking the Phenomenology of Human–Technology Relations," p. 394.
27 Ihde, Don: *Technology and the Lifeworld: From Garden to Earth*, Bloomington, IN: Indiana University Press 1990, p. 99.

cannot "dismount" from the avatar if we still want to experience the gameworld that is mediated by it.

Rune Klevjer thinks of the hermeneutical clash between the avatar as tool and the avatar as character as a clash between diegesis and embodied telepresence. But we also can conceive it as a relationship with a technological other or quasi-subject and as embodied relation at the same time. A relationship similar to the one between rider and horse: The horse never ceases to be an autonomous subject, but might be employed as an instrument. Therefore, we arrive at a very similar conclusion. As Klevjer states:

"One of the things that I find attractive about the action-adventure genre, is that there can be a companionship across the ontological gap, a felt resonance between your own experiences, and a slow realization that the two of you are, after all, travel companions and brothers in arms."[28]

This quote, I believe, foregrounds that there is more to the video game experience than a simple instrumental relation, which alone would justify conceptualizing the player as cyborg. In the process of playing a video game, a new entity comes about. A composite of flesh and technology that forms "a single cyborg consciousness."[29] This entity, the player, is no longer entirely human, but an inseparable mixture of technological and bodily relations with the gameworld. A cyborg, if you like.

LITERATURE

Clark, Andy: "Re-Inventing Ourselves: The Plasticity of Embodiment, Sensing, and Mind," in: *Journal of Medicine and Philosophy* 32, 3 (2007), pp. 263-82.
Friedman, Ted: "Civilization and Its Discontents: Simulation, Subjectivity, and Space," in: Greg M. Smith (ed.), *On a Silver Platter: CD-ROMs and the Promises of a New Technology*, New York: NYU Press 1998, pp. 132-150.
Ihde, Don: *Technics and Praxis*, Dordrecht: Reidel 1979, p. 18.

---

28 Klevjer, Rune: "Telepresence, Cinema, Role-Playing. The Structure of Player Identity in 3d Action-Adventure Games," Invited talk at The Philosophy of Computer Games 2011, Athens, https://runeklevjer.files.wordpress.com/2013/01/runeklevjerathenstalk.pdf

29 Friedman, Ted: "Civilization and Its Discontents: Simulation, Subjectivity, and Space," in: Greg M. Smith (ed.), *On a Silver Platter: CD-ROMs and the Promises of a New Technology,* New York: NYU Press 1998, pp. 132-150.

Ihde, Don: *Technology and the Lifeworld: From Garden to Earth*, Bloomington, IN: Indiana University Press 1990, p. 99.

Klevjer, Rune: "Enter the Avatar: The Phenomenology of Prosthetic Telepresence in Computer Games," in: John Sageng/ Hallvard Fossheim/ Tarjei Mandt Larsen (eds.), *The Philosophy of Computer Games*, New York: Springer 2012, pp. 17-38.

Klevjer, Rune: "Telepresence, Cinema, Role-Playing. The Structure of Player Identity in 3d Action-Adventure Games," *Invited talk at The Philosophy of Computer Games 2011, Athens,* https://runeklevjer.files.wordpress.com/2013/01/runeklevjerathenstalk.pdf

Leino, Olli Tapio: "Untangling Gameplay: An Account of Experience, Activity and Materiality within Computer Game Play," in: John Sageng/ Hallvard Fossheim/Tarjei Mandt Larsen (eds.), *The Philosophy of Computer Games*, New York, NY: Springer 2012, pp. 57-75.

Loomis, Jack. M.: "Distal Attribution and Presence," in: *Presence* 1, *1* (1992), pp. 113-19.

Merleau-Ponty, Maurice: "Eye and Mind," in: James Edie (ed.), *The Primacy of Perception: And Other Essays on Phenomenological Psychology, the Philosophy of Art, History and Politics*, Evanston, IL: Northwestern University Press 1964, pp. 121-149.

Merleau-Ponty, Maurice: *Phenomenology of Perception*, New York, NY: Routledge 2012.

Newman, James: "The Myth of the Ergodic Videogame. Some Thoughts on Player-Character Relationships in Videogames," in: *Game Studies* 2, *1* (2002), http://gamestudies.org/0102/newman

Shusterman, Richard: "The Silent, Limping Body of Philosophy," in: Taylor Carman/Mark B.N.Hansen (eds.), *The Cambridge Companion to Merleau-Ponty*, Cambridge: Cambridge University Press 2005, pp. 151-180.

Verbeek, Peter-Paul: "Cyborg Intentionality: Rethinking the Phenomenology of Human–Technology Relations," in: *Phenomenology and the Cognitive Sciences* 7, *3* (2008), pp. 387-395.

Wirman, Hannah/Olli Tapio Leino: "For Interface, against Regression!: An Exploratory Surgery of the Transhuman Umbilical Cord," in: *Proceedings of ISEA 2008: The 14th International Symposium on Electronic Art*, 2008, pp. 461-463.

LUDOGRAPHY

GRAND THEFT AUTO: SAN ANDREAS, (Rockstar Games 2004, O: Rockstar North)

Player Perception of Gameworlds and Game Systems: Load Theory as Game Analytic Tool

Nicolay Mohammad-Hadi

Introduction

In this paper, I intend to make the case that a video game influences its players' actions by changing its audiovisual presentation. The goal of this paper is to connect a few previously unrelated concepts to explain where perceptive processes are relevant during gameplay and how they influence player behavior.

In order to make sense of any video game phenomenon, it is worth reflecting on the ways in which this medium is unique. The topic being perception, I am here focusing on how video games are perceived differently than other audiovisual media. Since there has previously been much academic discourse on this topic,[1] I will avoid loaded terms such as *interactivity* and will not discuss the concepts of *fun* or *engagement*.[2] Instead, I will focus on this basic fact: for a video game to emerge meaningfully, a player is required to regularly give input in response to the game's output. This distinction is broad but sufficient to examine the role of perception in video games, as it addresses those aspects of the video game where perception is most important: the game's audiovisual output and the player's interpretation of this output to make decisions.

In the following, I will put forth a definition of perception and give a brief summary of *Load Theory* before expressing how a game's representation of its

---

1 Compare, for example, Juul, Jesper: "Games Telling Stories? A Brief Note on Games and Narratives", *Game Studies* 1, *1* (2001). http://www.gamestudies.org/0101/juul-gts
2 See Aarseth, Espen J.: *Cybertext: Perspectives on Ergodic Literature*, Baltimore, MD: Johns Hopkins University Press 1997.

systems influences player perception. Then, these points will be applied to a few video game case studies.

TERMS AND DEFINITIONS

The APA DICTIONARY OF PSYCHOLOGY, defines perception as

"the process or result of becoming aware of objects, relationships, and events by means of the senses, which includes such activities as recognizing, observing, and discriminating. These activities enable organisms to organize and interpret the stimuli received into meaningful knowledge and to act in a coordinated manner."[3]

This is a good definition to grasp key elements, as it encapsulates both the phenomenon of information reception as well as its further processing, and it even explains the reason for this: Perception is a method of information-gathering that influences decision-making. However, this definition, while suitable as a comprehensive explanation, conflates a three-step procedure consisting of sensation, perception, and cognition, into one. Separating those will allow for specificity in the analysis of what constitutes a player's immediate reaction and what is considered decision-making based on what the player perceives and processes. In any game, both kinds of player reactions occur, which makes the differentiation particularly important.

As mentioned before, perception can be defined as a three-step process comprised of sensation, perception, and cognition, as demonstrated by Celia Hodent in THE GAMER'S BRAIN. At the beginning of the perception process, "[r]eceptor cells receive stimuli"[4] (sensation), which are "turned into a mental representation of the world"[5] (perception) and then finally allowed "access to semantics,"[6] or, in other words, are intellectually processed (cognition). Understanding this differentiation allows for a more specific analysis of the individual points of a game that could exert influence on player behavior. For instance, picture a large engine room as a level in a hypothetical horror game. An area in this level might feature exceptionally loud mechanical noises and therefore seem to signal danger for multiple reasons. The loud noise might be intended to stress the player's auditory

---

3   See https://dictionary.apa.org/perception
4   Hodent, Celia. *The Gamer's Brain*. Boca Raton, FL: CRC Press 2018, p. 19.
5   Ibid.
6   Ibid.

perception or drown out characteristic noises of enemy characters, so it would be difficult to create an accurate mental image of the area. Or, the noise might act as a signal of an environmental hazard, causing the player character headaches and a loss of life energy.

In addition, this process does not occur in a strictly linear fashion. Hodent continues by saying that perception is influenced by cognition as follows:

"Although it could seem intuitive for this process to be bottom-up (first sensation, then perception, and lastly cognition), it is actually very often top-down, which means that your cognition (your knowledge and expectations about the world) will have an impact on your perception of it. Perception is therefore highly subjective because it is influenced by your past and present experiences."[7]

Returning to the example of the loud noise from the horror game, if a similar sound is used to signal that a monster is behind the player character off-screen, a player might flee before having properly perceived what they are running away from. This would more likely occur if the enemies in the game were exceptionally fast, and the player would potentially benefit from reacting quickly. Knowing this, a game designer might exploit this condition to pressure players into rash decisions before they even had the chance to accurately process their initial reaction.

In the context of psychology, I want to focus on basic concepts from Load Theory, which I believe to be particularly relevant for video games. This is because a large part of creating a video game experience consists of deciding the amount and manner of system information displayed for the player (more on the division between game system and representation below). Forster and Lavie summarize Load Theory in explaining that

"distractor processing critically depends on the availability of attentional capacity and can thus be prevented when the relevant-task processing involves sufficient high perceptual load to engage full attentional capacity. Evidence in support of this claim has been found in many studies demonstrating that distractor processing is significantly reduced with tasks of high (compared to low) perceptual load."[8]

To paraphrase, there is a certain amount of perceptual load that is suitable for a given task to a certain individual, which varies for each individual and each task.

---

7 H. Celia: *The Gamer's Brain*, pp. 19-20.
8 Forster, Sophie and Nilli Lavie: "Harnessing the Wandering Mind: The Role of Perceptual Load," in *Cognition* 111, *3* (2009), pp. 345–355, here p. 345.

From this theory, it follows in the video game context that certain amounts and modes of information are suitable to certain playstyles and preferences. In an action-focused sword-fighting game, a developer might choose to convey system information diegetically by focusing strongly on attack animations to emphasize attack speeds, whereas similar sword attacks in a massively multiplayer online role-playing game (MMORPG) might have their attack speeds signaled through explicit numbers in addition to the range of damage each attack does and any additional effects they might cause (including the chance of such effects to occur). In both instances, a near-identical action is performed, but only the more strategic MMORPG displays detailed system information, as it incentivizes its players to focus on performance optimization. The action game, conversely, may be designed to provide an escapist experience of immersion and to teach its players how to 'read' enemy behaviors.

GAME SYSTEM AND INTERFACE

Going forward, I want to utilize a description of video games by Christine Jørgensen, who states that video games are comprised of game system and gameworld. The game system is not visible to the players and consists of all the calculations and simulations inside the machine, whereas the gameworld is the interface with which we, as players, interact, and which the game uses to project its feedback to us:

"Gameworlds are world representations designed with a particular gameplay in mind and characterized by game-system information that enables meaningful player interaction [...] The gameworld and the game system are intimately connected and must be seen in context with each other rather than as distinct from one another. They operate together in order to provide the player with information about how to interact with the game."[9]

This notion is particularly helpful with investigating perception in video games, because it distinguishes the simulation from the representation of the simulation. Ultimately, it is the gameworld (i.e. the interface) which we perceive and with which we interact, as opposed to the actual game system:

"An interface is traditionally seen as the interconnection between different spheres and, in human-computer interaction, as the part of the system that allows the user to interact with

---

9 Jørgensen, Kristine: *Gameworld Interfaces,* Cambridge, MA: MIT Press 2013, p. 3.

the computer. In this context, the gameworld is exactly that: an environment that connects the player with the game system."[10]

Describing the game as a system with an interface highlights that players react to the representation of the simulation, not the simulation itself. Further, game developers do not only have to consider how to set up a coherent game system, but also how said system is presented to the players, i.e. creating the gameworld. It is worthy to draw this distinction as there are many elements in the gameworld that are not necessarily affected by the game system. A helpful example is, again, the depiction of enemy characters. For instance, a game could create an enemy that kills the player character immediately upon contact. Depending on whether this enemy is then displayed as a black hole into which the player character disappears or as a monster that eats the player whole, the player might attempt different escape strategies. If the enemy is a black hole, they might see no other option but to run in the opposite direction, but if it is a monster, they may choose to hide from or even fight it.

Viewing the gameworld as the interface to the game system, it follows that game developers can influence player action by changing the interface without having to make the game react mechanically. Since game design is so often about enticing, incentivizing, and suggesting, this can be considered an additional tool to adjust isolated parts of the game without having to change the system itself – which potentially leads to unintended consequences.

In the following I will summarize the previous concepts and combine them into one simple model that can be used to analyze video games. The aim is to provide a perspective of how a game is perceived by players, taking into account that they interact with the game system through the gameworld.

The video game artifact itself consists of two halves, the first being the game system, in which agents are simulated according to rules. The interface between game system and player is the gameworld which is represented through various means (on the screen, through the speakers, with controller vibration, etc.). The gameworld is the space in which the game system displays all necessary information to the player, the precise amount and manner determined by the developer. This is the actual level on which players can perceive the game, perception being the main method of gathering information to assist decision-making.

The player perceives in a process comprised of three steps: 1) sensation, the receiving of sensory stimulation, 2) perception, or the creation of a mental model, and 3) cognition. The last step describes the processing of information and actually has the potential to influence the other two steps, where, for instance,

---

10 J. Kristine: *Gameworld Interfaces*, pp. 3-4.

previous experience can lead to a false mental model. In this section, I will briefly investigate a few games from various genres with the above-mentioned notions in mind to demonstrate the type of information they provide.

Quest for Glory

Quest for Glory (1992) is a hybrid of puzzle-solving adventure and role-playing game, in which players take control of a young, nameless hero to help various people in the medieval fantasy world of Spielburg. The tone of the game is humorous and friendly, even though it is possible for the player character to die in many different ways. Close to the end of the game, players have to infiltrate the fortress of a gang of bandits. This is a series of self-contained, small point-and-click puzzles; a condensed, intensified execution of the game's overall mechanics.

In the middle of this sequence, the bandits discover the hero entering a dining hall and begin their chase. Now, the player has to perform a series of timed actions in order to advance without getting caught. However, unlike previous segments, they are not told what to do and have very little time to react. Instead, the player has to observe how the situation unfolds and get caught, resulting in the scene restarting. From this experience, the player needs to deduce how to proceed in each and every step after re-loading a save game. For instance, at first, players have to close the door through which they came, then barricade another one at the opposite end of the room. Failing to do so results in bandits capturing the hero. Next, players need to fend off the bandits by forcing them into a detour, assuming correct positioning, placing a trap, and activating it within a small time-frame.

Failure is virtually guaranteed in the first attempt of each step, as the developers made the puzzle unpredictable and omit required information. Players are thus tasked with ascertaining the necessary information through trial-and-error. This puzzle design might ordinarily lead to a frustrating play experience, as the game demands the quick and perfect execution of actions that the player could not possibly foresee. Regarding only the game system, this is a series of timed puzzles with no hints as to their solution and harsh punishment as a consequence of failure ("Game Over"-type fail state).

However, in the gameworld, humor is used to alleviate potential frustration on a cognitive level, i.e. the last stage of perception, when information is intellectually processed. On screen messages after each failure contain jokes, whimsical animations are played as characters interact, and some of the bandits are designed to look like the three stooges (highlighting the slapstick nature of this segment). The humorous elements of the gameworld add a layer of rewarding exploration onto the inherently unfair game system. In addition, the jokes suggest that players do not actually have to perform flawlessly at first, even though the game system punishes the slightest misstep as harshly as it can. Focusing exclusively on the game system while overlooking the gameworld would fail to adequately analyze this segment.

THE LAST OF US

In THE LAST OF US (2013), players travel throughout the USA in a post-apocalyptic scenario, fending off both monsters and other humans. A major part of this third-person shooter is spent engaging in combat very deliberately and carefully as ammunition is scarce, enemies are powerful, and basic actions such as aiming are slow and difficult to execute.

A section in the middle of the game forces the player into combat. After carefully traversing a small, abandoned town, the player character triggers a booby-trap and finds himself hanging from a rope by his foot. Now dependent on his partner to set him free, the game is depicted upside down, mimicking the player character's perspective. At this point, a pack of enemy monsters appears, attracted by the noise. As in the rest of the game, players defend themselves with a gun, but now have to fight while fixed to one point in space, experiencing the scene upside down.

In this section, the developers have changed the rules of the game system by forcing players to remain in one spot. They have also altered the representation of the gameworld by flipping the in-game camera on its head. This does not change how aiming works in this game, but the change in perspective can nevertheless cause disorientation and add extra difficulty to aiming and shooting, as the first two steps of perception (sensation of the gameworld and creation of the mental representation of the game system) are literally turned upside down. The sudden increase in difficulty might have been too steep for the developers' original intent, though, as they temporarily grant players an infinite amount of ammunition in this section, mitigating the punishment for missed shots.

REZ

The previous examples have focused on game segments changing their mode of representation or the dynamics of the game system (or both) in the middle of the game, but this last example is intended to examine how regular play is influenced by the perception of its gameworld. In this rail shooter, the player assumes the role of a hacker infiltrating a computer system through the control of a polygonal, anthropomorphic avatar that flies through cyberspace shooting at geometric shapes, which symbolize protection software

REZ'S (2002) blend of background sound and imagery with unique effects for every agent (i.e. player and enemy characters in this example) is of particular interest for this analysis. The game's background visuals and music themselves do not form a purposeful gameworld. It is mostly comprised of a few colorful shapes on simple backgrounds without many moving objects, and audio is restricted to slight rhythmic beats and melodies without effects. This does not make for a strong representation of the game's systems. However, the gameworld becomes much more meaningful as the agents within this space interact. This is because sound and visual effects are designed to blend with the background in a manner that creates a more compelling experience than observing these elements on their own.

On a systemic level, enemies are capable of spawning, attacking, and being destroyed. In the gameworld, each enemy is represented by a particular visual and sound effect. The same approach to effects applies to the player, who can attack in one of two ways: firing individual shots, which introduces sound and visuals with each button press, or charging their attack for a multi-shot attack, adding sound and visual effects at a strong rhythmic pace. The game system does not differentiate sharply between single shots and multiple shots; aside from their firing rhythm, these attacks are systemically identical.

This results in the gameworld changing drastically depending on how far the player has advanced. More layers to background music and visuals are added, but just as importantly, a gradual escalation in the game's difficulty leads intrinsically to a higher count of visual and sound effects, as stronger and more numerous enemies naturally require more player attacks. This leads to the emergence of unique visuals and soundscapes, and to a dynamic in which players are incentivized to act either in sync with the music they are perceiving, or to create a beat and suitable visuals of their own. The incentive comes in the form of added layers to the player's sensation, as ever more effects lead to a more spectacular gameworld, akin to a fireworks display increasing in intensity. This playful approach to REZ is encouraged further in its lowest difficulty setting, which allows for play without failure.

FURTHER RESEARCH

The goal of this paper was to connect some concepts from the fields of game studies and psychology to provide an accurate, broadly-applicable perspective with which to analyze video games. The brief analyses provided here exemplify some focal points, but a more committed investigation of many different games with the three-step perception process, Load Theory, and the division between game system and gameworld in mind could prove highly productive. I hope to have exemplified above how the game situations described were changed by alterations to the gameworld as opposed to the game system. It might also be worth evaluating the addition of other concepts from psychology and game studies, such as gestalt principles, self-determination theory, or how the concepts of the gameworld interface and world-building can be aligned with one another.

Humans perceive the world vastly differently from one another despite our (genetic) similarities and it is not always easy to comprehend each other's views. As playful computer simulations, video games offer unique zones for experimentation, which can be conducted safely to gain understanding of our capabilities and limitations, as well as our unique perspectives.

LITERATURE

Aarseth, Espen J. *Cybertext: Perspectives on Ergodic Literature*, Baltimore, MD: Johns Hopkins University Press 1997.
Forster, Sophie and Nilli Lavie: "Harnessing the Wandering Mind: The Role of Perceptual Load," in: *Cognition*, 111, *3* (2009), pp. 345–355.
Hodent, Celia: *The Gamer's Brain*, Boca Raton, FL: CRC Press 2018.
Jørgensen, Kristine. *Gameworld Interfaces*, Cambridge, MA: MIT Press 2013.
Juul, Jesper: "Games Telling Stories? A Brief Note on Games and Narratives," *Game Studies 1*, *1* (2001), http://www.gamestudies.org/0101/juul-gts

LUDOGRAPHY

THE LAST OF US (Sony Computer Entertainment 2013, O: Naughty Dog).
QUEST FOR GLORY I: SO YOU WANT TO BE A HERO (Sierra On-Line 1992, O: Sierra On-Line).
REZ (SEGA 2001, O: United Game Artists).

ONLINE RESOURCES

APA Dictionary: "Perception." https://dictionary.apa.org/perception, retrieved June 3, 2019.

On Character Analysis and Blending Theory
Why You Cried at the End of THE LAST OF US[1]

NATALI PANIC-CIDIC

VIDEO GAMES, LITERATURE, AND COGNITIVE NARRATOLOGY

"The player has the same relationship to Ellie as Joel does. And we can take our time to build a relationship between these characters. And if we do it right, then, the player would be feeling that same growth that Joel does and kind of mirroring the emotional relationship between the two."[2]

THE LAST OF US (2012) (TLOU) is arguably one of the most successful games to date regarding the quality of storytelling and the player's relationship to the story and its characters.[3,4,5,6,7] It did not take long for the game to gain academic inter-

---

1   This is the short version of the article. Please visit my ResearchGate profile page for the extended version, which includes sections on Cognitive Literary Studies, Cognitive Narratology, and Ellie's character analysis: researchgate.net/profile/Natali_Panic-Cidic
2   Neil Druckman in: GROUNDED: THE MAKING OF THE LAST OF US (Area 5 2013, D: Jason Bertrand et al.).
3   McHendry, Gavin: "Why 'The Last of Us' Was the Greatest Game of the Last Console Generation," in: *Vice*, March 03, 2016, https://www.vice.com/en_uk/article/av9yv4/why-the-last-of-us-was-the-greatest-game-of-the-last-console-generation-450, retrieved 2019.

est. Some scholars focus on linguistic properties, such as Colăcel[8] in his study on speech acts. However, his study only shows how speech acts might support a player's world-building process. Instead, Colăcel would benefit from an in-depth analysis of *what* the effect of these speech acts is on the player. Here, the level of interaction should be considered as the game narrative unfolds through interaction and visualization. This is what Farca and Ladevéze[9] did with their study.

They explore the game as a critical dystopia to our society and focus on the game's aesthetics that trigger the player involvement with the story which transcends the virtual world of the game.

Their research provides a promising insight into the genre of critical dystopia, French philosophy, and the role of game environment, yet it does not quite explain how players are able to feel affected or immersed into the sublime world of TLOU and its characters. This is what I call the affectional perspective that seems to be disregarded to this point. It elucidates why story-driven games such as TLOU allow players to feel the growth Neil Druckman is talking about.

Therefore, I argue that in TLOU, (1) there is a high emotional bond between the player and the characters that (2) depends on the narrative structure which is (3) embedded in Joel's and Ellie's character development. In order to prove this three-fold thesis, I will use the framework of cognitive narratology.

In the upcoming sections, the cognitive framework of blending is used for theoretical-analytical examination of Joel and his character perspectives, as this paper focuses on the game's characters. Blending is a mental information processing system that is necessary for meaning making. In the concluding section, the results are summarized and evaluated.

---

4   Hanson, Kyle: "How The Last of Us is Still One of the Greatest Games of All Time," in: *AOTF*, September 11, 2018, attackofthefanboy.com/articles/the-last-of-us-proves-is-still-one-of-the-greatest-games-of-all-time/, retrieved 2019.

5   Horth, Samuel: "How The Last of Us raised the bar for video game narratives," in: *Techradar*, August 04, 2018, https://www.techradar.com/news/how-the-last-of-us-raised-the-bar-for-video-game-narratives, retrieved 2019.

6   Metacritic: "The Last of Us Remastered," July 29, 2014, www.metacritic.com/game/playstation-4/the-last-of-us-remastered

7   Metacritic: "The Last of Us," June 14, 2013, www.metacritic.com/game/playstation-3/the-last-of-us, retrieved 2019.

8   Colăcel, Onoriu: "Speech Acts in Post-Apocalyptic Games: *The Last of Us* (2014)," in: *Messages, Sages and Ages* 4 (2017), pp. 41-50.

9   Farca, Gerald/Ladevéze, Charlotte: "The Journey to Nature. *The Last of Us* as Critical Dystopia," DiGRA Conference 2016; http://www.digra.org/wp-content/uploads/digital-library/paper_246.pdf, retrieved 2019.

BLENDING THEORY

"It has become clear that readers do not only perceive characters as signs or symbols, but also form holistic representations, i.e so-called 'mental models' [...] of those individuals and their fictional minds. These files are constantly updated during the reading process and serve as a means of representing and storing all textual and inferred information about a particular character."[10]

Imagine yourself playing a round of RAINBOW SIX SIEGE (2015) with your friends. Before the mission starts, you discuss the tactics for this round. You say to one of the teammates, "please stick to this plan and don't go Leeroy Jenkins!"[11] Here, mental processes play into the understanding of this metaphor and the process of understanding can be called blending.

Developed by Fauconnier and Turner in 2002 as Conceptual Integration Network (Fig. 1, Fig. 2), blending is a mental model that we constantly run in our heads while reading, playing, buying furniture, or talking by activating sets or frames of information. These are referred to as mental models or mental spaces. There can be at least two mental spaces. In the Rainbow Six Siege example, 'stick to this plan' and 'Leeroy Jenkins' are such input spaces, where the teammates understand it by projecting the information of what plans are good for and the act of Leeroy Jenkins. This example characterizes that battle tactics are there for preventing such unfortunate events.

---

10 Hartner, Markus: "Cognitive Approaches to Narrative. Blending Theory and the Analysis of Character Perspective in Jackie Kay's Trumpet," in: Vera Nünning (Ed.), *New Approaches to Narrative. Cognition-Culture-History*, Trier: WVT 2013, pp. 57-71, here p. 58.
11 Leeroy Jenkins refers to a player who instead of listening to his teammate's battle plan prepared a meal. After returning and blindly running into the battle, his teammates are killed because of his mistake.

Figure 1: The Basic Diagram of Blending.

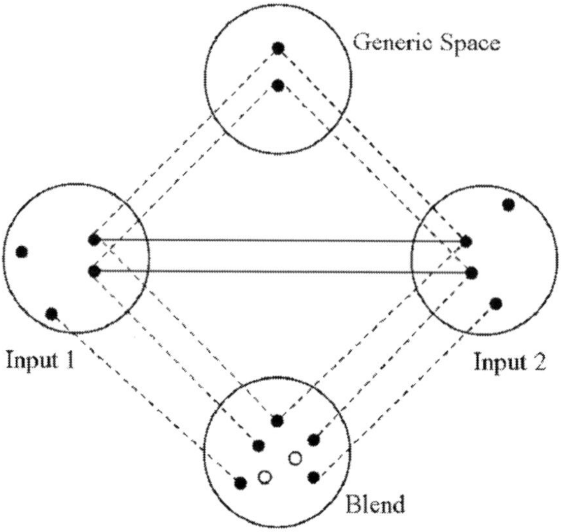

Source: G. Fauconnier, and M. Turner: *The Way We Think,* p.46.

There is an analogy between the two input spaces that is stored in the generic space, although they are two different ideas. Before the analogous elements find their way into the generic space, they are first identified as counterparts in the cross-space mapping (see Fig. 2). This generic space later allows blending to connect input points in the blended space. As Fauconnier and Turner point out, blending involves compression of information. Such compressions can be executed on various dimensions, as the following quote shows for time and space:

"When we see a Persian rug in a store and imagine how it would look in our house, we are compressing over two different physical spaces. We leave out conceptually all of the actual physical space that separates the real rug from our real house. When we imagine what answer we would give now to a criticism directed at us several years ago, we are compressing over times."[12]

For the Leeroy Jenkins example, the generic space stores the shared elements of 'defeat' and 'failed team play.' A plan is necessary to avoid unpleasant encoun-

---

12 Fauconnier, Gilles, and Mark Turner: *The Way We Think. Conceptual Blending and the Mind's Hidden Complexities*, New York: Basic Books 2003, p. 113.

ters. In a team, it is beneficial to coordinate individual movements and actions to enhance a positive outcome – win a match. Nonetheless, a plan can always fail. There is a high chance of being defeated because you play against players you never encountered before. Playing as a team, the chances of winning increase provided none of the teammates plays like Leeroy Jenkins.

Figure 2: Blending of Character Perspectives.

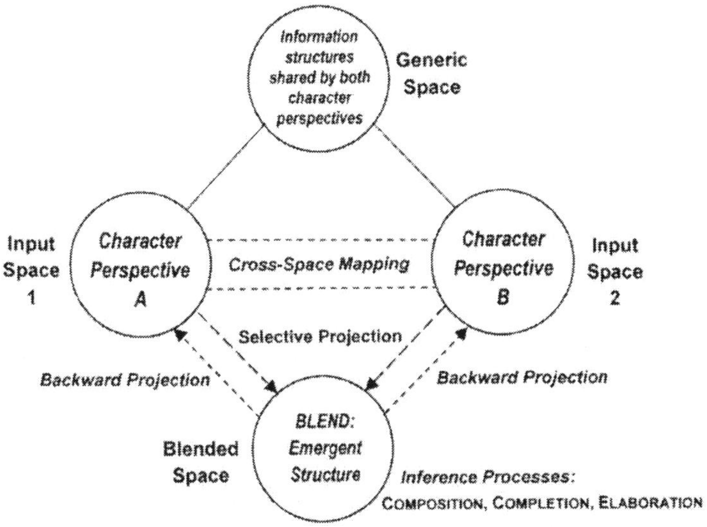

Source: M. Hartner, "Cognitive Approaches to Narrative," p. 62.

Based on this idea of shared elements, the generic space is projected onto the blended space where the emergent structure arises. In this structure, the concern of losing a match because of one teammate's recklessness becomes a reality, which you want to avoid.[13] Through the backward projection, you then associate that one player with Leeroy Jenkins.

According to Fauconnier and Turner, the emergent structure "is generated in three ways: through *composition* of projections from the inputs, through *completion* based on independently recruited frames and scenarios, and through *elabo-*

---

13 Schneider, Ralf: "Blending and the Study of Narrative: An Introduction," in: Ralf Schneider and Marcus Hartner (Eds.), *Blending and the Study of Narrative. Approaches and Applications*, Boston: De Gruyter 2012, pp. 1-30, here p. 5.

ration."[14] Composition joins elements of input spaces that appear to be different, such as the link of defeat and failed teamplay between a plan and Leeroy Jenkins. Completion uses our world knowledge and the existing frames. The metaphor only works if all players share the same frame of a plan and the concept of Leeroy Jenkins. As Schneider points out, "frames are the structures organizing the information projected into the blend."[15] Lastly, elaboration can be seen as a program which "runs the blend,"[16] as Fauconnier and Turner express it, in form of a simulation where you can elaborate on the metaphor by seeking a potential solution to the problem. The solution in the example calls for the player to listen and act according to the plan.

If you are familiar with RAINBOW SIX SIEGE and Leeroy Jenkins, think about how long it took to understand this metaphor and how long to read this section. Assuming you understood it, the process of understanding happens instantaneously leaving the question of how a mental model can be used for character analysis. As Hartner in the first quote of this subsection points out and Schneider elaborates more, "[i]n reading a narrative, we continually have to recruit mental spaces we fill with our knowledge of the world on the one hand, and spaces filled with aspects of the imaginary world elicited by the narrative we read (or listen to, watch, etc.) on the other."[17]

Additionally, in video games the unique element of interactivity contributes to the blending process by establishing a mental connection between players and game narrative. The player is aware of a distance between their avatars and themselves but the magical power of narrative and interactivity invites the player to reflect on their in-game actions the longer they play. Still aware of their distance, they start to understand avatar's personality, motivation and their actions. At some point, players can see their character's actions are in fact their own; pushing buttons on a controller to execute actions becomes player's choice of performing certain actions: "Game players are not simply directing their attention but are physically or mentally becoming part of the gaming experience itself through active participation."[18] Each players acquires their own individual meaning. This individual meaning will then have impact on the way how a narrative is being blended, therefore, interactivity contributes to the blending process.

---

14 G. Fauconnier, and M. Turner: *The Way We Think,* p.48. Emphasis in original.
15 R. Schneider: "Blending and the Study of Narrative: An Introduction," p. 7.
16 G. Fauconnier, and M. Turner: *The Way We Think,* p.48.
17 R. Schneider: "Blending and the Study of Narrative: An Introduction," p. 11.
18 Bostan, Barbaros: "Player Motivation: A Psychological Perspective," in: *Computers in Entertainment* 7, *2* (2009), pp. 1-26, here p. 1.

The difference between non-interactive media and video games is that video games can offer players a closer connection to a medium because they are interactive. Even though the example game has a linear narrative and gives players no choice on that part, it is still interactive enough for each type of player to experience the game in their own pace and style.

In theory, an emotional attachment to the characters of TLOU is possible because the narrative unfolds through interaction but is processed through the character development, and narrative and gameplay agree in terms of characters. Therefore, it is only sensible to track a character's development from the start to the end of the game by isolating crucial input points, their differences, interpreting the blend, and in the backward projection analyzing the results. To prove this, the next section works with the theory of blending in application to TLOU's character Joel.

BLENDING THEORY IN APPLICATION

In the epilogue, the dialogue between Ellie and Joel marks, on the one hand, the ending of their journey and on the other, their psychological transformation. The players can feel the same transformation that is only possible if an agreement between narrative and gameplay exists, where the character undergoes a natural character development. The importance of a steady pace development lies in the interactive nature of video games.

Everything on the narrative level is gradually revealed to, and by, the player. Joel and Ellie are narrative carriers through which the player reveals the narrative pieces. These feed into the mental spaces that are used to comprehend the actions. The players are constantly in the process of conceptual blending. The knowledge from the blend reflects what they already know about the narrative and characters. At this stage, the players can tell how their characters will act to a specific encounter and can directly spot a ludonarrative dissonance.[19] The latter leads to a failed or weak emotional bond.

In the process of comprehending the actions and narrative, the players are (sub)consciously developing a connection to their fictional characters. As Neil

---

19 Please refer to Clint Hocking, who coined the term, for definition: Hocking, Clint: "Ludonarrative Dissonance in Bioshock," in: *Click Nothing*, October 07, 2007, https://clicknothing.typepad.com/click_nothing/2007/10/ludonarrative-d.html, retrieved 2019.

Druckman explains,[20] the narrative and the story world of TLOU is embedded in the characters and he wants the player to connect to those two characters emotionally.

This confirms what Keen assumes about the narrative structure. She suggests that "aspects of plot structure and narration [...] might have a role in invoking reader's empathy."[21] However, not all players are the same and there can be various individual reasons for the player to establish a connection with their character but, in the case of TLOU, the obvious type is empathy.

Based on these ideas and statements, this section adapts the framework of blending to retrace character's development. This analysis will provide possible explanation towards the high emotional bond between the player and the character.

Figure 3: Joel's Character Perspectives

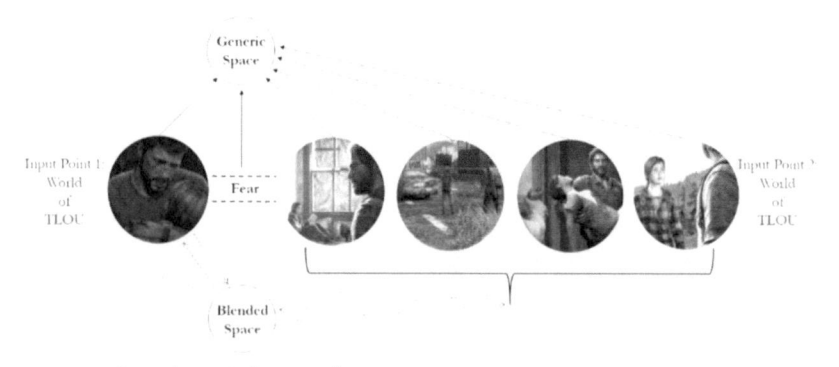

Joel

Joel is a psychologically a much different man at the end of the game, then he was at the beginning of it. The circumstances the player is introduced to at the start of the game in comparison to the end also change drastically. In the epi-

---

20 Neil Druckman in: GROUNDED: THE MAKING OF THE LAST OF US (Area 5 2013, D: Jason Bertrand et al.)
21 Keen, Suzanne: "A Theory of Empathy," *Narrative* 14 (2006), pp. 207-236, here p. 207.

logue, the player witnesses Joel lying to Ellie about an important event. But, as I will argue below, they are likely to agree with Joel's controversial decision. This is because players understand what Joel has been through; they experienced firsthand various events challenging, changing, and shaping the characters. "[C]haracters [...] manifest themselves as circumstances change,"[22] hence the usage of the framework of blending for Joel's character development.

Hartner is one of the scholars adapting this model for analysis on multiperspectivity to investigate narrative character perspectives. In this model (Fig. 2), mental spaces are labeled as character-perspectives with input spaces. In this first attempt to analyze a character development in a video game, five interconnected character perspectives (abbr. CP) are chosen.

The first CP (Fig. 3) marks Joel's disturbance of character at the start of the game. In this scene, the player experiences a tragic moment at the start of the end of the civilized world, witnessing the death of Joel's daughter, Sarah. This prologue sequence shows Joel as very vulnerable and sad, albeit creating a picture of a caring father. Without a doubt, this is the most important scene that has impact on Joel's decisions and choices that he makes around Ellie, hence, the first CP-A.

As this section is interested in Joel's development over the course of the game, there is one CP-A and four CP-Bs as they are all compared to the CP-A. Furthermore, at all times, these five CPs are influenced, or rather shaped by a world surrounded by death, disease, destruction, and constant struggle for surviving.

What these CPs share through the cross-space mapping is Joel's fear of losing loved ones and the unwillingness of suffering any further loss. The scene for CP-B1 visualizes this fear and the dialogue below explains the nature of Joel and Ellie's relationship. Initially, Joel is only supposed to deliver Ellie to the laboratory of the Fireflies (a group fighting to find a cure against the virus), however over the course of the game, they develop a mutual respect for each other. The players can see how Joel becomes very protective of Ellie and vice versa. They build a father-daughter relationship, which is evident from scenes such as the one printed below. When Ellie runs away from Joel because she overhears that he is leaving her with his brother Tommy, Joel has a chance to reflect his decision in an intervention with Ellie:

---

22 G. Fauconnier, and M. Turner: *The Way We Think,* p. 249.

> "Joel: Do you even realize what your life means? Huh? Running off like that. Putting yourself at risk...it's pretty goddamn stupid.
> Ellie: Well, I guess we're both disappointed with each other then.
> J: What do you want from me?
> E: Admit that you wanted to get rid of me the whole time.
> J: Tommy knows this area better than...
> E: Agh, fuck that.
> J: Well, I'm sorry, I trust him better than I trust myself.
> E: Stop with the bullshit. What are you so afraid of? That I'm gonna end up like Sam? I can't get infected. I can take care of myself.
> J: How many close calls have we had?
> E: Well, we seem to be doing alright so far.
> J: And now you'll be doing even better with Tommy.
> Ellie: I'm not her, you know."[23]

The player starts twenty years after Joel's tragic loss and is introduced to a careless smuggler. In this dialogue, he clearly shows a change of character by taking the second chance in life with Ellie and starting to care again. In CP-B2, at the bus depot, he even makes plans with her:

> "Joel: Look. Hospital. This is where we get off. Let's go, kiddo. Feel that breeze, huh? I tell you, on a day like this, I'd just sit on my porch, pick away at my six string. Yeah, once we're done with this whole thing, I'm gonna teach you how to play guitar. Yeah, I reckon you'd really like that. Whaddya say, huh?"[24]

Riding on the "breeze" of a new beginning, he is optimistic for the first time after the death of Sarah, which is very unlike his character from the beginning of the game. Given this and the previous knowledge the player gathers across different events with Joel and Ellie, Joel's decision to save Ellie (CP-B3) and deprive the Fireflies of existence may be drastic, but it is justified. In the epilogue (CP-B4), he lies to Ellie because he blends Ellie with Sarah. This is what Fauconnier and Turner call "double-scope identity blend"[25] that makes him save one life instead of millions of others. Interestingly, Joel or Ellie never communicate

---

23 THE LAST OF US (Sony 2012, O: Neil Druckman, Bruce Straley/Naughty Dog).
24 Ibid.
25 G. Fauconnier, and M. Turner: *The Way We Think,* p. 259.

their feelings directly to each other in the game, and yet, the player understands why Joel did not want to continue his journey with Ellie in CP-B1, why he has changed his mind (CP-B2), why he saved one life for the millions of others (CP-B3), and why he is dishonest to Ellie (CP-B4).

The player can see the absence of a ludonarrative dissonance because of the blending process. Blending brings out everything that is not directly communicated to the player. It helps to see the "concrete manifestations" of an "essence, which is itself abstract and invisible."[26] When the player creates the blended space from the generic space, an emergent structure arises. The player can see that a father-daughter relationship frame has emerged. Again, nowhere in the game is this communicated. The rule for this structure or frame to appear requires a character change.[27] As we have seen, Joel occupies different frames in the five perspectives that he gradually alters and even redeems himself:

"In literary, dramatic, and cinematic representations of redemption, the protagonist frequently hesitates at just the instant when he failed before, but this time does the right thing. We do not take such a plot as the story of a person who failed once and succeeded once, with equal weight given to the two events. Instead, we take the second event as the one that reveals the essence of the protagonist and proves that the first was a fluke. The success does not simply neutralize the failure, setting the scale back to zero. It restores the protagonist's identity, making him "whole once again."[28]

Joel holds himself responsible for failing Sarah and in this process loses himself just to have a chance at redemption with Ellie.

If the narrative structure invokes the reader's empathy, then it is important that the players can recognize the plot pattern. In the case of TLOU, they should be able to identify Joel and Ellie as narrative conduits. Only then can they run the right process of blending. By blending, which engages not only in-game logic but also player's real world-knowledge, they will develop a very clear understanding of the characters they are playing. In the written narrative media, blending helps the readers make meaning out of a text or blend various character perspectives. As in written sources blending is used in video games, too, but because of the interactive level, the players are not only reflecting and processing characters actions but also their own. Hence, if they can participate in a gradual character development, they are likely to show empathy towards their fictional counterparts.

---

26 Ibid.
27 G. Fauconnier, and M. Turner: *The Way We Think,* p. 253.
28 Ibid., p. 259.

Character Development and the Unbreakable Bond

In summary, the players are not identifying with the characters but are experiencing the same emotional roller coaster as Joel and Ellie because of the interactive nature of games. They can feel empathy and be affected by everything that concerns the two characters, due to the gradual character development which at the same time is the narrative element. This calls for an ongoing blending process. Only through blending, which is the cognitive process of meaning-making, is the player able to process the highly emotional events and consciously experience a relationship building towards and between the characters.

The answer to the question 'Why many players are conflicted with the ending of the game?' is simply because they are humans and care. Of course, being able to feel for fictional characters involves high-quality storytelling and narrative elements that support a gradual, unforced character development in order to avoid a ludonarrative dissonance.

Critique of the Methodology and Analysis

Doubtlessly, the framework of blending offers a multiperspective, transmedial, and flexible usage even to scholars who are unfamiliar with it. For game designers and literary scholars, blending helps to uncover the way the players think, hence, the way they perceive a narrative. Especially for game designers who are aiming for a story-driven video game, knowing how your players are processing the narrative input is of paramount importance. In general, the conducted analysis is based on the logical cognitive meaning processing. However, there are three flaws that need to be pointed out.

First, the process of meaning-making in the blended space and the emergent structure, in fact, happen unconsciously and once the meaning is established, we can only see it from this one paradigm, as Fauconnier and Turner[29] and Schneider[30] point out. How can we be sure that what we see as right is right?

Second, there are many blends possible because each player brings their individual world-knowledge to the emergent structure as there are different types of players. Some are interested in the story, others only play the multiplayer part

---

29 G. Fauconnier and M. Turner: *The Way We Think,* p. 263.
30 R. Schneider: "Blending and the Study of Narrative: An Introduction," p. 7.

where you never have any contact with the story or the characters. Furthermore, every analysis might be affected by the observer's paradox.[31]

Lastly, while a theoretical-analytical approach proved to be very fruitful with significant results, empirical studies still need to be conducted. Cognitive Literary Studies (CLS) (where blending is situated) are known for their encouragement and call for empirical studies. The gathered results should now be tested out on players. Ideally, you would closely observe players gameplay and after each session, you would conduct an interview about their perceptions of the game. This would further provide factual information on the thesis.

LITERATURE

Bostan, Barbaros: "Player Motivation: A Psychological Perspective," in: *ACM Computers in Entertainment* 7, 2 (2009), pp. 1-26.

Colăcel, Onoriu: "Speech Acts in Post-Apocalyptic Games: *The Last of Us* (2014)," in: *Messages, Sages and Ages* 4, 1 (2017), pp. 41-50.

Farca, Gerald, Charlotte Ladevéze: "The Journey to Nature. The Last of Us as Critical Dystopia," in: *DiGRA Conference*, 2016, http://www.digra.org/wp-content/uploads/digital-library/paper_246.pdf, retrieved 2019.

Fauconnier, Gilles and Mark Turner: *The Way We Think. Conceptual Blending and the Mind's Hidden Complexities*, New York: Basic Books 2003.

Hartner, Markus: "Cognitive Approaches to Narrative. Blending Theory and the Analysis of Character Perspective in Jackie Kay's Trumpet," in: Vera Nünning (Ed.), *New Approaches to Narrative. Cognition-Culture-History*, Trier: WVT 2013, pp. 57-71.

Keen, Suzanne: "A Theory of Empathy," *Narrative* 14, 3 (2006), pp. 207-236.

Labov, William: *Sociolinguistic Patterns*, Philadelphia: University of Pennsylvania Press 1972.

Schneider, Ralf: "Blending and the Study of Narrative: An Introduction," in: Ralf Schneider and Marcus Hartner (eds.), *Blending and the Study of*

---

31 Observer's paradox is a term coined by William Labov (1972) in *Sociolinguistic Patterns*, Philadelphia: University of Pennsylvania Press, p. 209, and it defines that "the aim of linguistic research in the community must be to find out how people talk when they are not being systematically observed; yet we can only obtain these data by systematic observation." This is what researchers need to look out for, if they do not want to influence the results or studies with their biases.

Narrative. Approaches and Applications, Boston: De Gruyter 2012, pp. 1-30.

LUDOGRAPHY

TOM CLANCY'S RAINBOW SIX SIEGE (Ubisoft 2015, O: Ubisoft Montreal)
THE LAST OF US (Sony 2012, O: Neil Druckman, Bruce Straley/Naughty Dog)

FILMOGRAPHY

GROUNDED: THE MAKING OF THE LAST OF US (Area 5, 2013, D: Jason Bertrand)

ONLINE MEDIA

Hanson, Kyle: "How The Last of Us is Still One of the Greatest Games of All Time," in: AOTF, September 11, 2018; www.attackofthefanboy.com/articles/the-last-of-us-proves-is-still-one-of-the-greatest-games-of-all-time/ retrieved 2019.

Hocking, Clint: "Ludonarrative Dissonance in Bioshock," in: Click Nothing, October 07, 2007; https://clicknothing.typepad.com/click_nothing/2007/10/ludonarrative-d.html, retrieved 2019.

Horth, Samuel: "How The Last of Us raised the bar for video game narratives," in: *Techradar*, August 04, 2018; www.techradar.com/news/how-the-last-of-us-raised-the-bar-for-video-game-narratives, retrieved 2019.

Metacritic: "The Last of Us," June 14, 2013; www.metacritic.com/game/playstation-3/the-last-of-us, retrieved 2019.

Metacritic: "The Last of Us Remastered," July 29, 2014, www.metacritic.com/game/playstation-4/the-last-of-us-remastered, retrieved 2019.

McHendry, Gavin: "Why 'The Last of Us' Was the Greatest Game of the Last Console Generation," in: *Vice*, March 03, 2016; www.vice.com/en_uk/article/av9yv4/why-the-last-of-us-was-the-greatest-game-of-the-last-console-generation-450, retrieved 2019.

Depression and Digital Games

An Investigation of Existing Uses of Therapy Games

LEONIE WOLF

INTRODUCTION

Depression: An illness of modern society, its causes and treatment methods

Depression, or Major Depression Disorder, is a common mental disorder characterized by persistent depressed mood, loss of interest in most activities, and feelings of loneliness, hopelessness and worthlessness. People suffering from depression usually have a deep-rooted, insubstantial negative perception of their own personality and the world around them. Additionally, people with depression can experience low appetite, poor concentration, reduced energy, sleeping disorders and anxiety. More than 300 million people worldwide suffer from Major Depression Disorder and it is expected to be one of the three leading causes of disability by 2030.[1,2] Depression can affect people of all ages and ethnic backgrounds. It has various causes, like stress and the inability to cope with loss or traumatic experiences, such as childhood traumas or accidents.

---

1 WHO. "Depression." Who.int. http://www.who.int/en/news-room/fact-sheets/detail/depression
2 Mathers, C.D./Loncar, D.: "Projections of Global Mortality and Burden of Disease from 2002 to 2030," https://doi.org/10.1371/journal.pmed.0030442, p. 2022.

Treatment methods include psychotherapy, pharmacotherapy, neuromodulation, art therapy, exercise therapy, acupuncture, and yoga, among others.[3] Successfully conducted studies on Virtual Reality exposure therapy (VRET) to treat phobias during the 1990s led to further research on the clinical effectiveness of this method for other mental conditions, like PTSD, anxieties or addictions.[4,5] Over the last fifteen years, digital game therapy has gained the interest of researchers and therapists alike.

Digital games have the potential to intensify therapeutic approaches based on how players perceive their content. Patients of game therapy, who can relate or identify with parts of the game world or narrative, will potentially change their perception about themselves along with the actions in the game. Digital games are cersatile tools that ca be shaped to a patient's individual needs, pick up on their starting point and lead them towards a healthier self-perception. To date, numerous forms of digital game treatment have been successfully tested with depressed patients,[6] such as serious games, exergames, VR games, digital psychotherapy, and games with cognitive control.[7]

---

3   Kessler, R.C. et al.: "The Use of Complementary and Alternative Therapies to Treat Anxiety and Depression in the United States," in: *The American Journal of Psychiatry* 158, no. 2 (2001), p. 291.

4   Botella, C. et al.: "Virtual reality treatment of claustrophobia: a case report," in: *Behaviour Research and Therapy* 36 (1998), pp. 243-244.

5   Mishkind, M.C. et al.: "Review of Virtual Reality Treatment in Psychiatry: Evidence Versus Current Diffusion and Use," in: K. Shore (Ed.), *Psychiatry in the Digital Age*, Springer US 2017, p.1.

6   Fleming et al.: "SERIOUS GAMES FOR THE TREATMENT OR PREVENTION OF DEPRESSION: A SYSTEMATIC REVIEW," in *Revista de Psicopatología y Psicología Clínica* 19, no. 3 (2014), pp. 227-242 and Li, J./Theng, Y./Foo, S.: "Game-Based Digital Interventions for Depression Therapy: A Systematic Review and Meta-Analysis," in: *Cyberpsychology, Behavior, and Social Networking* 17, no. 8 (2014), pp. 519-527 and Li, J./Theng, Y./Foo, S.: "Effect of exergames on Depression: A Systematic Review and Meta-Analysis," in: *Cyberpsychology, Behavior, and Social Networking* 19, no. 1 (2016), pp. 34-41.

7   Richardson, T./Stallard, P./Velleman, S.: "Computerised cognitive behavioural therapy for the prevention and treatment of depression and anxiety in children and adolescents: a systematic review," in: *Clinical Child and Family Psychology Review* 13 (2010), pp. 275–290 and Spek, V. et al.: "Internet-based cognitive behaviour therapy for symptoms of depression and anxiety: a meta-analysis," in: *Psychological Medicine* 37 (2007), pp. 319–328: quoted after: Li et al.: "Effect of exergames on Depression: A Systematic Review and Meta-Analysis," p. 34 and Schoneveld, E.: "MindLight –

This paper demonstrates how digital game therapy can inherit the therapeutic value of art therapy and exercise therapy, and how *play* affects mental health in games. It is hoped that this analysis inspires researchers to further investigate digital game therapy as well as contribute to its establishment as a form of therapy.

THE ARTISTIC AND PLAYFUL CHARACTERISTICS OF GAME THERAPY

Common treatment methods have a long history and have proven helpful for many patients suffering from depression.[8] In psychotherapy patients work on understanding negative thinking loops and strive to adopt healthier and more functional behaviors.[9] Pharmacotherapy focuses on using antidepressant drugs to restore the neurotransmitter activity in malfunctioning brain circuits caused by mental disorders.[10] Neuromodulation works in a similar way but instead of using antidepressants, short electrical pulses are applied to the patients scalp to create seizures that alter the neurotransmitters of the brain.[11]

However, less than 50 % of people affected by depression actually receive such treatments due to lack of resources or trained healthcare providers and the social stigma that is associated with mental disorders.[12] Additionally, common treatment methods are often human intensive and highly expensive.[13] Negative

---

Childhood Anxiety Prevention." Gemhlab.com. https://gemhlab.com/projects/anxiety/mindlight-childhood-anxiety-prevention/ (accessed 07.06.18).

8   American Psychological Association. "Understanding psychotherapy and how it works." Apa.org. http://www.apa.org/helpcenter/understanding-psychotherapy.aspx

9   American Psychiatric Association. "What is Psychotherapy?" Psychiatry.org. https://www.psychiatry.org/patients-families/psychotherapy

10 Ceskova, E.: "Current pharmacotherapy of depression – focused on multimodal/multifunctional antidepressants," in: *Expert opinion on Pharmacotherapy* 17 (2016), p. 2.

11 University of Michigan Depression Center. "Electroconvulsive Therapy (ECT)." Depressiontoolkit.org. http://www.depressiontoolkit.org/treatmentoptions/neuromodulation/ect.asp

12 WHO. "Depression." Who.int. http://www.who.int/en/news-room/fact-sheets/detail/depression

13 Cai, H. et al.: "A Virtual-Reality Based Neurofeedback Game Framework for Depression Rehabilitation using Pervasive Three-Electrode EEG Collector," in: *Chi-*

side-effects from antidepressant drugs or neuromodulation can also complicate remission.[14] This creates a barrier for those seeking help and can cause patients to quit their therapy.

Digital game therapy for depression is very versatile and flexible in its application. It is an attractive treatment method for people of all ages[15] and can be executed in various settings.[16] Therapy games can be designed to fit a patient's needs and can provide a combination of different types of treatment. In contrast to common treatment methods, playing video games can improve cognitive functions, specifically in attention and processing speed by hyper-stimulating the regions of the brain which reduce in depressed patients over time.[17,18] To persuade affected people to start a treatment at all is the first step to initiating recovery. Digital games offer an interesting form of therapy that appears much more accessible and motivational than common treatment methods.

However, to provide a patient with a therapy game, the patient needs access to a game system and a suitable therapy game, which might not have been developed yet. There have been attempts to create tools for therapists to develop

---

neseCSCW '17 *Proceedings of the 12th Chinese Conference on Computer Supported Cooperative Work and Social Computing* (2017), p. 173.

14 University of Michigan Depression Center. "Electroconvulsive Therapy (ECT)." Depressiontoolkit.org. http://www.depressiontoolkit.org/treatmentoptions/neuromodulation/ect.asp

15 Hoelscher, K. quoted after: Berjaoui, D.: "Exploring Active Video Games (AVGS) as an Intervention Promoting Wellbeing as It Relates to Depression" (Senior Honors Thesis), Michigan: Honors College, 2013, p. 7.

16 Berjaoui, D.: "Exploring Active Video Games (AVGS) as an Intervention Promoting Wellbeing as It Relates to Depression," p. 3.

17 Green, S.C./Bavelier, D.: "Action video game modifies visual selective attention," in: *nature* 423 (2003), pp. 534-537 and Dye at al.: "Increasing Speed of Processing with Action Video Games," in: *Current Directions in Psychological Science* 18 (2009), pp. 321-326: quoted after: Kühn et al.: "Fighting Depression: Action Video Game Play May Reduce Rumination and Increase Subjective and Objective Cognition in Depressed Patients," p. 2.

18 Davie, M.: "Chronic depression shrinks brain's memories and emotions." Theguardian.com. https://www.theguardian.com/society/2015/jun/30/chronic-depression-shrinks-brains-memories-and-emotions and Naranjo, C.A./Tremblay, L.K./Busto, U.E.: "The role of the brain reward system in depression," in: *Progress in Neuro-Psychopharmacology and Biological Psychiatry* 25 (2001), p. 784.

therapy games but, so far, they prove to be quite limited.[19] Digital games as a treatment for depression seems to be most effective for mild and moderate depression. Patients with severe depression or suicidal tendencies will most likely require additional forms of therapy. It is also not recommended for patients who experience video game addiction, even if a therapy game does not exhibit addictive features.[20]

Exercise Therapy

Research has proven that exercise therapy can help improve mental health conditions and provide a feeling of well-being. When used for the treatment of mild or moderate depression, exercising can be as effective as antidepressants or psychotherapy. Exercising releases endorphins and enkephalins into the body, which are chemicals known to promote feelings of well-being and pain relief.[21]

Exergames are video games that require physical activity from the player in order to be played. While most ordinary digital games receive input from finger movements on controllers, players need to apply full body motion to participate in exergames.[22] Research shows that exergames are among the most popular and most successfully tested games to achieve depression remission. The reason for this is the combination of physical activity, audiovisual feedback, and the joy of engaging in digital game playing.[23]

Studies have shown that VR games for the treatment of stroke survivors are especially motivating as a form of therapy because the system is programmed so that patients see a normally-functioning body on the screen, thus diverting focus from their affected limbs.[24] Another advantage of VR exergame therapy is that

---

19 Desai, N. et al.: *Creating Video Games to Treat Chronic Depression*, Alberta: University of Alberta 2010, pp. 2-3.
20 Carrasco, Á.E.: "Acceptability of an adventure video game in the treatment of female adolescents with symptoms of depression," p. 16.
21 MENTAL HEALTH FOUNDATION: *Up and running: exercise therapy and the treatment of mild or moderate depression in primary care*, London: Mental Health Foundation 2005, pp. 25-26. https://www.mentalhealth.org.uk/sites/default/files/up_running_report.pdf
22 American College of Sports Medicine: "Exergaming." Acsm.org/public-information/brochures, https://www.acsm.org/docs/brochures/exergaming.pdf
23 Li et al.: "Effect of exergames on Depression: A Systematic Review and Meta-Analysis," p. 34.
24 Burdea, G.C./Polistico, K.: "A Review of Integrative Virtual Reality Games for Rehabilitation," pp. 734-735.

the system can automatically save the progress and create a report, which gives therapists more time to tend to their patients instead of evaluating the data manually.[25] A different study showed a 20 % reduction of pain intensity and improvements in depression for post-cancer surgery patients after 16 sessions of treatment.[26]

When testing a VR exercise game on women with osteoarthritis in 30-minute sessions three times a week for a total of four weeks, the results showed that depression levels decreased significantly among the participants compared to the control group.[27] The initiators of the study argue that the positive results are based on the functionality and task-oriented activity of exercise games.

Exergames can be especially valuable to inpatient units because healthcare facilities often limit patients from trying something new to reduce their depression.[28] Additionally, they do not require much space, can be included as sessions in a daily or weekly program, and are not human-intensive. Exergames do not require much space, can be included as sessions in a daily or weekly program, and are not human-intensive. The success of exergames can partially be explained by the effect that leisure activity has on physical and mental health.[29] Those who experience improvement in their mental health will likely continue playing exergames after their release from their inpatient unit.[30] Having such a hobby gives released patients a daily structure, an interest that could help them connect with other people, and a gateway to societal reintegration.

---

25 Ibid., 736.

26 House, G. et al.: „A feasibility study to determine the benefits of upper extremity virtual rehabilitation therapy for coping with chronic pain post-cancer surgery," in: *British Journal of Pain* 10, no. 4 (2016), pp. 186-197: quoted after: Burdea/Polistico: "A Review of Integrative Virtual Reality Games for Rehabilitation," p. 736.

27 Wi, S.Y./Kang, J.H., Jang, J.H.: "Clinical Feasibility of Exercise Game for Depression Treatment in Older Women with Osteoarthritis: a Pilot Study," in: *Journal of Physical Therapy Science* 25 (2013), p. 166.

28 Berjaoui, D.: "Exploring Active Video Games (AVGS) as an Intervention Promoting Wellbeing as It Relates to Depression" p. 7.

29 Tinsley, H. E. A./Eldredge, B. D.: "Psychological benefits of leisure participation: A taxonomy of leisure activities based on their need-gratifying properties," in: *Journal of Counseling Psychology* 42, no. 2 (1995), pp. 123-132: quoted after: Berjaoui, D.: "Exploring Active Video Games (AVGS) as an Intervention Promoting Wellbeing as It Relates to Depression" p. 21.

30 Berjaoui, D.: "Exploring Active Video Games (AVGS) as an Intervention Promoting Wellbeing as It Relates to Depression" p. 3.

A systematic review by Li et al. revealed that demographic factors, depression severity, and game type influence the effectiveness of exergame therapy.[31] Gender, age, and ethnicity also need to be considered when designing exergames for depression treatment. The results of Li et al. demonstrate that active gaming can be effective for all ages and not just young adults. Furthermore, exergames high in playfulness have a significantly larger effect on improving depression than those low in playfulness.[32] It is not clear yet how this form of therapy will perform over long periods of time because long-term studies on game therapy have not been conducted yet.

Art Therapy

Art therapy focuses on the creation of art with numerous materials, across disciplines such as painting, clay modeling, sculpting, drawing, and crafting.[33] The positive effect art therapy has on mental health issues is based on the act of creation itself and being able to lose oneself in an activity whilst taking the mind off problems.[34] Art created during therapy can then be used as a visual representation of a patient's self-perception and discussed with a therapist to detect negative thinking loops.[35] On a neurological level, the success of art therapy is explained by the relationship of serotonergic and dopaminergic neurotransmitter systems and the origin of creativity.[36] These neurotransmitters also play a role in mental health conditions.

By observing the choice of materials for the therapy and the process of art creation, it is possible for both the patient and the therapist to identify negative thinking loops and even help identify suicidal tendencies in a patient.[37]

---

31 Li et al: "Game-Based Digital Interventions for Depression Therapy: A Systematic Review and Meta-Analysis," pp. 519–527.
32 Ibid, 39.
33 Farokhi, M.: "Art Therapy in Humanistic Psychiatry," in: *Procedia – Social and Behavioral Sciences* 30 (2011), p. 2089-2091.
34 Makin, S./Gask, L.: "'Getting back to normal': the added value of an art-based programme in promoting 'recovery' for common but chronic mental health problems," in: *Chronic Illness* 8, no. 1 (2011), p. 71.
35 Martius, P./Marten, D.: "Kunsttherapie," in: *Psychotherapeut* 59, no. 4 (2014), p. 331.
36 Reuter, M. et al.: "Identification of first candidate genes for creativity: a pilot study," in: *Brain Research* 1069, no. 1, (2006), pp. 190–197: quoted after: Martius /Marten: "Kunsttherapie," p. 335.
37 Bronisch T./Spreti F.: "The role of paintings in suicide prevention," in: Wassermann, Danuta/Wassermann, Camilla (eds.), *Oxford Textbook of Suicidology*, Oxford: Oxford

Art therapy can also help reveal if patients experienced deficits in their play behavior during childhood. Lev S. Vygotsky states that creativity and imaginative thinking are linked to childhood play.[38] Reproductive imagination originates in childhood play and then evolves into more complex and mature thinking processes. If this process does not take place in childhood, adolescents will struggle to produce higher cognitive functions and thoughts.

Many game designers make use of the symbolism of colors and shapes that is also used in art therapy to elicit a certain mood in the player. Dark and less saturated colors are generally perceived in the context of negative emotions while light and vibrant colors resemble happiness and inner peave.

The game world of LIMBO (2010), for example, is completely monochrome with a heavy use of black and white. The color scheme of the game conveys emotions of loneliness and unease and supports the narrative of the game. There are many interpretations of the plot but most of them revolve around topics like grief, death, abuse, and phobias.[39,40]

In JOURNEY (2012) the player travels through different environments with changing color schemes, which create feelings of peace and comfort, energy and zest for action, melancholy, and depression. The story of JOURNEY is discovering the meaning of life through the journey.[41] The gameplay portrays the different stages and emotional states experienced in the span of a (human) lifetime.

The color theory in FLOWER (2009) is very strong. The vibrant blue sky and green grassland in combination with the colorful flower petals represent liveliness and joy in contrast to the dark and gloomy urban environment, which is

---

University Press 2008, pp. 445–453: quoted after: Martius/Marten: "Kunsttherapie," p. 336.

38 Vygotskij, L.S.: *Imagination and Creativity* quoted after: Smolucha, F.: "The relevance of Vygotsky's theory of creative imagination for contemporary research on play," in: *Creativity Research Journal* 5, no. 1 (2009), pp. 69–76: quoted after: Blomdahl et al.: "Meeting oneself in inner dialogue: a manual-based Phenomenological Art Therapy as experienced by patients diagnosed with moderate to severe depression," p. 23.

39 Wikipedia. „Limbo (video game)." Wikipedia.com. https://en.wikipedia.org/wiki/Limbo_(video_game)#Presentation (accessed June 1, 2018).

40 Kotaku. „The Most Depressive Theories On What *Limbo* Means." Kotaku.com. https://kotaku.com/the-most-depressing-theories-on-what-limbo-means-1724276367 (accessed June 1, 2018).

41 Gameinformer. "The Meaning Behind Journey." Gameinformer.com http://www.gameinformer.com/blogs/members/b/le_hannibal_blog/archive/2012/04/13/the-meaning-behind-journey.aspx (accessed June 5, 2018)

shown at the beginning of the game. Many players reported that the game had a therapeutic effect on their mood.[42] This also comes from the act of "creating" within the game, as the grass sprouts and the game world flourishes, quite literally, at the hands of the player.[43] Harnessing motion control input, the player manipulates the wind to guide flower petals to dry patches in the countryside. When successful, the player revives the dried up landscape, transforming it into a lush, green pasture.

In ABZÛ (2016) the soothing tones of an underwater setting are used to communicate with the player and evoke emotion. The player comes across differently colored environments that convey specific moods. The game uses a drastic color scheme to indicate safe or dangerous areas in the game world. DEEP (2015) is a VR game for people with anxiety and depression that has a similar setting. The artist, Niki Smit, explains that he researched color psychology to design the game world.[44]

Just like colors, shapes also have an impact on emotions. Round shapes and circles are generally considered soft, dynamic, and "flowy," while strong and edgy shapes like triangles and spikes can convey agression and danger. An explanation for what shapes "feel like" is the way children experience them when they use their sense of touch to explore the world. When a child touches a sharp object and experiences pain, this feeling of danger will be remembered and associated with sharp objects in the future.[45] To return to ABZÛ here again, the developers frequently made use of shapes in combination with colors. The player comes across sharp triangular architecture and objects in bright red and black colors, which portray aggression and harm. The shape and color of these objetcs clearly indicate danger and resemble the "bad" of the game world. There are countless examples of games that use this shade and color 'code' to appeal to players' personal and cultural experiences and guide their perception of the narrative.

---

42 Suellentrop, C.: "In Bloom." Slate.com. http://www.slate.com/articles/technology/gaming/2009/02/in_bloom.html?via=gdpr-consent (accessed June 1, 2018).

43 IGN. "Flower PS4 Review." Ign.com http://www.ign.com/articles/2013/11/13/flower-ps4-review (accessed June 1, 2018).

44 Deep VR: A VR game that's good for you (USA, 2016, D: Engadget) https://www.youtube.com/watch?v=7T_iQsOseAg

45 Solarski, C.: "The Aesthetics of Game Art and Game Design." Gamasutra.com. https://www.gamasutra.com/view/feature/185676/the_aesthetics_of_game_art_and_.php?print=1

THEORIES OF PLAY

"The opposite of play [...] is not work, [...] it is depression."[46] This quote by Brian Sutton-Smith is the main inspiration for this paper. It underlines the theory that play is related to our mental well-being and deeply rooted within our human nature.

There are many attempts to define the term *play*, but none of them is definite. Brian Sutton-Smith says about defining play: "Something about the nature of play itself frustrates fixed meaning."[47] One difficulty in defining play is that some philosophers and writers separate "play" and "playing a game" while others do not make this distinction. Bernard Suits defines gameplaying as "[...] playing a game is the voluntary attempt to overcome unnecessary obstacles," while he calls *play* itself a 'leisure activity.'[48,49] Vygotsky states that there is a paradox in play among children since "playing by rules" gives them the most pleasure although they could play without rules entirely.[50]

Many researchers argue that play behavior originates in an attempt to learn and develop in childhood and they compare it with animal play.[51] However, this does not explain why adults play, considering that adults are "all grown-up" and do not to need to acquire basic living skills. While Sutton-Smith suggests that adult play is a kind of pleasant way of killing time,[52] Bernard Suits goes as far as claiming that if humankind lived in Utopia, playing games would be the only activity that would make life worth living.[53] Even Plato presumes play as the highest priority in life and does not look at it as an activity solely for children and animals to learn and develop.[54]

---

46 Sutton-Smith, B.: *The Ambiguity of Play*, Harvard University Press, 1997, p. 198.
47 Sutton-Smith, B.: Play theory: "A personal journey and new thoughts," in: *American Journal of Play*, 1, no. 1 (2008), p. 81.
48 Suits, B.: *The Grasshopper*, Canada: Broadview Press Ltd 2014, p. 43.
49 Ibid., 17.
50 Vygotsky, L. S. *Imagination and its Development in Childhood*. In: The collected works of L. S. Vygotsky. New York: Plenum Press, 1987: quoted after: Ferholt, B.: *Gunilla Lindqvist's theory of play and contemporary play theory*. Unpublished paper, 2007, p. 7. http://lchc.ucsd.edu/Projects/PAPER1%20copy-1.pdf (accessed May 28, 2018).
51 Cf. Sutton-Smith: *The Ambiguity of Play*, p. 22.
52 Ibid., 48.
53 Suits: *The Grasshopper*, pp. 188-189.
54 In Huizinga, J.: *Homo Ludens*, London: Routledge & Kegan Paul Ltd 1949, p. 18-19.

Play often has characteristics that fall into the category of exercise. When animals play, they usually engage in physical competition, like play fighting. Sports are good examples of competitive play in humans. Winning over others promises a feeling of self-worth and empowerment, which positively influences one's emotional state. In contrast to this, the catharsis theory by Ellies says that physical play is particularly helpful with releasing negative emotions.[55]

While there are similarities between the play of animals and the play of humans, play does not seem to fulfill the same function for both. For example, the theory that play is a way to discharge superfluous energy may be true for animals but cannot be applied to human play, since humans are known to play not only when they have energy left to do so, but also when they are supposed to direct their energy to activities that are not play.[56]

Other researchers link the development of creatitivity to the act of playing, especially in childhood. Lev S. Vygotsky states that the ability to develop creativity is based on functional or dysfunctional play behavior.[57] He defines creativity as "[the] ability to combine elements to produce a structure, to combine the old in new ways [...]."[58] Vygotsky also states that everything we can imagine is taken from reality and influenced by emotions that we have towards reality. Therefore, emotions can shape imagination, but imagination also satisfies emotional needs.[59] The end result is then a creative thought which was based on reality but altered by emotions according to individual needs.

Vygotsky argues that this cognitive process depends on experience and, therefore, needs to be practiced.[60] The means to practice this development is found in play. If a child is restricted in their play behavior, they cannot practice the ability to think creatively, which then might influence the brain structures that combine creativity and mental health on a hormonal level.

Although there are many different opinions on what the functions of play might be, they all consider the idea that the drive for play is the enjoyment of play itself. Humans invest time and energy, which could be used for activities

---

55 Ellis: Why people play: quoted after: Lane: The Meaning of Play for Adults from a Rehersal Theory Perspective, p. 24.
56 Suits: *The Grasshopper*, p. 224.
57 Vygotsky, L. S.: "Imagination and Creativity in Childhood", in: *Journal of Russian and East European Psychology* 42, no. 1 (2004), pp. 7-97: quoted after: Ferholt.: *Gunilla Lindqvist's theory of play and contemporary play theory*. p. 11. http://lchc.ucsd.edu/Projects/PAPER1%20copy-1.pdf
58 Ibid.
59 Ibid., 12-13.
60 Ibid., 14.

that ensure survival, to experience play, because play itself justifies this behavior.[61] Huizinga indicates that playing is an enjoyment of means and less dedicated to particular ends: "[...] we might call it a free activity standing quite consciously outside 'ordinary' life as being 'not serious,' but at the same time absorbing the player intensely and utterly. It is an activity connected with no material interest, and no profit can be gained from it."[62] Sutton-Smith supports this theory: "Play is fun [...] It is worth considering that the main adaptive function of play may be the generation of positive emotional states."[63] And referencing Sutton-Smith, Greta Fein says "I do not think play is about cognition and I don't think playing makes kids especially smarter. It most likely makes them happier [...] Little kids who do not play are usually very unhappy."[64] This explains why games which feature more playful interactions have a greater effect on the emotional states of players than games which do not.

Just as there seems to be a connection between play and fun, there seems to be a connection between mental health issues and a deprivation of play.

In THE POWER OF VULNERABILITY, Brené Brown explains that investigating the lives of people who committed school shootings revealed that many of them were restricted in their play behavior during childhood.[65] Peter Gray explains in his Ted Talk THE DECLINE OF PLAY how researchers discovered that young rats and monkeys become emotionally crippled when they are deprived of play.[66] He states that over the course of the last 50-60 years, play opportunities for children have declined due to a growth of school-imposed restrictions, irrational security fears, and the view that peer-play is a waste of time. This play deprivation results in increased anxiety and depression, a rise in narcissism, and a decline of empathy, creative thinking, and self-control.

Lous et al. investigated the play behavior of 3 to 6-year old depressed children and compared it to the play behavior of non-depressed children of the same

---

61 Suits: *The Grasshopper*, p. 225.
62 Huizinga.: Homo Ludens: A study of the play element in culture: quoted after: Lane: The Meaning of Play for Adults from a Rehersal Theory Perspective, p. 16.
63 Ibid., p. 32.
64 Fein, G. quoted after: Sutton-Smith: *The Ambiguity of Play*, p. 32.
65 Brown, B.: "The Power of Vulnerability: Teachings of Authenticity, Connection, and Courage" (Audible, 2012, 5:19:37 – 5:22:25).
66 Gray, P.: "The decline of play." Youtube.com https://www.youtube.com/watch?v=Bg-GEzM7iTk (accessed 07.06.18).

age.[67] The study revealed that depressed children show significantly less play behavior than non-depressed children and that depressed children changed between play and non-play behavior more often than non-depressed children.[68] This could be explained by a developmental delay in depressed children, which leads to less independence. Additionally, play behavior requires more attention and internal control which depressed children cannot muster.[69]

The research shows that play and depression influence each other. A deficit of play behavior in childhood can cause difficulties in concentration and internal control. It can also lead to difficulties in developing one's imagination and other creative faculties. Play combines the perception of the outside world with personal emotions and culture and lets players live out these combinations in a safe context.

HOW THE STIGMA OF DIGITAL GAMES IS HINDERING THERAPY GAMES

Most studies on digital games and depression seem to focus on the idea that games have addictive characteristics instead of exploring their therapeutic possibilities. In this context, it is necessary to take a close look at the various game genres and the differences between online and offline games. The 'addiction prejudice' mainly focuses on the same genre of online games, such as MMORPGS. While it is questionable whether games can cause addiction at all, it is necessary to investigate if the game world and gameplay are actually responsible for causing addiction or if some players find themselves addicted to the social aspect of online games. If this is true, the question must be raised if online games are much different than social media platforms.

The claim that excessive game playing leads to depression is not only unfounded but it could also be used to make the opposite point, as research on video game addiction often features field reports of patients who use games and other media to escape the already present issues in their lives. Game therapy will have to face this stigma and produce positive results to sufficiently convince society and researchers of its value.

---

67 Lous, A.M. et al.: "Depression and Play in Early Childhood: Play Behavior of Depressed and Nondepressed 3- to 6-Year-Olds in Various Play Situations," in: Journal of Emotional and Behavioral Disorders 8, no. 4 (2000), pp. 249-260.
68 Ibid., 253.
69 Ibid., 256.

Conclusion

Digital games offer a rich medium to combine several successfully tested forms of depression therapy. This includes a variety of elements that can influence a patient's mood positively, like meaningful task-fulfillment, healthy escapism, social interation, and engagement in active and creative activities. The immersive features of digital games can be used to shape a patient's perception of themselves and guide their inner emotions towards a healthier self-image. One of its most valuable features is to motivate people who are affected by depression to seek professional help.

Compared to common depression treatment, game therapy is less human intensive and more flexible in its execution, while bearing a smaller risk of negative side effects. It can also be modified to meet the needs of individual patients, but such systems have not been developed yet and the research on game treatment is still relatively new.

Many people continue to believe that gaming can cause addiction and promote an unhealthy lifestyle. This prejudice must be overcome before game therapy can be fully established.

The interest in the effectiveness of game therapy has been growing over the last two decades, but most studies are carried out within short time periods. To fully reveal the potential of game therapy, more long-term studies are needed. The current research is spread out very broadly and the results are difficult to compare. Some researchers fail to make full use of the video game medium; rather than desiging game therapy systems, these researchers merely gamify common treatment methods.

This study shows the potential of game therapy as an alternative and/or addition to common depression treatments for mild and moderate depression. With the improvement of VR and AR, digital interventions will become more immersive and useful in therapeutic environments. Therapy games will profit from this development as well and hopefully reach more people that suffer from depression as an adequate treatment method in the future.

Literature

Berjaoui, Dania: "Exploring Active Video Games (AVGS) as an Intervention Promoting Wellbeing as It Relates to Depression" (Senior Honors Thesis), Michigan: Honors College, 2013.http://commons.emich.edu/cgi/viewcontent.cgi?article=1332&context=honors

Blomdahl, Christina/Wijk, Helle/Guregård, Rusner, Marie: "Meeting oneself in inner dialogue: a manual-based Phenomenological Art Therapy as experienced by patients diagnosed with moderate to severe depression," in: *The Arts in Psychotherapy* 59 (2018), pp. 17-24. DOI: 10.1016/j.aip.2017.08.006

Botella, C./ Baños R. M./ Perpiñá, C./ Villa, H./ Alcañiz, M./ Rey, A.: "Virtual reality treatment of claustrophobia: a case report," in: *Behaviour Research and Therapy* 36, no. 2 (1998), pp. 239-246. DOI: 10.1016/S0005-7967(97)10006-7

Bronisch, T./Spreti, F.: The role of paintings in suicide prevention. In: Wassermann, Danuta/Wassermann, Camilla (eds.), *Oxford Textbook of Suicidology*, Oxford: Oxford University Press 2008, pp. 445–453.

Brown, Brené: "The Power of Vulnerability: Teachings of Authenticity, Connection, and Courage" (Audible, 2012, 5:19:37 – 5:22:25).

Burdea, Grigore C./Polistico, Kevin: "A Review of Integrative Virtual Reality Games for Rehabilitation," in: *E-Health and Bioengineering Conference (EHB)* (2017), pp. 732-736. DOI: 10.1109/EHB.2017.7995528

Cai, Hanshu/Wang, Ziyang/Zhang, Yanhao/Chen, Yunfei/Hu, Bin: "A Virtual-Reality Based Neurofeedback Game Framework for Depression Rehabilitation using Pervasive Three-Electrode EEG Collector," in: *ChineseCSCW '17 Proceedings of the 12th Chinese Conference on Computer Supported Cooperative Work and Social Computing* (2017), pp. 173-176. DOI: 10.1145/3127404.3127433

Carrasco, Álvaro E.: "Acceptability of an adventure video game in the treatment of female adolescents with symptoms of depression," in: *Research in Psychotherapy: Psychopathology, Process and Outcome* 19 (2016), pp. 10-18. DOI: 10.4081/ripppo.2016.182

Ceskova, Eva: "Current pharmacotherapy of depression – focused on multimodal/multifunctional antidepressants," in: *Expert opinion on Pharmacotherapy* 17 (2016), pp. 1835-1837. DOI: 10.1080/14656566.2016.1219340

Desai, Neesha/Szafron, Duane/Sayegh, Liliane/Greiner, Russ/Turecki, Gustavo: *Creating Video Games to Treat Chronic Depression*, Alberta: University of Alberta 2010.

Dye, Matthew W.G./Green, Shawn C./Bavelier, Daphne: "Increasing Speed of Processing with Action Video Games," in: *Current Directions in Psychological Science* 18, no. 6 (2009), pp. 321-326.DOI: 10.1111/j.1467-8721.2009.01660.x

Farokhi, Masoumeh: "Art Therapy in Humanistic Psychiatry," in: *Procedia – Social and Behavioral Sciences* 30 (2011), pp. 2088-2092. DOI: 10.1016/j.sbspro.2011.10.406

Fleming, Theresa M./ Cheek, Colleen/ Merry, Sally N./ Thabrew, Hiran/ Bridgman, Heather/ Stasiak, Karlina/ Shepherd, Matthew/ Perry, Yael/ Hetrick, Sarrah: "SERIOUS GAMES FOR THE TREATMENT OR PREVENTION OF DEPRESSION: A SYSTEMATIC REVIEW," in *Revista de Psicopatología y Psicología Clínica* 19, no. 3 (2014), pp. 227-242. DOI: http://dx.doi.org/10.5944/rppc.vol.19.num.3.2014.13904

Green, Shawn C./Bavelier, Daphne: "Action video game modifies visual selective attention," in: *nature* 423 (2003), pp. 534-537. https://www.nature.com/articles/nature01647.pdf

House, Gregory/Burdea, Grigore/Grampurohit, Namrata/Polistico, Kevin/Roll, Doru/Damiani, Frank/Hundal, Jasdeep/Demesmin, Didier: „A feasibility study to determine the benefits of upper extremity virtual rehabilitation therapy for coping with chronic pain post-cancer surgery," in: *British Journal of Pain* 10, no. 4 (2016), pp. 186-197. DOI: 10.1177/2049463716664370

Huizinga, Johan: *Homo ludens: A study of the play element in culture*. Boston, MA: Beacon Press, 1955.

Kessler, Ronald C./Soukub, Jane/Davis, Roger B./Foster, David F./Wilkey, Sonja A. ... Eisenberg, David M.: "The Use of Complementary and Alternative Therapies to Treat Anxiety and Depression in the United States," in: *The American Journal of Psychiatry* 158, no. 2 (2001), pp. 289-294. DOI: 10.1176/appi.ajp.158.2.289

Kühn, Simone/Berna, Fabrice/Lüdtke, Thies/Gallinat, Jürgen/Moritz, Steffen: "Fighting Depression: Action Video Game Play May Reduce Rumination and Increase Subjective and Objective Cognition in Depressed Patients", in: *Frontiers in Psychology* 9, (2018), pp. 1-8. DOI: 10.3389/fpsyg.2018.00129

Lane, Linda: *The Meaning of Play for Adults from a Rehersal Theory Perspective*, University of Arkansas, 2013. http://scholarworks.uark.edu/cgi/viewcontent.cgi?article=1843&context=etd

Li, Jinhui/ Theng, Yin-Leng/ Foo, Schubert: "Game-Based Digital Interventions for Depression Therapy: A Systematic Review and Meta-Analysis," in: *Cyberpsychology, Behavior, and Social Networking* 17, no. 8 (2014), pp: 519-527. DOI: https://doi.org/10.1089/cyber.2013.0481

Li, Jinhui/ Theng, Yin-Leng/ Foo, Schubert: "Effect of exergames on Depression: A Systematic Review and Meta-Analysis," in: *Cyberpsychology, Behavior, and Social Networking* 19, no. 1 (2016), pp. 34-41. DOI: https://doi.org/10.1089/cyber.2015.0366

Lous, Annemieke M./de Wit, Cees A. M./de Bruyn, Eric E. J./Riksen-Waldraven J. Marianne/Rost, Henk: "Depression and Play in Early Childhood: Play Behavior of Depressed and Nondepressed 3- to 6-Year-Olds in Various Play Situations," in: *Journal of Emotional and Behavioral Disorders* 8, no. 4 (2000), pp. 249-260. DOI: https://doi.org/10.1177/106342660000800405

Makin, Sally/Gask, Linda: "'Getting back to normal': the added value of an art-based programme in promoting 'recovery' for common but chronic mental health problems," in: *Chronic Illness* 8, no. 1 (2011), pp. 64-75. DOI: 10.1177/1742395311422613

Mathers, Colin D./Loncar, Dejan: "Projections of Global Mortality and Burden of Disease from 2002 to 2030," in: PLOS Medicine 3, no.11 (2006), pp. 2011-2030. http://journals.plos.org/plosmedicine/article?id=10.1371/journal. pmed.0030442#s1

Martius, Philipp/Marten, Diana: "Kunsttherapie," in: *Psychotherapeut* 59, no. 4 (2014), pp. 329-343. DOI: 10.1007/s00278-014-1055-3

MENTAL HEALTH FOUNDATION: *Up and running: exercise therapy and the treatment of mild or moderate depression in primary care*, London: Mental Health Foundation 2005, pp. 25-26. https://www.mentalhealth.org.uk/sites/default/files/up_running_report.pdf

Mishkind, Matthew C./Norr, Aaron M./Katz, Andrea C./Reger, Gred M.: "Review of Virtual Reality Treatment in Psychiatry: Evidence Versus Current Diffusion and Use," in: J. Shore (Ed.), *Psychiatry in the Digital Age* 19, no. 80 (2017), pp. 1-8. DOI: 10.1007/s11920-017-0836-0

Naranjo, Claudio A./Tremblay, Lescia K./Busto, Usua E.: "The role of the brain reward system in depression," in: *Progress in Neuro-Psychopharmacology and Biological Psychiatry* 25 (2001), pp. 781-823. DOI: https://doi.org/10.1016/S0278-5846(01)00156-7

Reuter, Martin/Roth, Sarah/Holve, Kati/Hennig, Jürgen: "Identification of first candidate genes for creativity: a pilot study," in: *Brain Research* 1069, no. 1 (2006), pp. 190–197. DOI: https://doi.org/10.1016/j.brainres.2005.11.046

Richardson, Thomas/Stallard, Paul/Velleman, Sophie: "Computerised cognitive behavioural therapy for the prevention and treatment of depression and anxiety in children and adolescents: a systematic review," in: *Clinical Child and Family Psychology Review* 13, no. 3 (2010), pp. 275–290. DOI: https://doi.org/10.1007/s10567-010-0069-9

Smolucha, Francine: "The relevance of Vygotsky's theory of creative imagination for contemporary research on play," in: *Creativity Research Journal* 5, no. 1 (2009), pp. 69–76. DOI: http://dx.doi.org/10.1080/10400419 209534423

Spek, Viola/Cuijpers, Pim/Nyklíček, Ivan/Riper, Heleen/Keyzer, Jules/Pop, Victor: "Internet-based cognitive behaviour therapy for symptoms of depression and anxiety: a meta-analysis," in: *Psychological Medicine* 37 (2007), pp. 319–328. DOI: https://doi.org/10.1017/S0033291706008944

Suits, Bernard: *The Grasshopper*, Canada: Broadview Press Ltd 2014.

Sutton-Smith, Brian: Play theory: "A personal journey and new thoughts," in: *American Journal of Play*, 1, no. 1 (2008), pp. 80-123. https://files.eric.ed.gov/fulltext/EJ1068966.pdf

Sutton-Smith, Bian: *The Ambiguity of Play*, Harvard University Press, 1997.

Tinsley, H. E. A./Eldredge, B. D.: "Psychological benefits of leisure participation: A taxonomy of leisure activities based on their need-gratifying properties," in: *Journal of Counseling Psychology* 42, no. 2 (1995), pp. 123-132.

Vygotsky, Lev S. *Imagination and its Development in Childhood*. In: The collected works of L. S. Vygotsky. New York: Plenum Press, 1987.

Vygotsky, Lev S.: "Imagination and Creativity in Childhood", in: *Journal of Russian and East European Psychology* 42, no. 1 (2004), pp. 7-97.

Wi, Sam Yeol/Kang, Jong Ho, Jang, Jun Hyeok: "Clinical Feasibility of Exercise Game for Depression Treatment in Older Women with Osteoarthritis: a Pilot Study," in: *Journal of Physical Therapy Science* 25 (2013), pp. 165-167. DOI: https://doi.org/10.1589/jpts.25.165

LUDOGRAPHY

ABZÛ (505 Games 2016, O: Giant Squid Studios)
DEEP (Owen Harris/ Niki Smit 2015, O: Owen Harris/ Niki Smit)
FLOWER (Sony Interactive System 2009, O: Thatgamecompany)
JOURNEY (Sony Interactive System 2012, O: Thatgamecompany)
LIMBO (Playdead/ Microsoft Game Studios 2010, O: Playdead)

ONLINE SOURCES

American College of Sports Medicine: "Exergaming." Acsm.org/public-information/brochures https://www.acsm.org/docs/brochures/exergaming.pdf

American Psychological Association. "Understanding psychotherapy and how it works." Apa.org http://www.apa.org/helpcenter/understanding-psychotherapy.aspx (accessed May 7, 2018).

American Psychiatric Association. "What is Psychotherapy?" Psychiatry.org. https://www.psychiatry.org/patients-families/psychotherapy (accessed May 7, 2018).

Davie, Melissa. "Chronic depression shrinks brain's memories and emotions." Theguardian.com. https://www.theguardian.com/society/2015/jun/30/chronic-depression-shrinks-brains-memories-and-emotions (accessed May 10, 2018).

Ferholt, B.: *Gunilla Lindqvist's theory of play and contemporary play theory.* Unpublished paper, 2007, p. 7. http://lchc.ucsd.edu/Projects/PAPER1%20copy-1.pdf (accessed May 28, 2018).

Gameinformer. "The Meaning Behind Journey." Gameinformer. http://www.gameinformer.com/blogs/members/b/le_hannibal_blog/archive/2012/04/13/the-meaning-behind-journey.aspx (accessed June 5, 2018).

IGN. "Flower PS4 Review." Ign.com http://www.ign.com/articles/2013/11/13/flower-ps4-review (accessed June 5, 2018).

Kotaku. „The Most Depressive Theories On What *Limbo* Means." Kotaku.com. https://kotaku.com/the-most-depressing-theories-on-what-limbo-means-1724276367 (accessed June 1, 2018).

Schoneveld, Elke: "MindLight – Childhood Anxiety Prevention." Gemhlab.com. https://gemhlab.com/projects/anxiety/mindlight-childhood-anxiety-prevention/ (accessed June 7, 2018).

Solarski, Chris: "The Aesthetics of Game Art and Game Design." Gamasutra. https://www.gamasutra.com/view/feature/185676/the_aesthetics_of_game_art_and_.php?print=1 (accessed June 5, 2018).

Suellentrop, Chris: "In Bloom." Slate. http://www.slate.com/articles/technology/gaming/2009/02/in_bloom.html?via=gdpr-consent (accessed June 1, 2018).

University of Michigan Depression Center. "Electroconvulsive Therapy (ECT)." Depressiontoolkit.org. http://www.depressiontoolkit.org/treatmentoptions/neuromodulation/ect.asp (accessed May 6, 2018).

Wikipedia. „Limbo (video game)." Wikipedia.com. https://en.wikipedia.org/wiki/Limbo_(video_game)#Presentation (accessed June 1, 2018).

World Health Organization. "Depression." Who.int. http://www.who.int/en/news-room/fact-sheets/detail/depression (accessed May 6, 2018).

VIDEOS

Deep VR: A VR game that's good for you (USA, 2016, D: Engadget) https://www.youtube.com/watch?v=7T_iQsOseAg

The decline of play (Unknown production country, 2014, D: TEDx Talks) https://www.youtube.com/watch?v=Bg-GEzM7iTk

Perceived Behaviors of Personality-Driven Agents

ALBERTO ALVAREZ & MIRUNA VOZARU

INTRODUCTION

The discussion regarding the believability of video game characters in the fields of game analysis and artificial intelligence research has taken many forms over the years, generally focusing on appearance and behavior.[1,2,3] In the paper at hand, we will present a study in which we chose to focus on behavioral believability.

The pervading notions related to the degree of character believability seem to be their awareness, reaction capabilities, and adaptability to the events taking place around them.[4] These factors seem to be connected to the mental schemas

---

1 Lankoski, Petri/Björk, Steffan: "Gameplay design patterns for believable non-player characters," in: *Proceedings of the 3rd Digital Games Research Association International Conference*, 2007.
2 Umarov, Iskander/Mozgovoy, Maxim: "Believable and Effective AI Agents in Virtual Worlds: Current State and Future Perspectives," in: *International Journal of Gaming and Computer-Mediated Simulations* (IJGCMS) 4, 2, pp. 37-59.
3 Lee, Michael Sangyeob/Heeter, Carrie: "What do you mean by believable characters?: The effect of character rating and hostility on the perception of character believability," in: *Journal of Gaming & Virtual Worlds* 4, 1 (2012), pp. 81-97.
4 Warpefelt, Henrik: "Analyzing the Believability of Game Character Behavior Using the Game Agent Matrix," in: *Proceedings of the sixth bi-annual conference of the Digital Games Research Association: Defragging Game Studies*, 2013.

activated by the visual depictions of characters and the game world.[5] This made us question how the believability of an agent would be affected by the absence of anchoring references. Stripping away referential visual depictions, narrative, and the relevance of affordances to the traversal of the game world, we sought to understand the narratives that observers create around an ambiguous entity acting within an abstract environment.

In this paper, we will first present our reasoning and the theoretical background of the research design, the technical aspects of the AI agent that served as our character, and the responses that participants provided following the viewing of several films depicting the actions of the agent. Finally, we will discuss our conclusions and implications for future research and game development.

Theoretical Background

The purpose of this research is to analyze the means through which the viewer makes sense of ambiguous behavior in the absence of corresponding mental schemas. To do this, we needed to understand the means by which information is perceived and integrated, and what the observer uses to fill in the blanks when the stimulus is too ambiguous to fit into pre-existing information. New information, such as that presented by the behavior of an observed game character, is integrated within the pre-existing mental schemas of the observer, which are used to shape the meaning of the new information and make predictions about future developments. For instance, in the video game PORTAL (2007), the portal gun activates the mental schemas corresponding to previously encountered guns in video games. Namely that it can shoot, it is a tool for progressing in the game, and it damages enemies. When the portal gun is used, instead of damaging an enemy, it creates a gateway that the player can use to traverse the game. This result does not match pre-existing knowledge, which will force a schema modification concerning the video game gun functionality. The visual representation affords the integration of the portal gun within the player's previously acquired knowledge; it is referential, descriptive, and concrete. The differences become apparent once the observed functionality does not match expected performance.

---

5   Stein, Dan J.: "Schemas in the cognitive and clinical sciences: An integrative construct," in: *Journal of Psychotherapy Integration* 2 (1992), pp. 45-63.

Affordance theory, popularized in design by Donald Norman, describes the action and use possibilities that an entity, object, or environment possesses.[6] This theory has been widely appropriated by game design, due to the designer's needs to communicate briefly, clearly, and coherently the means through which a player can traverse a game. Affordances can be tied to previously acquired knowledge, but also be assigned meaning derived strictly from their application within the game world. They are used to telegraph the ways in which the players can use the different elements at their disposal to navigate the game world and to constrain the situational role of the elements.

That being said, the perception of use and role is not a necessary factor in the perception of agency and attribution of specific behaviors. In a study conducted by Heider and Simmel, participants were shown a brief video in which the actors were a circle, a large triangle, and a small triangle.[7] The shapes were depicted in various types of motion, seemingly interacting with each other and the environment. The participants were then prompted to describe the events taking place in the video. All of the participants, with the exception of one, described the events of the video as part of a narrative, whether it was as two parents fighting in front of their child, or two people finding themselves in a romantic situation and then being interrupted by a third. This led us to conclude that the perception of self-directed motion transforms the interpretation of a pattern into one involving an agential entity.[8]

So far, we can conclude that the believability of the agent hinges on its recognizable visual representations, as well as the affordances displayed within the game world. By stripping these factors and endowing a visually ambiguous object with self-directed motion, it will be interpreted as an entity with perceived agency.

Personality traits have generally been viewed as probabilistic determinants for the predictability of a certain type of behavior mediated and moderated by the current situation.[9,10,11,12] The Cybernetic Big 5 model, henceforth CB5T,

---

6   Norman, Donald A. *The Design of Everyday Things*, New York, NY: Basic Books 2002.
7   Heider, Fritz/Simmel, Marianne: "An Experimental Study Of Apparent Behavior," in: *American Journal of Psychology* 57 (1944), pp. 243–59.
8   Harris, John/Sharlin, Ehud: "Exploring the Effect of Abstract Motion in Social Human-Robot Interaction," in: *IEEE* (Ed.), 2011 RO-MAN, New York, NY: IEEE 2011, pp. 441–448.
9   McCrae, Robert R./John, Oliver: "An Introduction to the Five-Factor Model and Its Applications," in: *Journal of Personality* 60 (1992), pp. 175–215.

treats personality-endowed agents as goal-based entities perpetually engaged in goal attainment loops.[13] The goal loops are divided into stages, with personality traits exerting their influence on each stage of the loop. Traits are manifested through characteristic adaptations, which, unlike personality, are constructed based on individual life experiences and are thus not universal. For instance, the manifestation of the trait compassion can take different characteristic adaptations, such as volunteering or monetary donations, which are dependent on the individual's socio-cultural environment

While our intentions steer clear of transforming the research into a projective test,[14] we decided to use personality factors as behavior determinants for our AI agents. Our hypothesis was that in the absence of other anchoring visual primers, the observers would integrate the perceived behavior within familiar characteristic adaptations. While we used Heider and Simmel's experiment as a starting point, our research was also informed by the similarity-attraction hypothesis, which states that individuals grant more positive appraisals to responses that match their own personality traits.[15] The agents were given the same traits as the corresponding observer. We used an AI agent instead of a pre-rendered movie, due to the options it offered in terms of personality customization. We distinguish our purposes from the creation of narratives surrounding ambiguous agents. To clarify, our purpose was not the exploration of the participants' creation of narratives surrounding the ambiguous behavior of an agent, but to explore the participants' propensity to recognize behaviors with which they are most familiar – the ones they have observed in themselves.

---

10 Mischel, Walter/Shoda, Yiuchi: "A Cognitive-Affective System Theory of Personality: Reconceptualizing Situations, Dispositions, Dynamics, and Invariance in Personality Structure," in: *Psychological Review* 102 (1995), pp. 246–68.
11 Tett, Robert P./Guterman, Hal A.: "Situation Trait Relevance, Trait Expression, and Cross-Situational Consistency: Testing a Principle of Trait Activation," in: *Journal of Research in Personality* 34 (2000), 397–423.
12 Costa, Paul T./MacRea Robert: *Advanced Personality*, Boston, MA: Springer 2012.
13 Deyoung, Colin G.: "Cybernetic Big Five Theory," in: *Journal of Personality* 56 (2014), pp. 35-58.
14 A projective test is a psychological assessment during which participants are asked to interpret ambiguous stimuli with the assumption that the interpretation will reveal insights regarding their personality traits.
15 Byrne, Bonn/Griffitt, William/Stefaniak, Daniel: "Attraction and Similarity of Personality Characteristics," in: *Personality and Social Psychology* 5 (1967), pp. 82–90.

AGENT BEHAVIOR AND DESIGN

The following section will cover the psychological and visual design of the AI agent, its personality, emotions, and affective behavior, as well as the reasoning behind the aesthetic choices we made.

As mentioned above, the CB5T model moves away from previous models and classifies traits as global influencers of the goal attainment loop, which is broken down into five stages: goal activation, action selection, action, outcome interpretation, and goal comparison. As a result of the ongoing process of receiving, perceiving, and filtering environmental stimuli, multiple goals can be active at the same time. The first and second phases are internal and generally comprised of parallel processes. The third phase presents a bottleneck to the goal loop, due to the fact that, while a person can hold multiple goals in their memory at the same time, actions are generally performed in sequence. In the fourth phase, the result of the action is measured against the intended results, which will generate a match or a mismatch. This will in turn inform the next goal and the subsequent cycle. Personality traits exert their influence in concert at every stage of the goal loop, becoming moderators to the goal attainment stages. For a better understanding of the goal loop, we can consider the following situation: The AI agent feels hungry, and in the process of trying to obtain food it realizes that it must jump over an obstacle. While both goals exist in its memory, the fact that it can perform only one action at a time determines that it must first perform the jump. This is the action selection phase. The agent jumps and fails to overcome the obstacle. The actual result and the intended result do not match, and its personality score will influence its reflection on this failure.

The CB5T model was coupled with a simplified version of the Ortony, Clore, and Collins model of emotions (henceforth OCC), "The OCC model revisited."[16] The reasoning behind the combination of personality and emotion models was derived from the need to visually depict the results of the internal processes taking place during the goal attainment phases. The influence exerted by personality traits on the goal attainment loop materializes in affective behavior, where the emotional valence and intensity is dependent on the personality score.

---

16 Steunebrink, Bas R./Dastani, Mehdi/Meyer, John-Jules Ch.: "The OCC Model Revisited," in: (Ed.), *Proc. of the 4th Workshop on Emotion and Computing*. Association for the Advancement of Artificial Intelligence, Location: Publisher 2009.

Figure 1: Simulation environment.

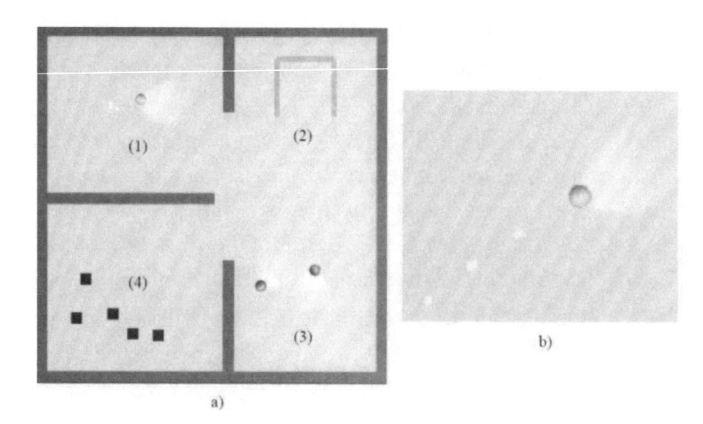

(a) Example environment that was presented to users, containing the personality-driven agent (1), and three different situations that the agent will encounter (2,3,4).

(b) Agent trail and view.

Intentionality and attention presented a large part of the concretization of personality-derived behavior. The agent's attention and intentions were depicted by a cone of light in front of it, maintaining the ambiguity of the stimulus but strengthening the perception of agency. Similarly, the trail the agent leaves behind signifies its movement speed which is dependent on its emotional arousal. The affective behavior exhibited by the agent had to be contextualized in specific situations, in order to be granted environmental referentiality. We created several situations, including but not limited to: positive and negative social situations, environmentally challenging situations, and situations that could produce distractions.

AGENT ARCHITECTURE AND SIMULATION

Human-like behavior is a complex subject and one that cannot be approached by using only one model or technique. Rather, different approaches use a compendium of specialized modules—for instance, emotional, personality, memory, or social modules that have various responsibilities in order to simplify the decision-making process.

The TOK architecture represents an agent as a set of different modules that handle the perception, reactivity, goals, emotions, and social behaviors. TOK is divided into three main components: (1) HAP, the goal-based reactive engine, (2) EM, the emotional model, and (3) Glinda, the natural language system.[17]

Figure 2: Observable Behavior.

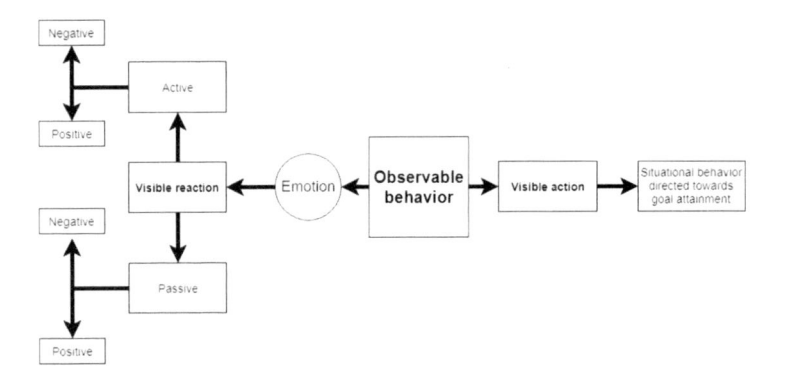

The observable behavior by the users is based on the set of actions provided by the encountered situation, which results in an emotional reaction. The reaction is based on the outcome interpretation phase, where the agent will choose the respective emotion (active/passive and negative/positive), intensity and reactive behavior.

Our model assimilates to HAP and EM, in that HAP selects an action based primarily on the agent's goals, emotions and perception by using the CB5T model, and with EM it calculates the emotional valence of the agent by comparing environmental stimuli with goals, possible actions with standards, and environmental objects with attitudes.

The agent's goals have a dynamic weight and a priority. The weight is determined by the agent's moment-to-moment actions and reflect its progression and perception of environmental cues. The priorities indicate the goal type, and

---

17 Bates, Joseph A./Loyall, Bryan/Reilly, W. Scott: "An Architecture for Action, Emotion, and Social Behavior," in: al Cimino (Ed.), *Proceedings of the Fourth European Workshop on Modeling Autonomous Agents in a Multi-Agent World* (1992), pp. 55-68.

their influence on survival and self-actualization. To exemplify, "hunger" is a priority 1 goal, and its weight will increase according to the presence of food in the agent's proximity and the time they spend roaming around the environment.

Subsequently, according to the outcome of the situation, the agent will feel pleased or displeased in accordance with the match or mismatch between the desired outcome and the actual one. The combination of the outcome difference and the personality traits trigger different emotional reactions. As presented in figure 2, the agent can perform several actions in specific situations and the consequence of the selected action entails not only different emotions but also different levels of arousal.

Table 1

Situation type	Event type	Agent type
Negative/Positive	Displeased/pleased	Standards
Passive/Active	Neuroticism	Neuroticism
LOW/MID/ HIGH	Goal weight	Neuroticism level
Inner choice	Situation target	Situation target

The Reaction table used to choose the respective emotional reaction. First, we choose the agent's emotion by choosing if active/passive and negative/positive as presented in figure 2, with the addendum that if more than one option is viable, the choice will be based on the situation's target. Finally, the intensity is calculated.

The way in which different emotional reactions occur was modelled in a table which is live queried to extract the agent's reaction. Table 1 illustrates how a reaction is chosen based on the two types of situations presented in our simulation.

SIMULATION

In order to control the agent's decisions, we built a decision tree that uses personality traits, perceived situations, and the current goal weight as inputs. The decision tree allows the agent to acquire its next goal, perform the action, and exhibit the corresponding emotional reaction. Therefore, the decision tree has five steps: (1) sense the environment, (2) reason about the possible actions based on their goals, (3) engage with the situation, (4) reflect on the outcome, and (5) produce an emotional reaction.

The agent constantly senses its surroundings to gather encountered entities, it inventories the situations they generate and compares them to its inner goals, and then chooses the situation that would satisfy the primary goal. To simulate the attraction towards novelty, every situation the agent engages in becomes less novel every time it is chosen. Once a specific type of situation becomes ordinary (i.e. not novel), the agent will give more weight to other types of situations.

Each situation has its own set of afforded behaviors. For instance, in a situation in which the agent can encounter other agents, it can approach them, give objects to them, or perform other context-specific actions. This allowed us to simplify the agent's decision-making step by allocating complexity to each situation.

Situations are divided into two main categories: environmental challenges and social challenges. For instance, the agent might *encounter an obstacle*, and finding out what is on the other side of it will satisfy its curiosity goal. Or it might engage in a situation where other agents are *having fun*, which in turn would satisfy the *social acceptance goal*.

Although the agent is given a set of behaviors to perform, there are cases where the agent will simply not perform the action, due to not having the necessary resources, being physically unable to do it, or due to a conflict with its personality traits. For instance, the agent might not be able to give any object to collecting agents, as the agent has not found anything yet, or to jump a gap due to low levels of assertiveness and high withdrawal.

Once the situation has been resolved, the agent compares the actual outcome to the expected one and the respective weight is modified accordingly. This final step triggers the agent's emotional reaction, defined by the Figure 2 process and reached by the queried information from the reaction table (Table 1). Finally, the agent goes back to its ordinary state and repeats the goal attainment loop.

Participant Assessments and Responses

Participants were selected using a snowball method. Both the selection method and the low number of participants (n=6) preclude us from generalizing results. Participants were informed that they would take part in a study focusing on behavior perception in a virtual environment. In the first stage of the research, the participants were asked to fill out a personality evaluation questionnaire. The questionnaire was comprised of 50 items, taken from the International Item Pool, and tailored to the CB5T.[18]

The scores were subsequently calculated and assigned to an individual agent. The agents were placed in the same environment and recorded while acting within the given environment. Consequently, the recordings were shown to the participants, who were asked to describe the behavior of the agent and what they thought the actions represented, without being aware of the specific traits given to the agent.

While the small number of participants does not allow us to draw generalizable conclusions, the responses indicate the recognition of the agent as an entity with directed behavior and agency, to which they attributed familiar characteristic adaptations. One of the participants described their agent's behavior as follows:

"[...] the agent is similar to a person that works in an office. He is engaging in conversation with his co-workers/superiors and tries to do his day-to-day tasks. As I see it, the agent has a lot of work to do, as he is in a continuous movement. I think he should take a break from time to time."

We can see that the ambiguous movement of the agent is identified with a specific characteristic adaptation, and the environment is given characteristics that e replace abstract representations with imagery from an everyday office space. The participant also evaluates the agent in a sympathetic manner, which we can consider a byproduct of the contextualization within a familiar characteristic adaptation.

A different participant, viewing the behavior of their own agent in the same environment, described the behavior as follows:

---

18 Goldberg, Lewis R./Johnson, John A./Eber, Herbert W./Hogan, Robert/Ashton, Michael C./Cloninger, C. Robert/Gough, Harrison G.: "The International Personality Item Pool and the Future of Public-Domain Personality Measures," in: *Journal of Research in Personality* 40 (2006), pp. 84–96.

"He's pretty anxious, he isn't sure of himself, of what he's going to do (with the box). At first he seemed a bit shy, he basically wanted to avoid the other two, and I think he didn't even say hello to them [...]"

We can see that the agent's movements of approach and withdrawal are described here through the lens of common human social behavior of greeting and social avoidance. The agent is also given specific, human-like traits, which signal recognition and contextualization of behavior.

The responses also reflect drawbacks in our aesthetic choices, but strengthen the hypothesis that, when confronted with ambiguous cues, the participants will appeal to their most readily available mental schema. One participant wrote:

"This agent looks like it's sweeping the ground for something with a metal detector. It checks both sides of the box but looks like it doesn't find anything."

While the cone of light was intended to be a signifier of attention and intention, it was interpreted in this case as a concrete object, a metal detector. However, the participant's interpretation that grounds the agent's behavior as exploratory is consistent with our hypothesis of the need to concretize ambiguous behaviors.

We can see the ways in which the participants interpret, and ascribe meaning to, the ambiguous behaviors of the agent. While remaining in the realm of the abstract, the motions and actors could be described as "the dot got closer to the other dots and then got further away." However, the participants attributed emotion and reasoning to the entity.

Conclusion

This pilot experiment explored the ways in which people attribute known and familiar behaviors to an AI agent in the absence of other anchoring visual cues. Participants who, unknowingly at the time, contributed to the creation of the AI by providing data regarding their personality traits, largely interpreted ambiguous behavior by association with their own characteristic adaptations. Future research into this area could explore the interpretation of behavior exhibited by AI agents that have different personality traits than those of the observers. While stripping visual cues from the environment and characters is not a valid aesthetic choice for most video games, the central take-away of this experiment should be the importance of missing information, whether deliberate or not.

The behavior descriptions reflect the participant's propensity for filling in blanks with their own familiar characteristic adaptations. When presented with merely a few rectangles and spheres, one participant saw an office, while another saw a social situation that the protagonist was trying to avoid. These results point to an important value that should be considered in the design, critique, and analysis of digital games: the ambiguity variable.

One of the key missing pieces of this research was the capability of the participants to execute actions within the environment. This would have given the agent in-world affordances, allowing the players to integrate their own intentionality and project their characteristic adaptations onto the performed actions. However, at this stage we did not want to assess the participants' projection of personal actions, but rather their perception of ambiguous events and characters.

Our agent was a capsule, a dot on a two-dimensional plain. However, motion granted it the status of an entity and its ambiguous actions afforded it reasoning, motives, and personality (in the eyes of the participants). The participants were not aware of the personality traits that the agent had been given, but they were able to recognize the narrative around them. The results of the research underline that when ambiguity is present, the space will be filled by the viewer's characteristic adaptations. This research is just a pilot, and drawbacks such as the limited number of participants and lack of interactivity should be addressed in future iterations.

Acknowledgements

Miruna Vozaru ackowledges the financial support received from the European Research Council (ERC) under the European Union's H2020 ERC-ADG program (grant agreement No 695528).

Literature

Bates, Joseph A./Loyall, Bryan/Reilly, W. Scott: "An Architecture for Action, Emotion, and Social Behavior," in: al Cimino (Ed.), *Proceedings of the Fourth European Workshop on Modeling Autonomous Agents in a Multi-Agent World* (1992), pp. 55-68.

Byrne, Bonn/Griffitt, William/Stefaniak, Daniel: "Attraction and Similarity of Personality Characteristics," in: *Personality and Social Psychology* 5 (1967), pp. 82–90.

Costa, Paul T./MacRea Robert: *Advanced Personality*, Boston, MA: Springer 2012.
Deyoung, Colin G.: "Cybernetic Big Five Theory," in: *Journal of Personality* 56 (2014), pp. 35-58.
Goldberg, Lewis R./Johnson, John A./Eber, Herbert W./Hogan, Robert/Ashton, Michael C./Cloninger, C. Robert/Gough, Harrison G.: "The International Personality Item Pool and the Future of Public-Domain Personality Measures," in: *Journal of Research in Personality* 40 (2006), pp. 84–96.
Harris, John/Sharlin, Ehud: "Exploring the Effect of Abstract Motion in Social Human-Robot Interaction," in: *IEEE* (Ed.), 2011 RO-MAN, New York, NY: IEEE 2011, pp. 441–448.
Heider, Fritz/Simmel, Marianne: "An Experimental Study Of Apparent Behavior," in: *American Journal of Psychology* 57 (1944), pp. 243–59.
Lankoski, Petri/Björk, Steffan: "Gameplay design patterns for believable non-player characters," in: *Proceedings of the 3rd Digital Games Research Association International Conference*, 2007.
Lee, Michael Sangyeob/Heeter, Carrie: "What do you mean by believable characters?: The effect of character rating and hostility on the perception of character believability," in: *Journal of Gaming & Virtual Worlds* 4, 1 (2012), pp. 81-97.
McCrae, Robert R./John, Oliver: "An Introduction to the Five-Factor Model and Its Applications," in: *Journal of Personality* 60 (1992), pp. 175–215.
Mischel, Walter/Shoda, Yiuchi: "A Cognitive-Affective System Theory of Personality: Reconceptualizing Situations, Dispositions, Dynamics, and Invariance in Personality Structure," in: *Psychological Review* 102 (1995), pp. 246–68.
Norman, Donald A. *The Design of Everyday Things*, New York, NY: Basic Books 2002.
Stein, Dan J.: "Schemas in the cognitive and clinical sciences: An integrative construct," in: *Journal of Psychotherapy Integration* 2 (1992), pp. 45-63.
Steunebrink, Bas R./Dastani, Mehdi/Meyer, John-Jules Ch.: "The OCC Model Revisited," in: (Ed.), *Proc. of the 4th Workshop on Emotion and Computing*. Association for the Advancement of Artificial Intelligence, Location: Publisher 2009.
Tett, Robert P./Guterman, Hal A.: "Situation Trait Relevance, Trait Expression, and Cross-Situational Consistency: Testing a Principle of Trait Activation," in: *Journal of Research in Personality* 34 (2000), 397–423.
Umarov, Iskander/Mozgovoy, Maxim: "Believable and Effective AI Agents in Virtual Worlds: Current State and Future Perspectives," in: *International*

Journal of Gaming and Computer-Mediated Simulations (IJGCMS) 4, 2, pp. 37-59.

Warpefelt, Henrik: "Analyzing the Believability of Game Character Behavior Using the Game Agent Matrix," in: *Proceedings of the sixth bi-annual conference of the Digital Games Research Association: Defragging Game Studies*, 2013.

LUDOGRAPHY

PORTAL (Valve Corporation 2007, Valve Corporation)

From Pixelated Blood and Fixed Camera Perspectives to VR Experience
Tracing the Diversification of Survival Horror Video Games and Their Altered Mode of Perception

CORNELIA J. SCHNAARS

THE SURVIVAL HORROR GENRE

The video game genre of survival horror is inextricably linked to players' experiences in scary game worlds and the resulting feeling of powerlessness and entrapment. Early survival horror games have significantly shaped the genre in terms of representation and gameplay. Nearly 21 years after the first RESIDENT EVIL was released in 1996, RESIDENT EVIL 7: BIOHAZARD[1] (2017) brings a new technology to the genre—namely, Virtual Reality (VR). What does this change in respect to the perceptions and playability of a survival horror game? Have early survival horror videogames become, in hindsight, less scary compared to more recent titles, which utilize modern graphics and controls? Are there some essential features of the older generation that contemporary horror games lack? What are the lasting benefits of these seemingly outdated videogame formats apart from feelings of nostalgia? And is it even possible to reproduce a similar gameplay experience despite technological innovation? By focusing on the groundbreaking game series of RESIDENT EVIL and SILENT HILL, this paper shall explore the mechanisms of the genre's evolution (perhaps more aptly described as a decline) and the corresponding changes in player perception.

The RESIDENT EVIL and SILENT HILL-series have been recognized as twin pillars of the survival horror genre. As a subgenre of Action-Adventure games,

---

1 Henceforth 'RE7.'

they managed to counterbalance action and exploration components while including diverse puzzle elements. Within this basic formula, they formed a horrific gameplay experience created out of fixed camera angles, clumsy controls, manual save points, limited resources, and obscure, maze-like game worlds featuring eerie music and unsettling sound effects.

The world design of RESIDENT EVIL was significantly influenced by the first ALONE IN THE DARK (1992). The latter features pre-rendered scenery which is visualized through fixed camera perspective (particularly cinematic high and low angles) that created blind spots, obscuring enemies lurking in the dark. Tanya Krzywinska concludes: "[t]he intrusive effect of pre-rendered camera angles within gameplay reminds the player that control is limited and that the gameplay is highly predetermined."[2] The third person perspective, pre-rendered environments, fixed camera, and even the fog in SILENT HILL were all consequences of technical limitations of the time.

"RESIDENT EVIL and SILENT HILL us[e] the negative aspects of other games to an advantage. While fixed camera angles, dodgy controls and clunky combat were seen as problematic in most games, the traditional survival horror took them as a positive boon [...] overlooking glaring faults in favor of videogames that could be genuinely terrifying."[3]

These visual and mechanical features are essential to gameplay, as they "create a player-avatar relationship that sacrifices control and predictability for perceptual unease and cinematic horror."[4] They create a setting in which you can never be sure what might be lurking behind the next door or around the next corner. Accompanied by unsettling music and sound effects, especially in SILENT HILL, the player has to navigate the avatar through uncanny, intricate spaces, and rely on inaccurate controls. Due to limited ammunition and health items, the player is forced to avoid confrontation with enemies unless absolutely necessary. They have to tiptoe around or rush past them, sometimes without remembering the last

---

2   Krzywinska, Tanya: "Hands-On Horror," in: *Spectator: The University of Southern California Journal of Film & Television* 22 (2002), pp. 12-23, https://cinema.usc.edu/assets/098/15877.pdf, here p. 15.

3   Sterling, Jim: "How Survival Horror Evolved Itself into Extinction," *Destructoid*, December 8, 2008, https://www.destructoid.com/how-survival-horror-evolved-itself-into-extinction-114022.phtml.

4   Klevjer, Rune: *What is the Avatar? Fiction and Embodiment in Avatar-Based Single-player Computer Games*, Bergen: University of Bergen, 2006, https://folk.uib.no/smkrk/docs/RuneKlevjer_What%20is%20the%20Avatar_finalprint.pdf, here p. 213.

time they saved their progress. In Bernard Perron's words, the genre of survival horror depends on:

"the vulnerability of the player character who, without the gun powder and the supply of ammunition found in shooter games, has to face or run away from monstrous foes while finding his way out of labyrinthine spaces, gathering various items, solving puzzles and overcoming obstacles. The survival horror is also notorious for its clumsy controls, which make the gamer's life even more difficult—both for combat and for movement through the game world."[5]

Taken together, this characterizes the typical perception of a survival horror game, as the player is constantly on edge and can never feel entirely safe. Nevertheless, technology has since developed considerably in terms of graphics, controls, and camera perspective, which has resulted in a predicament for survival horror: as "the game's strength is rooted in 'old' gameplay, evolution brings a risk of annihilation."[6]

THE GENRE'S PREDICAMENT

In a first for the genre, RESIDENT EVIL 4 (2005) employs a 360-degree controllable camera within a three-dimensional world. The controllable camera enables a three-dimensional view that can constantly be adjusted, granting players more control over the environment. Combined with abundant weaponry and improved combat and aiming systems, the player no longer feels as helpless—even when facing hordes of enemies. In contrast to previous games, you cannot stealthily sneak past enemies either.

"RESIDENT EVIL 4 is not a formulaic survival horror game because it allows players nearly unrestricted ammunition, allows for convenient saving, and the visual representation is actually three-dimensional. [...] While becoming a more normal action game, [...] it breaks with its own tradition by changing the rules it helped to create."[7]

---

5   Perron, Bernard: *The World of Scary Video Games: A Study in Videoludic Horror*, New York, London, Oxford i.a.: Bloomsbury Academic 2018, here p. 65.
6   J. Sterling: "How Survival Horror Evolved Itself into Extinction."
7   Taylor, Laurie N.: "Gothic Bloodlines in Survival Horror Gaming," in: Perron (ed.), *Horror Video Games* (2009), pp. 46-61, here p. 54.

While RESIDENT EVIL 4 is often praised as the best game of the series,[8] the game fatally shifted the series' focus towards more action and constitutes a milestone of the genre's decline. This development can also be observed in the SILENT HILL series. Whereas SILENT HILL 4: THE ROOM (2004) employed an experimentally dichotomous perspective that, alongside other design choices, broke with the series' traditions, SILENT HILL: HOMECOMING (2008) then introduced the rotatable camera in three-dimensional space and, like RESIDENT EVIL 4, compensated for this change with increased enemy difficulty. While, like a SILENT HILL title should do, both games evoked a sense of fear and dread, they simultaneously—and unfortunately—also evoked another emotion at the expense of fear and dread: pure frustration.

RESIDENT EVIL 5 (2012) and RESIDENT EVIL 6 (2017) further built on the action-oriented approach and reduced the survival horror aspect to absurdity. They have become outright shooter games, undeniable departures from the original survival horror atmosphere:

"[W]ith improved combat ability comes a decreased amount of fear – the better your in-game character is at fighting, the less you have to worry about. With full camera control, the developer's ability to frighten you with the unseen is significantly damaged. However, if you sacrifice usability in the name of fear, you'll simply alienate consumers who have come to expect RESIDENT EVIL 4 gameplay as standard."[9]

RESIDENT EVIL creator Shinji Mikami has repeatedly expressed his dissatisfaction with the increasing action aspect and attempted to return to the foundational features of early survival horror.[10] However, he ended up creating THE EVIL WITHIN (2014), which is a horror game full of intertextual references to the cinematic horror genre and the heyday of survival horror, but in and of itself is not precisely a survival horror game. The player can even open the menu in the middle of combat to craft more ammunition, while the action continues in slow-motion. In early survival horror, however, resources like ammunition and health

---

8   See for example, RESIDENT EVIL 4's official metascore of 96—which is by far the highest score of a RESIDENT EVIL game—and the corresponding reviews on *Metacritic.com* (https://www.metacritic.com/game/gamecube/resident-evil-4). For a short overview of the game's reception see B. Perron: *The World of Scary Video Games*, pp. 211-12.

9   J. Sterling: "How survival horror evolved itself into extinction."

10 Slabaugh, Brett: "Resident Evil Creator Explains Why the Series Stopped Being Scary," *The Escapist*, September 28, 2013, http://v1.escapistmagazine.com/news/view/128251-Resident-Evil-Creator-Explains-Why-the-Series-Stopped-Being-Scary

items had to be carefully managed at all times and could not be produced in combat situations. Much like the games Mikami criticized, THE EVIL WITHIN focuses strongly on action-oriented elements. Players might feel frightened at times, but by and large the game relies heavily on gore and jump scares, neglecting subtle atmospheric terror as well as an underlying fear of the unknown.

This begs the question: Is there such a thing as modern survival horror? How can it ensure its existence without contradicting the genre characteristics it previously established? Are there modern gameplay mechanics that can reproduce the original survival horror atmosphere?

The cancelation of SILENT HILLS might indicate the difficulties in a modern reinterpretation of a potentially outdated video game genre. Its playable teaser P.T. seemed to diminish a focus on action in favor of a puzzle-solving component. In fact, various modern conceptualizations of horror gameplay appear to compensate the stylistic device of fixed camera angles by employing different gameplay mechanics. Many independent games during the 2010s rely on a 'run-and-hide' mechanic as opposed to actual combat. Games that embody this shift include AMNESIA: THE DARK DESCENT (2010), SLENDER: THE EIGHT PAGES (2012), OUTLAST (2013), and LAYERS OF FEAR (2016). This was already the case in HAUNTING GROUND (2005), which supports the argument that some aspects of early survival horror are present in modern approaches.

In order to further define the line of early survival horror to contemporary games with horror aesthetics, I shall now take a closer look at the controversial RE7. Just as Shinji Mikami promised to go back to early survival horror with THE EVIL WITHIN, RE7's producer Masachika Kawata expressed a desire to return to the roots of the RESIDENT EVIL franchise.[11]

RESIDENT EVIL 7

RE7 was "the first full triple-A scary game sold for the PlayStation VR"[12] and, so far, approximately 15.4 % of all RE7 players have played the game in VR (as of May 2019).[13] VR attempts to maximize the illusion of the game world, encompassing the player's visual field so as to exclude as much from the outside

---

11 Hidalgo, Jason: "RE7: Capcom's Kawata Talks Building a Better Resident Evil," *Technobubble*, December 22, 2016, https://eu.rgj.com/story/life/2016/12/19/masachika-kawata-resident-evil-7-re7-interview-roots-technobubble/95602270/

12 B. Perron: *The World of Scary Video Games*, p. 282.

13 See official statistics on http://www.residentevil.net/en/sevenrecord.html

world as possible, and focus the player's senses almost exclusively on the game world.[14] Back in 2009, Bernard Perron described how the vibration function of the PlayStation DualShock controller intensified his own experience of playing SILENT HILL and remarked "[w]ith the family resemblance it shares with virtual reality (VR), the video game perfectly incarnates the digital technology in what becomes an extension of the body."[15] For this reason, it only seemed like a logical step for a horror video game to adopt VR.

There is no need to stress the truly immersive quality of a videogame experience in VR. The all-encompassing atmosphere is remarkably scary, especially in a horror context. As a player, you are thrown into the diegetic world and the boundary between you and your avatar is no longer visible: you can look around and everything is right in front of you; as if the experience were free of mediation.[16] In other words, it really feels as if it is you who is trapped inside the Baker residence. Yet, of course, you still know you are safe on the couch. Some things repeatedly remind you of this fact and, thus, disturb the sense of immersion. Since VR is still in its technological infancy, it is prone to errors and glitches and, like early survival horror games, it is saddled with technical limitations.

---

14 The game designers also offer players a scented candle, allegedly reeking of moldy, old timber, leather, sweat, and blood, in order to encompass even more perceptual stimuli.

15 Perron, Bernard: "The Survival Horror: The Extended Body Genre," in: Bernard Perron (ed.), *Horror Video Games* (2009), pp. 121-144, here p. 136.

16 The avatar-player relation has been the subject of many studies. Daniel Vella emphasizes that there is a disparity between the player's subjectivity inside and outside of a game world: "it is the 'I' to whom the player ascribes experiences of the gameworld and actions within the gameworld. It emerges, in the course of play, as a subjective identity the player experiences as 'herself', in the first-person – albeit, crucially, as a 'self' that is distinct from her own identity as a playing individual outside the gameworld, and that is in large part determined by the game itself through its structuring of the ludic subject-position." (Vella, Daniel: "Who Am 'I' in the Game?": A Typology of the Modes of Ludic Subjectivity", in: *Proceedings of 1st International Joint Conference of DiGRA and FDG*, https://e-channel.med.utah.edu/wp-content/uploads/2017/02/paper_234.pdf, pp.1-16, here p. 3). See also Rune Klevjer's analysis of prosthetic telepresence and notion of the avatar as the player's proxy in Klevjer, Rune: *What is the Avatar? Fiction and Embodiment in Avatar-Based Singleplayer Computer Games*, Bergen: University of Bergen 2006, https://folk.uib.no/smkrk/docs/RuneKlevjer_What%20is%20the%20Avatar_finalprint.pdf.

For instance, in RE7 the graphics are significantly scaled back compared to the standard console or PC version. Further, the edges of your peripheral vision are constantly blurred, and surfaces shimmer and flicker in an unnatural way. While these shortcomings do not disturb the atmosphere too much, some sensations still break the fourth wall; especially considering that VR only allows visual and auditory perceptions to be altered, meaning haptics and the general sense of being in the world can be easily undermined.

Figure 1: Left: Avatar's arm stump. Right: Arm floating next to the menu screen.

Source: Screenshots by author, highlights added around the arms.

For instance, very early in the game, the avatar's left hand is sawn off. The avatar is then holding his left arm stump with his right hand (see fig. 1). This rather believable behavior appears almost comical, however, because the upper left arm is missing too; it appears as if the player is carrying someone else's arm stump around, totally disconnected from any (and especially the player's own) body. This issue resurfaces when the player opens the game's menu screen: Ethan's detached lower arm floats in the air next to the inventory. Perron summarizes it as follows: "Ethan's body is not modeled in RESIDENT EVIL VII: BIOHAZARD and the arms, cut at the level of the forearm, are more like an unattached prosthesis; it diminished and even shattered the affects related to the body being mutilated."[17]

This is especially confusing as, by contrast, there are cutscenes that precisely do not show the avatar's arms when they would have been clearly visible.[18] To sum up, VR furthers the sensation of immersion in the first place via enhanced

---

17 B. Perron: *The World of Scary Video Games*, p. 283.
18 For example, the player has to use a bolt clipper from the inventory to cut an iron chain on a cell; here, the bolt clipper just operates magically in mid-air.

visual and auditory output. Yet it is also more susceptible than non-VR gaming experiences to (inadvertent) breakings of the fourth wall in terms of bodily representations.

SURVIVAL HORROR IN RESIDENT EVIL 7?

Irrespective of its VR compatibility—can we classify RE7 as a survival horror game? Since clunky controls and fixed camera perspective are no longer an acceptable option for a AAA title, developers must come up with new ways to make the player feel insecure, frightened, and powerless. RE7 makes use of three main devices to evoke fear in spite of technological progress. One of them is the shift to first-person perspective (and VR) as it puts the player closer to the in-game events:

"In first-person mode, there is increased visual proximity to what lurks within such shadowy places, heightening the sense of contact. This heightened proximity to potential danger builds disquietude and tension."[19]

Another element, which is very popular in first-person horror games in particular, is the jump scare. Especially in VR, it is an extremely powerful design tool utilized to startle the player. However, it becomes rather disappointing in its frequency and its pre-scriptedness. In early survival horror games, the limited perspective granted the potential of seemingly coincidental jump scares, because the player could not anticipate zombies waiting for them in blind spots or around the next corner. In RE7, jump scares are deliberately programmed as cutscenes featured in the linear progression of the story. They are often predictable and rely on popular horror film tropes.

The third gameplay element employed to induce fear is the reiteration of enemy encounters which tries to compensate for the lack of the survival horror mechanics of backtracking and spatial disorientation. Very early in the game, players learn that the protagonist's wife, whom he has come to rescue, is not quite herself anymore. Players have to face the fact that even though it appears as if she has been killed, she keeps turning up, very much alive. As game mechanic this induces uncertainty and terror in players, but it also works on the level of the narrative. It manifests an uncertain duality of good and evil, of alive and dead. A loved one who is only partly recognizable and who turns into a

---

19 T. Krzywinska: "Hands-on Horror," p. 16.

monstrous enemy trying to kill you, can be inherently uncanny and terrifying. In early survival horror, an area is almost never safe when entered again, because monsters respawn, leaving the player constantly on high alert. Similarly, several boss fights against Jack Baker teach players that they can never be sure whether or not Baker is truly defeated. As Tanya Krzywinska concisely emphasizes: "This evocation of helplessness in the face of an inexorable predetermined force is crucial to maintaining horror-based suspense."[20]

To further explore RE7's suitability for the survival horror realm, we need to visualize its overarching structure. At the beginning of the game, the protagonist Ethan—and thus the player—is thrown into an unfamiliar environment, not really knowing what to expect. Soon we get to meet the Baker family, each of them appears not quite human, as they cannot really be harmed by the avatar. We are chased through the farmhouse, constantly attempting to avoid Jack on our way to solving puzzles in order to escape. We are almost defenseless, after a while merely supplied with a pocket knife and later a handgun (for which we constantly lack ammunition). This part of the game is—despite the change of perspective—indeed very reminiscent of the traditional survival horror genre in its overall feeling.

As the game continues, we get more weapons and become more familiar with the game's mechanics and puzzles, thus strengthening our combat abilities. The boss fight against the third incarnation of Jack marks the climax and turning point of the game. Ethan has grown into his role and it feels like we have reached the game's end. This, however, is not the case. Everything that follows entails more and more combat, fighting against enemies which increase in number and difficulty. The game then comes to a close in a final battle against a monstrous creature towering over the house. This evolution towards combat renders a large part of the game unsuitable for survival horror. The overall structure signifies not only Ethan's character development (especially his improved combat skills) but can also be read as a 'chronology' of the RESIDENT EVIL series, as it moves from traditional survival horror to typical action gameplay, ending in a final David vs. Goliath fight. As in classic horror texts and films like GODZILLA and KING KONG, the protagonist—and likewise the viewer or player—is substantially smaller in comparison to the giant foe, ostensibly helpless in the face of the superhuman creature. Yet, because of its size, the enemy is often not as fast with its attacks and, in certain weak spots, vulnerable to damage from the player.[21] Since RESIDENT EVIL 4, the series' producers have not departed

---

20 Ibid.
21 Since the controllable camera in RESIDENT EVIL 4 brought with it the new task of aiming that could be used as a central gameplay feature, the boss fights of each subse-

from this basic combat formula. It puts a clear focus on players' aiming skills and overlooks creative tactics. Arguably, this paints a rather unimaginative picture for the future of the series' combat systems and its similar dramatic structure in each game.[22]

Conclusion

In reference to the first Resident Evil-games, RE7's strong suit lies in the necessity of resource management, including the constant lack of ammunition and health items. The evenly distributed proportions of puzzle and combat elements is only held up in the first half of the game. During these initial sequences, RE7 thus evokes a survival horror-feeling to some extent, however, this stands in stark contrast to its form of representation. Even though "the high degree of presence and the increased emotional involvement aimed for by VR is really suitable to create a scary experience,"[23] in this early stage of technological development, VR is still rather susceptible to errors in representation. Because of the accumulation of such representational flaws, VR—as it is today— is "not that different from the classical first-person view. Everything is still translated through tactile vision and not embodied."[24]

As a point of departure for further analysis, I argue that not only RE7 but practically every contemporary horror game cannot be considered as belonging to the survival horror genre due to a rather intricate combination of mechanical, narrative, and atmospheric elements that underpinned survival horror games around the millennium. The very gameplay experience cannot be replicated with modern technology since the evocation of this particular survival horror feeling is directly related to technical restrictions. This suggests that the genre's heyday is more or less confined to the 1990s and early 2000s. Even though contemporary independent horror games often have to cope with technical or financial limitations as well, games like Amnesia: The Dark Descent are not quite comparable to early survival horror games in terms of representation and mechanics.

---

quent game—the remake of Resident Evil 2 being no exception—mainly demand of the player to aim for giant eyes which spread over a boss's body.

22 "If bigger guns and more powerful means of extermination can easily make a better shooter [...], bigger monsters don't necessarily render a game scarier." (B. Perron: *The World of Scary Video* Games, p.79)
23 Ibid., pp. 284-5. See also ibid., p. 409.
24 Ibid., p. 283.

Hence, the perceptual effects on players differ. A major trend in independent horror games is the 'run-and-hide' mechanic and the concomitant defenselessness as it is the case in the OUTLAST-series.[25] By contrast, in AAA titles, the focus seems to have shifted to advancements in combat mechanics, item management, and crafting, as well as skill upgrades (for example in THE EVIL WITHIN-series). Both of these approaches of dealing with modern technology are clearly situated in the realm of horror games. Yet, even though it can be argued that the 'run-and-hide' mechanic is merely a logical development out of former technical limitations, and genre distinctions are by no means clear-cut, contemporary horror games belong to a different genre, since "the third-person perspective or point of view remains particularly important because the game design revolved around predetermined camera angles."[26] The perspective in combination with spatiality strongly influences how a game is perceived. Only through the use of fixed, cinematic framing do otherwise predictable situations such as enemy encounters often appear unforeseeable. Thus, blind spots indirectly render enemies and other hazards more dangerous than they would be without fixed camera angles.[27] By such means of unsettling players, original survival horror is able to create a unique perceptual experience distinct from contemporary horror games.

---

25 The creation of an extensive combat and item management system is excluded and compensated for by the main item, the diegetic camera, for which batteries have to be obtained. Only with the aid of the camera's night vision is it possible to see in the pervasive darkness. In this sense, the battery level, which is always displayed in the top right of the camera's interface, assumes the role of the avatar's health status in a paradoxical interconnection of the camera and the avatar body, since light is essential for survival.

26 Ibid., p. 64.

27 The independent Spanish developer studio Protocol Games takes an approach including fixed camera angles in their current project SONG OF HORROR, thereby giving it at least a rather survival-horroresque look. I could, however, not determine, whether the game will be released in the near future—or at all.

Literature

Hidalgo, Jason: "RE7: Capcom's Kawata Talks Building a Better Resident Evil," *Technobubble*, December 22, 2016, https://eu.rgj.com/story/life/2016/12/19/masachika-kawata-resident-evil-7-re7-interview-roots-technobubble/95602270/

Klevjer, Rune: *What is the Avatar? Fiction and Embodiment in Avatar-Based Singleplayer Computer Games,* Bergen: University of Bergen 2006, https://folk.uib.no/smkrk/docs/RuneKlevjer_What%20is%20the%20Avatar_finalprint.pdf

Krzywinska, Tanya: "Hands-On Horror," in: *Spectator: The University of Southern California Journal of Film & Television* 22 (2002), pp. 12-23, https://cinema.usc.edu/assets/098/15877.pdf

Perron, Bernard (ed.): *Horror Video Games: Essays on the Fusion of Fear and Play*, Jefferson, NC: McFarland 2009.

Perron, Bernard: *The World of Scary Video Games: A Study in Videoludic Horror*, New York, London, Oxford i.a.: Bloomsbury Academic 2018.

Perron, Bernard: "The Survival Horror: The Extended Body Genre," in: Bernard Perron (ed.), *Horror Video Games* (2009), pp. 121-144.

Slabaugh, Brett: "Resident Evil Creator Explains Why the Series Stopped Being Scary," *The Escapist*, September 28, 2013, http://v1.escapistmagazine.com/news/view/128251-Resident-Evil-Creator-Explains-Why-the-Series-Stopped-Being-Scary.

Sterling, Jim: "How Survival Horror Evolved Itself Into Extinction," *Destructoid*, December 8, 2008, https://www.destructoid.com/how-survival-horror-evolved-itself-into-extinction-114022.phtml

Taylor, Laurie N.: "Gothic Bloodlines in Survival Horror Gaming," in: Perron (ed.), *Horror Video Games* (2009), pp. 46-61.

Vella, Daniel: "Who Am 'I' in the Game?": A Typology of the Modes of Ludic Subjectivity," in: *Proceedings of 1st International Joint Conference of DiGRA and FDG*, https://e-channel.med.utah.edu/wp-content/uploads/2017/02/paper_234.pdf, pp. 1-16.

Ludography

ALONE IN THE DARK (Infogrames 1992, O: Infogrames)
AMNESIA: THE DARK DESCENT (Frictional Games 2010, O: Frictional Games)
DREADOUT (PT Digital Semantika Indonesia 2014, O: Digital Happiness)

HAUNTING GROUND (Capcom 2005, O: Capcom)
LAYERS OF FEAR (Aspyr Media 2016, O: Bloober Team)
OUTLAST (Red Barrels 2013, O: Red Barrels)
OUTLAST 2 (Red Barrels 2017, O: Red Barrels)
PROJECT ZERO (Wanadoo 2002, O: Tecmo)
P.T. (Konami 2014, O: 7780s Studio)
RESIDENT EVIL Series (Capcom 1996-, O: Capcom)
  RESIDENT EVIL (Capcom 1996, O: Capcom)
  RESIDENT EVIL 2 (Capcom 2019, O: Capcom)
  RESIDENT EVIL 4 (Capcom 2005, O: Capcom)
  RESIDENT EVIL 5 (Capcom 2009, O: Capcom)
  RESIDENT EVIL 6 (Capcom 2012, O: Capcom)
  RESIDENT EVIL 7: BIOHAZARD (Capcom 2017, O: Capcom)
SILENT HILL Series (Konami 1999-2014, O: Konami)
  SILENT HILL (Konami 1999, O: Konami Computer)
  SILENT HILL 4: THE ROOM (Konami 2004, O: Team Silent)
  SILENT HILL: HOMECOMING (Konami 2008, O: Double Helix Games)
SLENDER: THE EIGHT PAGES (Parsec Productions 2012)
SONG OF HORROR (in development, O: Protocol Games)
THE EVIL WITHIN (Bethesda Softworks 2014, O: Tango Gameworks)
THE EVIL WITHIN 2 (Bethesda Softworks 2017, O: Tango Gameworks)

FILMOGRAPHY

GODZILLA (J 1954, D: Ishirô Honda)
KING KONG (USA 1976, D: John Guillermin)
SAW (USA 2004, D: James Wan)
THE TEXAS CHAINSAW MASSACRE (USA 1974, D: Tobe Hooper)

Survival Horror and Masochism

A Digression from the Modern Scopic Regime

SHUNSUKE MUKAE

Like many other research fields, game studies started as an extension of existing disciplines. Espen Aarseth's book CYBERTEXT: PERSPECTIVES ON ERGODIC LITERATURE,[1] now part of the game studies canon, is a good example of this phenomenon. Aarseth started his career as a scholar of literature which he bridged to video games by analyzing text-based adventure games as "ergodic literature."[2] This kind of scholarship—adapting theories of existing disciplines to the study of video games—continues to be popular today,[3] with game studies already long-established as a field. In this context, film studies is one of the most commonly cited fields. At the 2017 Clash of Realities conference, it was given special treatment by a panel on 'cineludic aesthetics,'[4] which considered the relation between video games and film with contributions from prominent film scholars such as Thomas Elsaesser.[5] And this connection is two-way: For example, video

---

1 Aarseth, Espen J.: *Cybertext: Perspectives on Ergodic Literature*, Baltimore Md.: Johns Hopkins University Press, 1997.
2 Ibid. p.1.
3 Freyermuth, Gundolf S.: *Games | Game Design | Game Studies*, Bielefeld: Transcript Verlag, 2015, pp. 11.
4 About the conference, see http://www.colognegamelab.de/research/clash-of-realities-conference/
5 Clash of Realities: "Clash of Realities. Conference Program November 14-16, 2016," 2016, http://www.clashofrealities.com/2016/wpcontent/uploads/2016/11/Program_ClashOfRealities20161.pdf, retrieved 2019. This is not the first time that Elsaesser discusses games (e.g., Elsaesser, Thomas and Buckland, Warren: Studying Contemporary American Film: A Guide to Movie Analysis, London: Arnold Publishers; New

games have been featured several times in CAHIERS DU CINEMA, one of the most influential film magazines, with special focus on graphics.[6] Le Diberder's 1996 article L'INTERACTIVITÉ, NOUVELLE FRONTIÈRE DU CINÉMA provides another good example of this connection.[7]

However, the experiences of playing a video game and watching a film should not be regarded as the same. This paper considers that point by analyzing the masochistic aspects of horror games, with an emphasis on perspective. Deleuze says, "[i]n masochism we find a progression from disavowal to suspense, from disavowal as a process of liberation from the pressures of the superego to suspense as incarnation of the ideal."[8] Games can be considered as activities based on this masochistic pleasure, which unfolds within the 'magic circle.'[9] I will then demonstrate how this characteristic places games outside of the modern scopic regime proposed by Martin Jay.[10]

WHAT DIVIDES FILM AND GAMES? TWO TYPES OF INTERACTIVITY

Film and games have often been linked by both film and game scholars, game developers, and players. The designers and producers of RESIDENT EVIL (1996), SILENT HILL (1999) and METAL GEAR SOLID (1998) declared that their titles were inspired by specific films.[11] Moreover, numerous games, including RESI-

---

York: Oxford University Press 2002.). He is one of the scholars who have comparatively early taken notice of the relation between game and film.

6 E.g., *Hors série cahiers du cinéma avril 2000: Contient entre autres: Aux frontières du cinema*, April 2000, pp. 38-49., *Hors-série cahiers du cinema: Spécial jeux vidéo*, September 2002.

7 Le Diberder, Alain: "L'interactivité, nouvelle frontière du cinéma," in: *Cahiers du cinema* 503, June 1996, pp. 122-126.

8 Deleuze, Gilles: *Masochism: Coldness and Cruelty*, New York: Zone Books 1991, p.127.

9 Salen, Katie/Zimmerman, Eric: *Rules of Play: Game Design Fundamentals*, Cambridge, Mass.: MIT Press 2003, p. 94.

10 Jay, Martin: "Scopic Regimes of Modernity," in: Foster, Hal (ed.), *Vision and Visuality*, Seattle: Bay Press, 1988, pp. 3-23.

11 Hideo Kojima, the director of METAL GEAR SOLID series, is widely known as a designer of filmic games. In his works he includes film-like title logos, staff roles, and

DENT EVIL and SILENT HILL, have been made into films. The connection between film and games has often manifested itself in cross-references such as these.

As I have already mentioned, CAHIERS DU CINEMA focused on video games in 1996. In their first feature, Alain Le Diberder, a French TV director, published the article L'INTERACTIVITÉ, NOUVELLE FRONTIÈRE DU CINEMA.[12] There, he discusses how to estimate the meaning of interactivity in the context of two-way communication between film capital that places games under their influence, and game developers that are aspiring to make film-like games. Although he insists that interactivity is not fundamentally compatible with narrative, he also admits that some kinds of interactivity have indeed been introduced in narrative media like film. He says that though the border between authors and readers was established along with the advent of written culture, previously, in oral culture, authorship and readership were not strictly divided. The porosity of the boundary between authors and readers renders narrative malleable in oral culture. We still see this today, for example, when parents read to their children: Depending on the dynamic and demands of narrator(s) and listener(s), the same story can be told in many different ways. Le Diberder lists the variation of folklore in Iranian film and contradictory explications of the same occurrence in RASHÔMON (1950) as typical examples of interaction in film. Whether we entirely agree with his statements or not, it is certainly possible to say that film also has some interactive aspects. However, Le Diberder confuses two different types of interactivity and, consequently, he obscures his argument.

Baba and Yamamoto, game designers at Sega and Koei respectively, explain that there are two dimensions of interactivity in games: that of interpretation and condition.[13] The former means that audiences do not affect the content of the artifact itself, but interpret its meaning; the latter means that any parameters, objects, or situations of the medium can be physically modified when subjects take action. The interactivity in film is the interaction of interpretation. Although it requires some kind of voluntary commitment, the role that spectators play in a cinematic system that they cannot modify is passive. On the other hand, players contribute crucially to construct the game world. The interactivity of condition makes this possible. Both of these interactivities can be compatible with each other in video games, but the interactivity of condition is the distinctive feature of the gaming experience.

---

    cinephilic characters who describe films that influenced the game they are in (e.g., Para-Medic in METAL GEAR SOLID 3).

12 Le Diberder, Ibid.

13 Baba, Yasuhito/Yamamoto, Takamitsu: *Gêmu no kyôkasho*, Tokyo: Chikuma shobô 2008, pp. 25-26.

Deleuzian Masochism in the Gaming Experience

These interactivities are of concern to a game's characteristics in a wider sense. Whether we consider video games as a form of art or play, all player input should be in accordance with the rules and take place in the designated field of play. Otherwise, the player will be excluded from the game. In this sense, gaming experiences can be seen as essentially masochistic. In order to enter the activity, the player/spectator needs to voluntarily agree to the rules and limitations of the experience. This agreement resonates with Deleuze's idea that the essence of masochism is trying to keep oneself inside the ritual space.

The Characteristics of Deleuzian Masochism

The general picture of Deleuzian masochism is too complex to explain here in detail. However, it is necessary to understand its essence to proceed with this argument. In this section, I explore the ritual and suspense of masochism—key concepts of this paper—which set Deleuzian masochism apart from Freudian sadomasochism.

According to Deleuze, in order to arrange the ritual space, a masochist has to persuade, cultivate, and contract his mistress to be his ideal torturer.[14] This torturer is not a sadist because she is trained by the masochist and subjected to him. In time, the contract changes, driving him to perform a rite; "[t]he masochistic contract generates a type of law which leads straight into ritual. The masochist is obsessed; ritualistic activity is essential to him, since it epitomizes the world of fantasy."[15]

Another aspect of Deleuzian masochism is suspense. He states that "[i]n Masoch's novels, it is the moments of suspense that are the climactic moments" because "the art of suspense always places us on the side of the victim and forces us to identify with him, whereas the gathering momentum of repetition tends to force us onto the side of the torturer and make us identify with the sadistic hero."[16] This also indicates the separation between sado and maso.

---

14 As Deleuze is faithful to Masoch, it is fixed that the victim is always a man and the torturer is a woman. Linda Williams points out this aspect from a gender studies perspective in, Williams, Linda: "Film Bodies: Gender, Genre, and Excess," in: *Film Quarterly* 44, 4 (1991): pp. 2-13. As I have no space here to discuss it, I will come back to this in the future study.

15 Ibid., p. 94.

16 Ibid. p.34.

In the space of video games, the masochistic rite resonates with the concept of the 'magic circle.'[17] Salen and Zimmerman offer an explanation of the term in their book RULES OF PLAY:

"As a player steps in and out of a game, he or she is crossing that boundary—or a frame—that defines the game in time and space [...] we call the boundary of the game the *magic circle*, [...] the term is used here as shorthand for the idea of a special place in time created by a game. [...] As a closed circle, the space it circumscribes is enclosed and separate from the real world. As a marker of time, the magic circle is like a clock: it simultaneously represents a path with a beginning and end. The magic circle inscribes a space that is repeatable, a space both limited and limitless. In short, a finite space with infinite possibility."[18]

We can find some passages in the explanation above which link the magic circle and the masochistic ritual space, such as the notion of limited and repeatable time; both contracts continue for a fixed period, and suspense is caused through repetition. However, the magic circle is not unique to video games. For example, we might rely on some kind of illusion to interpret two-dimensional pictures as three-dimensional worlds. In this context, a screen displaying moving images could be considered a magic circle of sorts. But now we need to remember the differences between the two interactivities. For any medium that only has the interactivity of interpretation, the circle needs to exist in advance for the subject to enter it.

In the case of games, which also feature interactivity of condition, the players themselves must construct a magic circle by using controllers, screens, and other materials. This is decidedly different from other media in that the subject must engage voluntarily and actively in every step.[19]

A masochist does not directly reach ecstasy. In fact, he might delay it ecstasy through repeated actions in the magic circle. Gaming and masochism are thus

---

17 While many scholars use this term, there are arguments against its existence because it implicates several meanings (e.g., Liebe, Michael: "There is No Magic Circle: On the Difference between Computer Games and Traditional Games," in: *Proceedings of The Philosophy of Computer Games Conference* 2008; https://publishup.uni-potsdam.de/frontdoor/index/index/docId/2558, retrieved 2019). Here we merely specify its meaning as the space and time in which games are played and are physically isolated from real world.
18 Salen/Zimmerman, Ibid, p. 95.
19 E.g., Suits argued this point, see Suits, Bernard: *The Grasshopper: Games, Life and Utopia*. Toronto: University of Toronto Press 1978.

further connected in the context of repetition. Players activate the two forms of interactivity at once and intentionally stay inside of the magic circle for as long as possible.

Is the Modern Scopic Regime Sadistic?

According to Martin Jay, there were different scopic regimes, including Cartesian perspectivalism, the art of describing, and the baroque. To summarize his point, even when a scopic regime dominated the world, alternative conceptions of perception persisted. What is more, we can even find competing modes within the dominant system.[20]

In contrast to Jay, Jonathan Crary looks at the period from the perspective of the human body.[21] He disagrees with Jay in that he pays attention to the apparatus with respect to Cartesian perspective and emphasizes its substantial impact on the scopic regime, clarifying that it was overturned by the emergence of physiology: The human body comes back to the field of optic cognition by paying attention to the retina afterimage.[22] However, seeing is undividable from the social and material system of each age. Crary says that a system of vision leads to the birth of the observer within it; while the 19th century 'spectator' implies "a passive onlooker at a spectacle,"[23] 'observare,' the root of 'observe,' doesn't originally contain the meaning "to look at."[24] It rather means "to conform one's action, to comply with" and "'observer' is embedded in a system of conventions and limitations."[25] The observer can only exist inside of the system but cannot destroy it like the (Deleuzian) sadist does. Observers merely accept sculptures, pictures and films. Any limitations unrelated to media themselves (such as fixed routes for appreciation, ropes closing off entry, the flow of the crowd, or closing time) and the subordination to the correct or preferable way for appreciating the artwork can be considered as sadism, which never accepts resistance. In short, within the collective experiences of modern visual media, it is not easy to have an individual connection with objects in the space for appreciation even if the action occurs through masochistic voluntary engagement.

---

20 Jay, Ibid., p. 11.
21 Crary, Jonathan: *Techniques of the Observer: On Vision and Modernity in the Nineteenth Century*, Cambridge, London: MIT press 1992, p. 5.
22 Crary, Jonathan: "Modernizing Vision," in: Foster, Hal (ed.), *Vision and Visuality*, Seattle: Bay Press 1988, pp. 33-34.
23 Crary, 1992, Ibid, p. 5.
24 Ibid.
25 Ibid, p. 6.

Therefore, visual media from Renaissance art to film partially contain sadistic aspects that force the observer to adopt specific positions. However, we are still able to find an element of masochistic pleasure in modern vision—that which is produced by subordination to the law within the place of appreciation. In other words, it is pseudo-sadism which derides superego within masochism. Video games, which require more active engagement and a personal contract with the object, differ from modern visual media in this respect.

FROM THE FILMIC VIEW TO NAVIGATION

As I have discussed above, players voluntarily construct a place called the 'magic circle.' The rite of playing a game, which is performed entirely with subordination to the law or rules inside of the magic circle and suspension, produced by eternal repetition, can be considered as a practice of Deleuzian masochism. In this chapter, I will give a detailed explanation of the problem of the body and points of view (POV) in three titles that demonstrate masochism in video games.

The RESIDENT EVIL series, a pioneering franchise of Japanese survival horror games, is a typical case in a transitional period when the survival horror genre shifted from imitating horror films to producing horror games which provided unique experiences. Throughout the over twenty titles of the series, the player's POV can be classified into three types: 1) Third-person view (TPV)—e.g., RESIDENT EVIL1 (1996), 2 (1998) and 3 (1999). 2) First-person view—e.g., the RESIDENT EVIL SURVIVOR series. 3) Third or first (sometimes mixed) person movable point of view—e.g., CODE: VERONICA, RESIDENT EVIL 4.

Fixed TPV in the original RESIDENT EVIL is similar to the typical perspective of a horror film. The camera doesn't follow the avatar's movement, but rather intermittently shows the avatar moving within a frame as if changing shots or jumping between security cameras. The avatar is often hidden by objects on the map, and sometimes enemies and traps are set in a blind spot. That is to say, while designers and players play fairly without hiding any information under the bird's eye view of 2D games, this kind of 3D game produces suspense by intentionally concealing such information as part of the level design. This method is as typical in horror films as the main enemy of this series—the zombie. Thus, RESIDENT EVIL provides a typical example of adopting the filmic view within the video game medium.

While the avatar's body is highlighted with striking angles and gushing blood effects, it intermittently disappears from the screen. This creates difficulties for certain players trying to control the avatar. Especially when the screen is blacked out during transitional moments, players might be confused because they cannot precisely imagine where exactly the avatar is on the new map. It is true that players will get used to guessing the avatar's location, but the accuracy of the forecast is not the problem here. It is the interval between the player's operation and the avatars' actual acts that suspends the gaming experience. It still occurs even after players become accustomed to controlling it; the avatar may go back to the former stage or the player inadvertently bumps the avatar into a sculpture because s/he continues to push a directional button. This is more noticeable in games than film though sometimes the former is modeled after the latter. On the other hand, players have been looking at the game world over the avatar's shoulder since RESIDENT EVIL 4 (2001), navigating from the avatar's POV. The game world now contains real space—the space behind the avatar overlaps with the player's in the real world—and dissolves the border between the screen and the player's 'real world' surroundings in the magic circle. In this way, RESIDENT EVIL decreases its affinity with film and emphasizes the gaming experience.[26]

Realistic representation of the body has also attracted interest as another remarkable point of the gaming experience. A typical instance is motion capture, which was introduced in fighting games such as VIRTUA FIGHTER (1993) in the early nineties and later in other genres such as RPGs, for example FINAL FANTASY VIII (1999).[27] It allowed not only for avatars to move realistically and have expressive faces, but also for smooth controlling. Independence between the controllability of the avatar's movements and operation of the POV changed the relation between body and eyes; the player can control them independently and integrally like we do with our bodies.[28]

---

26 Previous to it, RESIDENT EVIL GUN SURVIVOR (Capcom 2000) introduced DOOM-like FPV. Moreover, we can also find a shift away from film, for example, with the abandonment of the DVD-like 'director's cut' and real time selection of action in RESIDENT EVIL 3.

27 Besides the motion capture, face capture is also introduced and brought more realistic bodies in RESIDENT EVIL 6.

28 Analog sticks highly contributed to this tendency. Though FPS games like DOOM (1993) and ALIEN TRILOGY (1996) were very popular, the avatar cannot look other directions without moving body. However, even in later titles, a transitional period seemed to continue due to various reasons; in SILENT HILL, both fixed camera and a camera that trails the avatar were introduced for better controllability, yet the control of perspective is limited. After 2000, when PS2 and Game Cube required dual analogue sticks as standard, it finally became mainstream.

Operating and Changing POV: Repetition and Suspense

Unlike zombies in the RESIDENT EVIL series, the enemies in PROJECT ZERO (2001) are ghosts that are immune to physical attacks of any kind. The player fights them off by taking their picture with a spiritual camera called *Sya'eiki* (Camera Obscura). Taking pictures in the first person view introduces an aspect that is absent from the first trilogy of RESIDENT EVIL: the disappearance of the avatar's body. Linda Williams regards horror film as a kind of *body film* characterized by Freudian sadomasochism. It contains various 'excesses,' e.g., copious amounts of violence and blood.[29] Spectators accept these films corporeally from the perspectives of 'sadistic monsters' and 'masochistic victims.'[30] While zombies in RESIDENT EVIL embody the excess of violence with their bodies in the way Williams describes, ghosts are not literally embodied themselves. Moreover, even the avatar's body disappears from the screen when it looks into the finder in PROJECT ZERO. For the most part, the player's POV is a fixed TPV like the one found in RESIDENT EVIL, but the player's perspective overlaps with the avatar's point of view when using the camera. One of the characteristic differences between ZERO and most other survival horror games, including RESIDENT EVIL, is the system which implements the banishment of the avatar's body.

The essential border between the victim and the torturer is thus weaker in PROJECT ZERO than in the body film. Miku, the heroine, embodies this dynamic with a camera instead of a whip: Now that the tangible enemy—the essential torturer—is gone, it is the player who decides whether the avatar or the ghost is attacked by changing the POV. For this type of game, Deleuzian masochism is better suited than Freudian sadomasochism, which Williams adopted for the analysis of film. Deuleuze writes: "The beating woman represents the superego superficially and in the external world, and she also transforms the superego into the recipient of the beating, the essential victim."[31] As masochistic ego (the victim) and pseudo-sadistic superego (the torturer) are mixed within the space of the ritual (gaming), the player takes responsibility for both as a master of the rite.

---

29 Williams lists *The Texas Chainsaw Massacre*, *Halloween* and other splatter (house) films as examples.

30 Williams, Ibid. She lists several characteristics of body film. For example, bodily fluids such as tears for melodrama, sperm for porn, and blood for horror. They affect not only spectators' vision, but rather their somesthesis.

31 Deleuze, Ibid, p.125, as the protagonist of this game is a girl who uses camera instead of a whip, it might be better to say 'the shooting girl' here.

Selecting Masochism—Voluntary Extension

Though there are considerable differences between them, it is still possible to play both RESIDENT EVIL and PROJECT ZERO as a subjective player. In FORBIDDEN SIREN (2003), players enjoy multilayer perversion. In the SIREN series the player physically attacks zombie-like monsters called *Shibito*, like in RESIDENT EVIL. There are two choices for the player's POV—TPV and FPV—both of which control the avatar's movements. In addition to these two POVs, the series offers another: Second person's view (SPV), called "sight jacking," enables the player to see through the eyes of the enemy. It is modified for each title but can be used throughout the whole series. In SIREN: BLOOD CURSE (2008), players can simultaneously see the avatar's perspective and those of the enemies. In earlier titles, the entire screen displays the enemies' viewpoint and the avatar cannot move during sight jacking.[32] However, the screen is split in two while using sight jacking in SIREN: BC; the left displays the avatar's perspective and the right the enemy's. As the player has the avatar's eyesight, s/he can move the avatar with this system. Moreover, the player can even jack four POVs (of the avatar and three enemies) at the same time by restricting the avatar's movement. Both the eyes of the avatar and the enemies are marked on screen, and they sometimes cross each other. Since the first title, the SIREN series has gradually deepened the level of masochism: by merely jacking enemies' eyesight in FORBIDDEN SIREN, low-level interaction with jacked eyesight in FORBIDDEN SIREN 2, and finally the crossing perspectives of ego and superego in BC—which can be read as the climax of Deleuzian masochism.

The SIREN series enables communication with enemies in an alternative way: by foregrounding the act of being seen. In SIREN: BC, the player is simultaneously haunted by the avatar and the enemies. In other words, the player kills her/himself whether the avatar or enemies die. To be clear, players can continue the game without using sight jacking—a mechanic which is not required to beat the game. However, the masochistic player voluntarily uses this system, and witnesses the moment they are killed by themselves, perhaps in order to reach something like ludic ecstasy.

---

32 In FORBIDDEN SIREN 2, some avatars can move with someone's view or partially interact with it.

Conclusion

Although the gap between the paradigms they belong to is still debatable, scholars have often referred to preceding media, especially film, when discussing video games as I explained earlier. On the one hand, while the Cartesian perspective dominated the paradigm by renouncing the body, the modern scopic regime highlights its recurrence. Nevertheless, the subject still has to see through the fixed system. On the other hand, the interactivity in the survival horror genre, which remains on the ritual—masochistic—side, produces opportunities for changing the relation between the pseudo-sadistic superego and the masochistic ego. In video games, the player tries to remain in suspense through endless repetition in order to approach completion of the masochistic rite. And this pleasure denies the continuity between games and former media like film. With the multiple views of avatars and enemies in SIREN: BC, the player experiences the acme of masochism as they witness themselves being killed through the torturer's POV. The pleasure is mediated by the imaginary body, and it is delayed and suspended by limitless repetition. It is the visibility of the body which "never ceases to act and react *before the mind moves it*"[33] that produces this new form for pleasure. It allows the subject—the gamer—to experience media in a different way than the observer, who is subjected to the system. In this sense, we should consider video games not as a legitimate descendent of modern visual media, but a new horizon of our media experience.

Acknowledgments

Thanks to James Scanlon-Canegata, Chloé Paberz, Curtis Maughan, Federico Alvarez Igarzábal, and Michael S. Debus for comments and proofreading.

---

33 Deleuze, Gilles: "The Shame and the Glory: T. E. Lawrence," in: *Essays Critical and Clinical*, London: Verso 1998, p.123, italics in original.

Literature

Aarseth, Espen J.: *Cybertext: Perspectives on Ergodic Literature*, Baltimore Md.: Johns Hopkins University Press 1997.

Baba, Yasuhito/Yamamoto, Takamitsu: *Gêmu no kyôkasho*, Tokyo: Chikuma shobô 2008.

Crary, Jonathan: "Modernizing Vision," in: Foster, Hal (ed.), *Vision and Visuality*, Seattle: Bay Press 1988, pp. 29-44.

Crary, Jonathan: *Techniques of the Observer: On Vision and Modernity in the Nineteenth Century*. Cambridge, London: MIT press 1992.

Deleuze, Gilles: "The Shame and the Glory: T. E. Lawrence," in: *Essays Critical and Clinical*, London: Verso 1998, pp. 115-125.

Deleuze, Gilles: *Masochism: Coldness and Cruelty*, New York: Zone Books 1991.

Elsaesser, Thomas and Buckland, Warren: *Studying Contemporary American Film: A Guide to Movie Analysis*, London: Arnold Publishers; New York: Oxford University Press 2002.

Freyermuth, Gundolf S.: *Games | Game Design | Game Studies*, Bielefeld: Transcript Verlag, 2015.

Hors-série cahiers du cinéma avril 2000: Contient entre autres: Aux frontières du cinema, April 2000, pp. 38-49.

Hors-série cahiers du cinema: Spécial jeux vidéo, September 2002.

Jay, Martin: "Scopic Regimes of Modernity," in: Foster, Hal (ed.), *Vision and Visuality*, Seattle: Bay Press, 1988 pp.3-23.

Le Diberder, Alain: "L'interactivité, nouvelle frontière du cinéma," in: *Cahiers du cinema* 503, June 1996, pp. 122-126.

Liebe, Michael: "There is No Magic Circle: On the Difference between Computer Games and Traditional Games," in: *Conference Proceedings of The Philosophy of Computer Games* 2008; https://publishup.uni-potsdam.de/frontdoor/index/index/docId/2558

Salen, Katie/Zimmerman, Eric: *Rules of Play: Game Design Fundamentals*, Cambridge, Mass.: MIT Press 2003.

Suits, Bernard: *The Grasshopper: Games, Life and Utopia*. Toronto: University of Toronto Press 1978.

Williams, Linda: "Film Bodies: Gender, Genre, and Excess," in: *Film Quarterly* 44, 4 (1991): pp. 2-13.

FILMOGRAPHY

RASHÔMON (JP 1950, D: Akira Kurosawa)

LUDOGRAPHY

ALIEN TRILOGY (Acclaim Japan 1996, O: Acclaim Japan)
DOOM (id Software 1993, O: id Software)
FINAL FANTASY VIII (Square 1999, O: Square)
FORBIDDEN SIREN (Sony Computer Entertainment 2003, O: Sony Computer Entertainment Japan Studio)
FORBIDDEN SIREN 2 (Sony Computer Entertainment 2006, O: Sony Computer Entertainment Japan Studio)
METAL GEAR SOLID (Konami 1998, O: Konami Computer Entertainment Japan)
METAL GEAR SOLID 3 (Konami 2004, O: Konami Computer Entertainment Japan)
PROJECT ZERO (Tecmo 2001, O: Tecmo)
RESIDENT EVIL (Capcom 1996, O: Capcom)
RESIDENT EVIL DIRECTOR'S CUT (Capcom 1997 O: Capcom)
RESIDENT EVIL 2 (Capcom 1998, O: Capcom)
RESIDENT EVIL 3: NEMESIS (Capcom 1999, O: Capcom)
RESIDENT EVIL GUN SURVIVER (Capcom 2000, O: Tose)
RESIDENT EVIL CODE: VERONICA (Capcom 2000, O: Nextech)
RESIDENT EVIL 4 (Capcom 2005, O: Capcom)
RESIDENT EVIL 6 (Capcom 2012, O: Capcom)
SILENT HILL (Konami 1999, O: Konami)
SIREN: BLOOD CURSE (Sony Computer Entertainment 2008, O: Sony Computer Entertainment Japan Studio)
VIRTUA FIGHTER (Sega 1993, O: Sega-AM2)

ONLINE MEDIA

Clash of Realities: "Clash of Realities. Conference Program November 14-16, 2016," 2016, http://www.clashofrealities.com/2016/wp-content/uploads/2016/11/Program_ClashOfRealities20161.pdf, retrieved 2019.

Epiphany Through Kinaesthetics
Unfolding Storyworlds in Immersive Analog Spaces[1]

ÁGNES KAROLINA BAKK

If nowadays we mention immersive theatre or immersive experience, the concept of immersion reminds many of us of the sense of immediate magical transportation. But what makes an immersive performance actually "immersive" is a matter of much academic debate. Immersion is a widely used concept in cognitive skill development, language learning (encountered via the term "language immersion"), and especially when discussing the gameplay experience of video game players.[2] Nevertheless, it is still a rather unspecified term that does not always bear a valid definition. In art-related theories, the concept of immersion is often associated with video games and entertainment genres. Gordon Calleja discusses immersion as a multidimensional concept that has various experiential manifestations. He points out the difference between immersion as absorption (involvement into gameplay) and as transportation (the sense of being transported into another reality).[3] Marie-Laure Ryan, meanwhile, identifies two types of

---

1 This work was supported by a grant of the Ministry of National Education, CNCS – UEFISCDI Romania, project number PN-III-P4-ID-PCE-2016-0418.
2 Cummins, James: *Bilingualism and Education: Issues in Assessment and Pedagogy*, Celevedon, England: Multilingual Matters, 1984. Genesee, Fred: *Learning Through Two Languages: Studies on Immersion and Bilingual Education*, Belmont: Wadsworth Pub 1987.
3 Calleja, Gordon: *In-game. From Immersion to Incorporation*. Cambridge, MA: MIT Press 2011, p. 32.

psychological immersion: narrative and ludic; later she also identifies epistemic immersion, in which the search for knowledge leads the participant.[4]

In this paper, I aim to show that the creators of immersive theatre performances invite the audience to become an active participant and to experience epiphany (and through this various social emotions) during the performance by using the picturesque effects of New Horror and somaesthetic design concepts.[5] I will present an in-depth analysis of the performance DAS HEUVOLK (Strawpeople) by the Danish company SIGNA, which was presented in the summer of 2017 in Mannheim, Germany, during the Schillertage Festival. Within my theoretical framework, I will interpret their performance as a video game, relying especially on the mechanics they use in their world-building procedure and the non-linear open world story elements that unfold throughout the performance. By introducing the concept of "epiphany" into the video game discourse, I will also attempt to describe the sensation experienced by the audience.[6]

WHAT IS IMMERSIVE THEATRE?

Janet Murray defines immersion as "the sensation of being surrounded by a completely other reality, as different as water is from air, that takes over all of our attention, our whole perceptual apparatus."[7] As Murray also points out, immersion is not a concept that is only linked to video games but also to non-digital media. So the genre of immersive theatre has also started to become more and more widespread, especially in the UK, propagated mainly by the theatre group Punchdrunk. As Josephine Machon points out, similar tactics (what we call today "immersive") can be traced to the early Modernists and their continua-

---

4   Ryan, Marie-Laure: *Narrative as Virtual Reality*, Baltimore, MD: The John Hopkins University Press 2001, p. 16. Ryan, Marie-Laure: "From Narrative Games to Playable Stories," in: *StoryWorlds: A Journal of Narrative Studies*, 1, *1*, University of Nebraska Press 2009, p. 55.
5   See Ndalianis, Angela: *The Horror Sensorium*: Media and the Senses, Jefferson, NC: McFarland&Company 2012. Shustermann, Richard: "Somaesthetics: A Disciplinary Proposal," in: *The Journal of Aesthetics and Art Criticism* 57, *3* (Summer, 1999), pp. 299-313. Höök, Kristina: *Designing with the Body,* Cambridge, MA: MIT Press 2011.
6   Aarseth, Espen: *Cybertext. Perspectives on Ergodic Literature,* Baltimore, MD: The Johns Hopkins University Press 1997.
7   Murray, Janet H.: *Hamlet on Holodeck. The Future of Narrative in Cyberspace,* Cambridge, MA: MIT Press 1997, p. 101.

tion can be observed from the 1960's onward, starting with the sensual and interactive practice of performance artists such as Allan Kaprow or Richard Schechner. These tactics were once referred to as "total installations."[8] This fine art aspect is especially important, as it can help define immersive theatre against traditional theatre formats and practices. In the case of immersive performances, "the audience is 'thrown' (sometimes even literally) into a totally new environment [...] which [is] seemingly outside of 'everyday' rules and regulations and (the audiences) always have expectations of physical interaction."[9]

I distinguish two types of environments, in which I also include the presence of the performers or digitally-animated non-player or player characters: analog and digital immersive environments. The first type applies to non-digital media and the second to virtual environments. (1) In analog environments the audience encounters physical closeness and almost awkwardly intimates situations with the performers; (2) In digital environments, the audiences turn into 'experiencers'[10] as they gather various types of experiences enhanced by their participative status. They face the "magical" capacities of new technology, but this magic is framed by a rule system and these works "not only require activity on the part of their recipients, but they also orchestrate, control, and channel the resulting actions."[11] In the latter environments, a lack of spontaneity can be observed, as these systems cannot (yet) fully answer the expectations of the experiencers regarding immersion. The experiencers can observe the system from which these immersive digital experiences emerge but they can miss the sudden changes of hierarchy and power relationships (and also the intimacy the presence of live performers can offer). In the following analysis I will describe an example of analog immersive spaces, where the experiencer faces the picturesque and structural elements of horror combined with intimate situations with the performers, accompanied by pre-designed (or guided) kinetics from the experiencer's side.

---

8   Machon, Josephine: *Immersive Theatres. Intimacy and Immediacy in Contemporary Performance*, London: Palgrave Macmillan 2013, p. 34.
9   Ibid., p. 27.
10 See Benford, Steve/Gabriella Giannachi: *Performing Mixed Reality*, Cambridge, MA: MIT Press 2011.
11 Kwastek, Katja: *Aesthetics of Interaction in Digital Art,* Cambridge, MA: MIT Press 2011, p. 262.

Analysis

The Danish-Austrian company SIGNA was founded in 2007 and usually stages performances in Germany or Austria. The two founders, Signa and Arthur Köstler, describe their works as performance installations: the setting of their productions are big houses or complexes, where 30 to 50 actors perform in an evening. When audiences enter the space, they immediately encounter the dramaturgical context of the performance.[12]

DAS HEUVOLK was presented in 2017 in Mannheim, Germany, in the frame of the Internationale Schillertage theater festival. It took place in the suburbs of Mannheim in Benjamin Franklin Village. While entering that suburb with the bus, one could already see a gathering of performers. When the bus stopped, the audience was welcomed by performers wearing costumes that resembled the solid monochrome dresses of cult members. The performers divided the audience members into several rooms where they received initiation training: they learned that they were there because Jack, the head of the cult, had recently died and the group was recruiting new members in order to find their missing gods. This was necessary for surviving the end of the world and becoming the "Himmelfahrer" (Ascencioners). The audience was told by the performers that they could encounter various rituals at certain times in the different rooms, where they could follow the cult members as they called upon the gods to return. There were also certain house rules that had to be obeyed (e.g. when entering or leaving a room one had to greet the mythological tricksters with a hand signal). After this, the audience could wander around in a two-level building that contained many thematic rooms where the performers carried out rituals. For example, one could enter a room filled with red, blue, and black carpets, heavy furniture, and drinks with high levels of alcohol. This was the *Peacock's Room* where men were fighting each other (in the frame of the ritual). The audience, in close proximity, experienced the weight of the punches and kicks, how the fighters were sweating from physical exertion, and how their skin was reddening from being struck. In the *Cowboy Room*, the audience faced a real life struggle, as they witnessed the "bull" (a performer) suffering from being possessed by a god.

After five hours spent in this house (which is not enough time to visit all of the rooms), the audience was guided into a nearby chapel. Here, everyone was seated near the walls forming a circle. A ritual started accompanied by songs about gratefulness, where the audience members could finally decide whether they wanted to join the cult or not. There was only one condition: they had to

---

12 See www.signa.dk/about as of March 28, 2019.

undress in the middle of the circle and join a washing ceremony. Those who chose this option could stay one hour longer (while the rest of the audience was brought back to the city with a bus) and attended a further performance. This final event was a private after party with the actors, where the old and new members of the cult sang together and embraced each other. The cult members appeared content, as they were able to recruit more members to help them with their search for the missing gods. If an audience member who joined the cult revisited the performance, they were greeted at the start as a member.

The above description of the performance does not focus on the narrative framework, but on how all the characters have a pre-established biography, with a set of characteristics and behavior. Within the community, everyone talks freely about other cult members, but a constant fear of the future can also be observed, while sometimes secrets are only partly revealed, encouraging the audience to gather further information. As an active audience, the experiencers can also choose which room to visit, with which performer to interact, how to act themselves, or whether they want to stop a certain act of violence.[13] Even though the spectators cannot have a direct influence on how the narrative path develops, they can have an effect on which experiences they gather throughout the evening. They can choose to have more (superficially) joyful moments or to investigate the dark side of this community. In these heavily themed rooms the experiencer engages with other people in various ways: they act together with the performers and other experiencers, and in this way they can encounter various social emotions such as guilt, disgust, embarrassment, or shame. These emotions emerge from the relationships that develop between the experiencers and performers. But all these emotions are encountered as having a triple identity: As Mühlhoff observes while analyzing himself as an audience member in a previous SIGNA production, one has to decide whether to act as a private person (as the audience members' real name and background is asked very frequently), as a guest (as the audience is always welcomed as a guest of a special community) or as a political subject opposed to the scenes of violence. This amalgam of the experiencer's potential roles, combined with an active attitude, can be a new sensation for the audience and can cause participants to enthusiastically seek out such situations where they might encounter a variety of experiences.

Being a member of the audience is also very similar to having a temporary avatar, which is formed by the triple identity described above. Here, it is useful

---

13 See Mühlhoff, Rainer: "Dark Immersion. Some Thoughts on SIGNA's Us Dogs," in: Doris Kolesch/Theresa Schütz/Sophie Nikoleit (eds.), *Strategies of Staging Spectators in Immersive Performances: Commit Yourself!* London and New York: Routledge 2019.

to borrow the concept of "a representation of a user" from De Zwart and Lindsay.[14] They define avatars not only as "any online representation of a user" but, going beyond the "online" qualifier, they argue that board game pieces, live-action role playing game personas, MMORPG (massively multiplayer online role-playing games) characters, and social virtual world characters or figures are all avatars. While having this unstable state of mind regarding which avatar to embody, the experiencers seek to find new ways to gain knowledge and experience about this new world.

Adam Alston interprets this avatar attitude as follows:

"Audiences are likely to find themselves functioning as something more than an audience, either as a character cast within a given world, or as some kind of hyper-self, even a pastiche of oneself once confronted with a range of participatory demands pining towards some kind of revelation."[15]

According to Alston, "(t)he non-reproducible element comes largely from the consumer narcissistically investing their own personality and desire."[16] But what actually creates this "hunting attitude" in the audience? In these performances, the experiences are unevenly distributed. The audience members, who are already familiar with the mechanics of the performance, continue to explore the environment, thus seizing the opportunity to experience more of the story world. Alston links this attitude to the rise of neoliberal ideologies: "Take responsibility upon yourself to make the most of what is available."[17] In a related way, the desire to take risks may be a contributing factor to the appeal of immersive theatre. And, building on Alston's hypothesis, I can add that in immersive theater some of these risks concern social emotions, such as guilt or shame, which audience members typically try to avoid in their everyday environments.

---

14   De Zwart, Melissa/Lindsay, David: "My self, my avatar, my rights? Avatar identity in social virtual worlds," in: Daniel Riha (ed.): *At the Interface/Probing the Boundaries. Frontiers of Cyberspace*, Leiden: Brill-Rodopi 2012, pp. 81-100, here p. 82.
15   Alston, Adam: "Audience Participation and Neoliberal Value. Risk, agency and responsibility in immersive theatre," in: *Performance Research: A Journal of the Perfoming Arts* 18, 2, pp. 128-138, DOI: 10/1080/13528165.2013.807177, here p. 131.
16   Ibid., p. 131.
17   Ibid., p. 133.

RISK IN A HORROR ENVIRONMENT?

In 2017, I had the opportunity to conduct an audience survey in cooperation with National Theatre Mannheim. In total, 201 audience members answered the questionnaire about the experiences they had during the performance of DAS HEUVOLK. For the purposes of this paper, it is not necessary to describe the outcome of the survey in detail, but it is interesting to mention that one of the questions was "to which genres would you compare the performance?" Several answers mentioned the genre of thriller and horror, both being based on the mechanism of epistemic immersion. Although only a few members of the audience gave these genre examples as answers, I'll scrutinize why this is nevertheless crucial to the analysis of DAS HEUVOLK. . The genre of horror films indeed has a multi-sensorial effect on the recipient. As Ndalianis states in her book *The Horror Sensorium*, "[t]he spaces of horror media not only fictionalize—in vividly sensory ways—their own sensorium, but they also demand that we cognitively and physiologically respond to their fictions by translating their sensorial enactments across our bodies."[18] But how exactly can the horror genre have this effect? Ndalianis explains that, "[a]s a genre, it's capable of intensifying the range of reactions and experiences in which we can become enmeshed when connecting with media texts and, over the last decade in particular, the proliferation of horror texts across media have amplified their focus on sensory encounters."[19] Film theorists often state that haptic exploration is not necessarily limited to the senses of touch, but can be connected to vision as well. In the case of the cinematic medium, the horror environment constitutes the "aesthetic of disgust."[20] In the case of DAS HEUVOLK, the player (the member of the audience) faces the challenges of this fictional world in a multisensorial environment, which is actually very effective as it makes use of "carnal elements" such as sweat, saliva mixed with dirt, real time violence, and also taxidermies. These sources of disgust boost the hunting attitude of the audience, and it is this attitude that actually guides the experiencer through the performance space and unfolding story. Experiencing disgust in one room can create the expectation of the next shocking element in another room. Just as in walking simulators, experiencers make choices that shape the form of the performance without drastically altering the storyline. In this way "the story becomes a personal experience for the player – an experience

---

18 Ndalianis, Angela: *The Horror Sensorium: Media and the Senses*, Jefferson, NC: McFarland&Company 2012, p. 3.
19 Ibid.
20 Ibid. p. 6.

defined by a challenge that could be intellectual, psychological, ethical, emotional, and/or physical."[21] And we can add that the situation makes the player more driven to achieve the highest peak of personalization of the game.

These horror elements, however, cannot be truly experienced merely by listening and seeing, rather they require kinesthetic and haptic experiences. The performance is designed in a way that the audience can move around freely, only occasionally accompanied by some of the performers. Being in the presence, and following the rules, of the community, an audience member might notice how they are embodying specific actions that are required to be a part of the community (like greeting the tricksters in each room). This bodily awareness is created by the environment through somaesthetics. As Shustermann states:

"Somaesthetics can be provisionally defined as the critical, meliorative study of the experience and use of one's body as a locus of sensory-aesthetic appreciation (aisthesis) and creative self-fashioning. It is therefore also devoted to the knowledge, discourses, practices, and bodily disciplines that structure such somatic care or can improve it."[22]

In this performance, the experiencers, by embodying and interiorizing prescribed actions, start to better understand the inner mechanics of the 'community,' in which they can also adapt to different roles. This adaptation can be considered as the peak point of such productions, which is comparable to the effect of epiphany in video games.

Why Epiphany?

Espen Aarseth defines epiphany as: "the sudden revelation that replaces the aporia, a seeming detail with an unexpected, salvaging effect: the link out. [...] The aporia-epiphany pair is thus not a narrative structure but constitutes a more fundamental layer of human experience from which narratives are spun."[23] What Aarseth means by this is that the epiphany is the solution of the problem and potentially the game. Immersive theatre guides experiencers to a gameplay-like epiphany by bringing them into a special mode of kinetic embodiment that

---

21 Thabet, Tamer: *Video Game Narrative and Criticism,* London: Palgrave Macmillan 2015, p. 41.
22 R. Shustermann: "Somaesthetics: A Disciplinary Proposal," p. 302.
23 Aarseth, Espen: *Cybertext. Perspectives on Ergodic Literature,* Baltimore: The Johns Hopkins University Press 1997, p. 91.

emerges from interaction with the actors and improvised dialogical situations. And it is not only that the audience is guided with the 'help' of the actors but, due to the deeply hyperrealistic setting that affects the olfactory and haptic sensoriums, the experiencers begin to take a physically active role in unfolding the storyworld of the performance. They discover various narrative elements through multisensorial experiences, thus enhancing immersion. In this way, the audience can experience the real epiphany of the immersive performances. If the members of the audience take a more passive attitude, then this passivity can be interpreted as a self-reflexive aporia that halts the experiencer from following one of the narrative paths.

Conclusion

Analyzing the nature of immersive performance, Adam Alston states that "it is not just that immersive theatre places audiences in an environment that surrounds them completely, but that they must invest something of themselves in this environment that builds toward the sense of an immersive world's cohesiveness."[24] In this paper I investigated how this investment from the audience's side can be described and how it can 'add' to the audience's experience, and how it makes use of the epiphany characteristics of video games. In these performances, the experiencers are hunting for new affects and emotions. Furthermore, in an immersive theater performance, the emotions of the experiencers are strengthened by experiencing all the sensory (e.g. haptic and even gustatory) inputs and undertaking kinaesthetically framed actions like walking.[25] In this way, participants do not delegate their blocks of affect to the actors, but they readily embody those feelings themselves. The audience is hunting to 'earn' more and more social emotions, just like a player hunts for more content in Massive Multiplayer Online Games. But in this type of immersive performance, experiencers also encounter the sensory elements of intimacy as a modality for epiphany.

These performances owe their immersion to the physical contact and spontaneity of the performers, as well as the audience's kinesthetic synchronization with the world of the performance. As Ndalianis states, reflecting on the dark ride attraction in theme parks, "the senses have no choice but to react to being thrown about in various directions and to being propelled forwards and back-

---

24 Alston, Adam: *Beyond Immersive Theatre,* London: Palgrave Macmillan 2016, p. 220.
25 See Alston, Adam: *Beyond Immersive Theatre*, p. 3.

wards."[26] From this point of view, it is important to consider why many immersive theatre performances use the aesthetics of horror—to amplify bodily reactions. But these bodily reactions are also used in performances where the audience needs spatial guidance through the experience. As Alston also mentions, the audience itself is actually used in the production of immersive theatre aesthetics.[27] This use is made possible through somaesthetic design concepts that are put into practice, which helps the audience to embody an avatar.

While in the case of video games (except some idle games) the agency on behalf of the audience is story-changing, in the case of immersive performances the audience members cannot change the storyline (as it is more of a story world than a linear narrative, even though the creators embedded a common goal for the participants in order to progress the leading storyline), but they can enhance agency through the multisensoriality of the environment and they can articulate their agency through kinesthetics.

Literature

Aarseth, Espen: *Cybertext. Perspectives on Ergodic Literature,* Baltimore: The Johns Hopkins University Press 1997.

Alston, Adam: "Audience Participation and Neoliberal Value. Risk, agency and responsibility in immersive theatre," in: *Performance Research: A Journal of the Perfoming Arts* 18, 2, pp. 128-138. DOI: 10/1080/13528165.2013.807177

Alston, Adam: *Beyond Immersive Theatre,* London: Palgrave Macmillan 2016.

Benford, Steve/Gabriella Giannachi: *Performing Mixed Reality,* Cambridge, MA: MIT Press 2011.

Calleja, Gordon: *In-game. From Immersion to Incorporation,* Cambridge, MA: MIT Press 2011.

Cummins, James: *Bilingualism and Education: Issues in Assessment and Pedagogy,* Celevedon, England: Multilingual Matters 1984.

De Zwart, Melissa/Lindsay, David: "My self, my avatar, my rights? Avatar identity in social virtual worlds," in: Daniel Riha (ed.): *At the Interface/Probing the Boundaries. Frontiers of Cyberspace,* Leiden: Brill-Rodopi 2012, pp. 81-100.

---

26 Ndalianis, Angela: *The Horror Sensorium: Media and the Senses,* Jefferson, NC: McFarland&Company 2012. p. 8.

27 Alston, Adam: *Beyond Immersive Theatre*. London, Palgrave Macmillan 2016. p.3.

Genesee, Fred: *Learning Through Two Languages: Studies on Immersion and Bilingual Education,* Belmont: Wadsworth Pub 1987.

Höök, Kristina: *Designing with the Body,* Cambridge, MA: MIT Press 2011.

Murray, Janet H.: *Hamlet on Holodeck. The Future of Narrative in Cyberspace,* Cambridge, MA: MIT Press 1997.

Kwastek, Katja: *Aesthetics of Interaction in Digital Art,* Cambridge, MA: MIT Press 2011.

Machon, Josephine: *Immersive Theatres. Intimacy and Immediacy in Contemporary Performance,* London: Palgrave Macmillan 2013.

Mühlhoff, Rainer: "Dark Immersion. Some Thoughts on SIGNA's Us Dogs," in: Doris Kolesch/Theresa Schütz/Sophie Nikoleit (eds.), *Strategies of Staging Spectators in Immersive Performances: Commit Yourself!* London and New York: Routledge 2019.

Ndalianis, Angela: *The Horror Sensorium: Media and the Senses,* Jefferson, NC: McFarland&Company 2012.

Ryan, Marie-Laure: "From Narrative Games to Playable Stories," in: *StoryWorlds: A Journal of Narrative Studies* 1, *1*, University of Nebraska Press 2009.

Ryan, Marie-Laure: *Narrative as Virtual Reality,* Baltimore, MD: The John Hopkins University Press 2001.

Shustermann, Richard: "Somaesthetics: A Disciplinary Proposal," in: *The Journal of Aesthetics and Art Criticism* 57, *3* (Summer, 1999), pp. 299-313.

Thabet, Tamer: *Video Game Narrative and Criticism,* London: Palgrave Macmillan 2015.

Authors

Alvarez, Alberto is a PhD student on Procedural Content Generation and Computer Science at the Faculty of Technology and Society at Malmö University, Sweden. His research focuses on AI assisted game design tools that support the work of designers through collaborating with them to produce content, either to optimize their current design or to foster their creativity. He holds an MSc in games technology from the IT University of Copenhagen and a Bachelor in game design and development from ESNE, Madrid. His research interests are on computational intelligence in games, evolutionary computation, co-creativity, and the development of believable agents. He can be contacted at: alberto.alvarez@mau.se

Bakk, Ágnes Karolina (1986). Ph.D. student at Moholy-Nagy Art and Design University, Budapest. Bakk graduated from the Theatre Studies and Hungarian-Finnish Department and received her M.A. degree in Theatre Studies. She is the founder of the performing arts & technologies blog: zip-scene.com. Currently she is the initiator and organizer of the immersive storytelling conference entitled Zip-Scene Conference in Budapest that takes place for the second time in November 2019. She is a member of the research project Rethinking Intermediality in Contemporary Cinema: Changing Forms of In-Betweenness, (Sapientia University, RO). Her latest publications can be found in ICIDS 2017 and EVA London 2018 conference proceedings. She is one of the founding members of Random Error Studio (randomerror.studio), a lab that supports various VR productions.

Boccia, Alex is a Master student in "Game Development and Research" at the Cologne Game Lab. He previously studied Computer Games Development at DePaul University, Chicago, and also earned a gap-year Business degree as part of a joint studyship between universities in France, Sweden, and the United

States. Now living abroad since 2013 and having visited more than 15 countries in that time, Alex remains dedicated to playing his part in a growing international community of game developers, academics, and future leaders. His preoccupation with computer games, geopolitics, economics, and education stems from a childhood of PC strategy gaming and a young adulthood of exploration, adaptation, and a curiosity about the fundamental mechanisms and historical events that brought society to its current state, and that now inhibit its further development.

Brandis, Rüdiger is currently studying "Game Development and Research" at the Cologne Game Lab while working for the Cologne based HTML5 game company Flying Sheep Studios as project manager and game designer. He originally graduated in History, German Literature and Cultural Anthropology at the University of Göttingen studying early documentary film, ethnographic film, and postmodern theory. His research focuses on player's choice, atmospheres, and game feel in linear narrative games. He is also a PhD candidate at the University of Göttingen working on his thesis "Historical Simulacra in Digital Spaces. Methodological and Epistemological Implications of Digital Historical Simulations."

Ferguson, Christopher J. is a professor of psychology at Stetson University near Orlando, Florida. He has a Ph.D. in clinical psychology from the University of Central Florida and is licensed as a psychologist. His research work has focused extensively on media effects ranging from body image to suicide contagion, with the majority of it focused on video game effects. In addition to his work on violence in games, he recently has conducted several studies looking at the impact of sexualized representations of women in games. He is a fellow of the American Psychological Association. He coauthored a book on video game controversies: *Moral Combat: Why the War on Violent Video Games is Wrong* as well as a novel, *Suicide Kings*. He lives in Orlando with his wife and son.

Fetzer, Frank is a PhD candidate at the University of Vienna. He holds a master's degree in film studies from the same institution. His work focuses mainly on phenomenological and post-phenomenological theories. Key elements of his research are embodiment, human-technology relations, cyborgs, the ontology of virtual worlds, and, of course, the video game as such. In his dissertation project, he tries to disentangle the manifold relations between player and video game as technological artefact and extension of player and world.

Mohammad-Hadi, Nicolay. With a background in film production, he gained an undergraduate degree in literature at Philipps-University in Marburg, Germany before studying video games at the Cologne Game Lab in Cologne, Germany. Currently, he is working as producer at Remedy Entertainment in Espoo, Finland as he is finishing his MA thesis on the question how complementary elements of video games such as graphics, audio, and text contribute to a game's design and play experience.

Mukae, Shunsuke is a PhD student of game studies at the Graduate School of Core Ethics and Frontier Sciences at Ritsumeikan University in Kyoto, Japan. He is also a temporary assistant of RCGS (Ritsumeikan Center for Game Studies). He earned a master's degree in film studies from Kansai University, and wrote a paper on Japanese horror films: "J-Horror: Its Birth and the Theory behind It" (*Proceedings of the 3rd EU Workshop*, 2011, pp. 69-79). His current research focuses on the meaning of video game interfaces in the age of postmedia. His next paper about the relation between Japanese let's-play videos and gay pornography will be presented at the DiGRA 2019 conference in Kyoto.
Website: http://ri-search.ritsumei.ac.jp/field/001/1/004/0000000191/profile.html

Nguyen, Anh-Thu is currently a master's student in Media Studies and English Literature at the University of Cologne. In the past, she worked as a freelance editor in the German eSports industry. Now, she is fully dedicated to video games as an academic discipline and makes it a priority in her studies, as well as her work as a student associate at the University of Cologne. With a broad range of knowledge throughout media and arts, her research takes on an interdisciplinary approach. She has also spent a year at Sophia University in Tokyo to study Japanese art and film history. The next research project she is working on deals with intercultural negotiations in the video game franchise KINGDOM HEARTS.

Panic-Cidic, Natali is a passionate gamer, a scholar, and a Master student at the RWTH Aachen University. She has been researching games from multiple perspectives, including cognitive narrative sciences, meaning construction in video games through image schemas, and player-narrative interactions since 2013. Currently, she is working towards a PhD in Games User Research (GUR) and she is hoping to work within the video game industry to help create immersive video games. In 2019, she started working on her first board game inspired by her four feline friends.

Price, Derek is a PhD candidate at Vanderbilt University in German and Media Studies. During the 2018/2019 academic year, he is a Fulbright Research grantee associated with University of Cologne, where he is working on his dissertation entitled "Playing Economy: Leisure and Labor in German Gaming Cultures." His project considers the aesthetics, contexts, and material conditions of production, reception, and use of games that make industrial, agricultural, logistical, and public-service work playable. He is also the creator and co-host of "Scholars At Play," a podcast dedicated to the critical discussion of games in society and the academy (scholarsatplay.net).

Roth, Christian. Media psychologist, researcher, docent and consultant, specializing in the design of interactive experiences with a particular focus on their transformational potential in applied projects. Christian is currently a post-doc researcher at the University of the Arts, Utrecht (HKU), leading user experience studies at the Professorship Interactive Narrative Design. He also teaches narrative game design and research for design at the HKU school Games & Interaction. He has been involved in two FP7 interdisciplinary European projects. As part of the Department of Journalism and Communication Research (IJK) at the University of Music and Drama, Hanover, Germany, he participated in the design and analysis of studies measuring the player identification with video game characters for the project "Fun of Gaming - Measuring the Human Experience of Media Enjoyment" (FuGa). His measurement toolbox for the evaluation of interactive narrative user experiences, was developed during the course of his PhD thesis "Experiencing Interactive Storytelling" at the VU University Amsterdam and as part of the interdisciplinary European FP7 project "Integrating Research in Interactive Storytelling (IRIS)". He is one of the founders of GameCamp Berlin, an annual conference that brings together practitioners and game researchers from different disciplines. He is a lecturer on video game effects, a speaker, and a strong advocate of games for learning. His interest in investigating violence in video games began in 2005 with a user experience study of GRAND THEFT AUTO.

Schnaars, Cornelia J., is currently a master's student of Computer Game Studies at University of Bayreuth. She received a bachelor's degree in Media Culture and English Studies from University of Cologne. Besides the Young Academics Workshop in 2017 and 2018, she also presented a paper at the international workshop „Architectonics of Game Worlds – On Aesthetics and Mechanics, Spaces and Places, Rhythms and Philosophies", organized by Marc Bonner (Cologne, March 2019).

Vozaru, Miruna is a PhD student at the IT University of Copenhagen. Her work, part of the 'Making Sense of Games' project focuses on the development of a game analysis framework for the application in player oriented studies. She holds an MSc in game analysis and development from the IT University of Copenhagen and a Bachelor in Psychology from West University of Timisoara. Her research interests include player psychology, player typologies and game ontology. She can be contacted: at mivo@itu.dk

Wolf, Leonie is a 3D Game Artist based in Cologne, Germany. She studied digital games at the Cologne Game Lab of the TH Köln and received her Bachelor's degree in 2018. In her thesis she investigates how digital games can be used as a form of therapy to treat depression. Throughout her studies she has worked on a number of games that garnered attention at several Game Festivals. In 2017, she was awarded with the Künstlerinnenpreis NRW. Among other projects, she worked as the lead artist for KYKLOS CODE, a 3D action puzzler that was released on Steam in December of 2017. Aside from her occupation as a 3D Game Artist, Leonie has given public workshops and talks on game development, particularly for women and younger game makers. As part of the #FemDevsMeetup, a collective that brings together women in the German Game Industry, she helps with the organization of game related community events. Leonie will continue her studies at the Cologne Game Lab in the Master's program, where she is planning to deepen her research on digital games as a therapy tool in the Mental Health sector.